830396

796.33 Michelson, Herb.
MIC

Rose Bowl football
since 1902

ROSE BOWL FOOTBALL

SINCE 1902

Other books by Herb Michelson:

A Very Simple Game
Sportin' Ladies
Charlie O.

ROSE BOWL

SINCE

HERB MICHELSON

FOREWORD BY O.J. SIMPSON

FOOTBALL

1902
DAVE NEWHOUSE

S⅁ STEIN AND DAY/*Publishers*/New York

Library of Congress Cataloging in Publication Data

Michelson, Herb. Rose Bowl football: since 1902.

Includes index.
1. Rose Bowl Game, Pasadena, Calif.—History.
I. Newhouse, Dave, 1938–   joint author. II. Title.
GV957.R6M5 1977 796.33′272 77–8454
ISBN 0-8128-2168-8

Two poems by John Kieran © 1933 by The New York Times Company.
Reprinted by permission.

Photographs courtesy of Touchdown Publications, Inc.

To our wives:

Gloria Sumner-Michelson, who would have
preferred a novel, and
Patsy Newhouse, an orchid among roses.

ACKNOWLEDGMENTS

This book could not have been prepared without the kindness and cooperation of dozens of nice people—especially the athletes and coaches who participated in the Rose Bowl and were decent enough to take the time to share their recollections with us. Thanks, too, to sports information directors at several universities—particularly Jim Perry of USC and Gary Cavalli of Stanford. Also our gratitude to Tournament of Roses Association executives Walter Hoefflin and Forest W. "Frosty" Foster, magazine editor Dave Duncan, Dave Price, and Marsha Robertson of the Pacific-8 Conference and our typist, Liz Bertuccelli.

CONTENTS

FOREWORD BY
O. J. SIMPSON

Growing up in San Francisco, naturally I was a pro football fan as a kid. I saw my first football game in 1957 when I was ten, at Kezar Stadium, when the Detroit Lions made a fantastic comeback in the second half and knocked the 49ers out of the playoffs. Up until the time I left for USC in 1967, I never missed a 49er home game. But it was the Rose Bowl that decided in my mind about my going to USC.

The first Rose Bowl I saw was on television. It was the 1963 game, between USC and Wisconsin. I watched the parade before the game, saw all those expensive floats. You can imagine what all this looked like to a kid living in the ghetto. Then the game was something else! USC got a big lead. Pete Beathard threw a lot of touchdown passes, Hal Bedsole caught them, and Willie Brown was all over the field. Then Ron Vander-Kelen went out of sight and Wisconsin almost came back to win. It had to be one of the great games of all time.

But the one thing that sold me on USC came after the Trojans had scored first in that game. Their white horse came running down the field, with Tommy Trojan on top, waving his sword. The USC band was playing, "Fight On for Ol' SC." Right there I said to myself, "I want to go to that school!"

I didn't win a lot of honors at Galileo High School, but things started coming together for me as a football player after I went to City College of San Francisco. After I made all-America my first year, USC was recruiting me. I thought, "Here is the school I want to go to, and they're coming after me. Wow!"

It became pretty hectic after my next year of junior college, because the University of California got into the picture, too. There was pressure on me to stay in the San Francisco Bay Area and play in Berkeley, which was just across the bay. Willie Mays even phoned me, telling me not to rush into something, to make sure that the college I picked was the best one for me.

I made up my mind at three o'clock one morning. The phone had been ringing most of the night, and I couldn't sleep. I decided I was going to USC, because that's what I wanted to do all along. I could still remember that first game on television, and I knew I had a better chance of playing in the Rose Bowl if I became a Trojan.

I knew I'd made the right decision before I arrived at USC. USC has such a great athletic tradition, but especially in football. When you talk about USC, you're talking about great names like Howard Jones and Cotton Warburton. They'd been to the Rose Bowl and that appealed to me. The Rose Bowl was even more traditional than USC, the Big Ten, or what have you. It stood for tradition. After all, it's the granddaddy of all bowl games. And we went to the Rose Bowl both years I was at USC.

I remember the first game. We got off the bus, dumped our bags in the locker room and went out to see what the place really looked like. I thought about all the great people who had played in the Rose Bowl and all the great games that had taken place here since the 1920s. It was like, wow!, what else is there? USC against the Big Ten, before 100,000 people. Hey, this is it!

We beat Indiana, 14–3. We clinched the national championship with that victory. I had been named all-America after my first year of major college ball. I was player of the year in some polls, and I finished second to Gary Beban in the Heisman Trophy voting. Now I had scored both touchdowns against Indiana, was awarded the Player of the Game trophy, and everyone was taking my picture. That day was the zenith of my young athletic life. And to think, eleven months earlier, I had been living with my mother in a government project.

After the game, Marquerite, who then was my wife to-be, and I went over to the home of a teammate, Willard "Bubba" Scott. His mother cooked up some black-eyed peas, hog jowls, and ribs. I thought, this was it! The Rose Bowl was the championship of my world, more than winning the national championship or making all-America. At Bubba's house, I wondered how anything could get any better.

I ran eighty yards for a touchdown against Ohio State in the next Rose Bowl. But it didn't mean a thing because we lost, 27–16. Winning the Rose Bowl is one of the great moments possible; losing is just the opposite. But it gives you another picture of just how important the Rose Bowl is to those who have played and coached in the game.

I'm always there at the Rose Bowl if USC plays. If USC isn't playing, then I watch on TV. But I never miss a game; it's still a part of me. I've taken my son Jason to Rose Bowl games, so he can see what it is like for himself. This way I can tell him that his daddy played there, and he can understand some of the importance that it holds for me.

There are a lot of great football traditions. USC and UCLA. Ohio State and Michigan. Nebraska and Oklahoma. There are other bowl games, too. But the biggest game of them all, with the best tradition, is the Rose Bowl.

TRADITION

There were six minutes and thirty-eight seconds to play in the sixty-first Rose Bowl game. Ohio State and Southern California, both such frequent visitors to Pasadena they should consider establishing branch campuses there, were at it again—their third consecutive meeting in the most prestigious of the Bowls. It was January 1, 1975, and the Buckeyes had just gone ahead 17–10, the third time that afternoon the lead had changed hands. This time it was on the strength of Tom Klaban's 32-yard field goal for Ohio State. Only that 6:38 remained.

Pat Haden, Rhodes Scholar and Trojan quarterback, said later, "When they got that field goal, we decided that if we could score a touchdown, we'd go for a two-point conversion." For an 18–17 victory, not a 17–17 tie.

After Tom Skladany's kickoff, the Trojans took possession on their own 17. They'd have to march 83 yards without their top running back, Anthony Davis. "A. D.," as he was known, bruised his ribs in the first half and was out of the game. Instead, Allen Carter, Davis' caddy in the Trojan backfield for three years, would have to eat up the yardage.

On first down, Carter went for 5 yards on a sweep to the right. On second, it was Carter through right tackle for 8 and a first down at the SC 30. Then Dave Farmer went through the same hole for 9. Now Carter again, for 10 yards and a first down at the SC 49. The Trojans were eating up yardage, and the clock; now there were less than five minutes to play.

A new fellow on the squad, Ricky Bell, got the call from Haden and picked up 6 yards, again through the right tackle hole. Carter swept the right side for 2, left tackle for 1, right tackle for 4 yards and a first down at the Ohio State 38.

Only two and a half minutes left.

USC's split end had a familiar name: McKay. He was John Jr., son of the Trojan coach. He was also more than familiar to Haden: the two were playing together for their eighth year of playing for the same team; first high school ball in the L.A. megalopolis, and then Troy. This would be their last game, their last play together. The elder McKay called their number and this was their big play.

"We'd thrown that pass a million times," Haden confided later.

It was a corner pattern—young McKay digging across the middle, then slanting toward the end zone, where he caught Haden's pass. "I've seen him make catches like that for eight years," said the USC quarterback, who within two years would be playing regularly for the Los Angeles Rams of the National Football League (NFL). "When I threw it, John wasn't quite open. But after years of playing together, I know where he's going to be, and he knows where the ball is going to be."

And so now it was 17–16. Conversion time. A gamble, maybe. But with only two minutes and three seconds on the clock there was hardly time for another drive and a win.

This time the call went out to Shelton Diggs. The 6'2" sophomore flanker had seen little action as a freshman, with only four receptions in the regular season, and had suffered a shoulder separation in the 1974 Rose Bowl. And during the 1974 regular season he had hurt his foot and missed three games. But the Rose Bowl can pull the best out of you. He had only eight catches during that season and none at all in the early part of the 1975 Rose Bowl game. Not one, until . . .

"I had the option of running or passing on the conversion attempt," said Haden. "I had decided to run when the guy who was covering Shelton came toward me. So I threw it to Shelton." He caught it, just off the ground, for two points, for an 18–17 Trojan lead—and the national championship. A little curl pattern with dividends.

"I suspect," said Ohio State coach Woody Hayes, "that the difference between the teams was one point." And then he said, "I presume you will see me here next year."

They did. They saw Woody upset 28–10 by UCLA. And the omnipresent They got to see the same Mr. Diggs have a fine afternoon against Michigan in the 1977 Rose Bowl.

The annual game is, of course, an isolated event. Its tradition as much as its action provides the magic. Just ask anyone who's played there and he'll confirm that the Rose Bowl is the Everest of collegiate football participation. If it's only a game played by boys, it has become a phenomenon to be treated with modest reverence. It's a flower show gone Big Time, a parade with an immeasureable route, a pleasant day in a pleasant place.

You'll find most of the scoring statistics in the back of the book; the people come first. We've quoted extensively because the aura of those bygone games is best seen through the eyes of those who played them and those who watched them. We've sampled the decades, and the athletes, and the games. Not all of the decades were good, not all of the players stars, nor every single game ever played exciting. But all come together in the annual Rose Bowl in an encapsulated version of the American Dream.

HISTORY AND POMP

On January 1, 1977, an estimated one million, three hundred ninety thousand spectators lined a five and one-half mile parade route to gaze, for two morning hours, at a collection of sixty-one floats, thirty-four equestrian units and twenty-two marching bands. Then, early in the afternoon, some one hundred thousand folks filled a Pasadena football stadium in the same town to witness a game weighted with all the prestige three quarters of a century could lend it.

All in all, a day, as the *New York Times'* William Wallace observed, that "has been and remains a promotion, a hustle, but one disguised in the most genteel fashion."

Totally genteel, in fact.

The beginnings were simple, and civil. Before the turn of the century, the Valley Hunt Club represented the creme de la creme of Pasadena. There was a discussion among some of its members in the winter of 1889 about the absurdly frigid weather in the East. Rather than say, "Let them eat snow," Hunt Club figure Dr. Charles Frederick Holder and his friend Dr. F. F. Rowland suggested their colleagues count their blessings and stage a celebration, a festival to salute their land of sunshine, citrus and blossoms. Rowland named the event the Tournament of Roses.

Thus, on the first day of 1890, many of Pasadena's 4,882 citizens gathered at a local park for a day of fun and games, plus a small parade which featured flower-bedecked horses and carriages. Not to mention sporting events such as "tilting at the rings," burro races and what the day's master of ceremonies, C.C. Brown, called "a football race."

Bit by bit, year by year, the event just grew, to the obvious pleasure of the area's real

A modern Rose Parade float, a floral recreation of a San Francisco cable car.

estate gentry. A marching band was added in 1891, women riders in 1892, reviewing stands along the leveled dirt track parade route in 1894.

By 1895, the Hunt Club couldn't keep up with the growth of the affair and turned over the festival to a newly-formed group, called the Tournament of Roses Association. Soon there were floats, queens, marshals and more games.

An East-West gridiron affair was added in 1902, but after Michigan destroyed Stanford no team from the West was willing to submit to the possibility of such embarrassment again until 1916. Chariot racing seemed more calming.

But once football did dig in at Pasadena on New Year's, it stayed for keeps. The Tournament of Roses Association holiday game became the Rose Bowl, "the grand-daddy of them all."

"An event," wrote John Underwood. "One of a kind."

And always, under the direction of the white-suited Association members (fourteen hundred who work on thirty-two different committees for as long as a quarter of a century), very, very genteel.

As one of them said in 1977, "I've never seen anything as tightly run or as well-organized in my life."

The entire Tournament is a volunteer professional operation. There is no reason it will not go on forever. Here are the components:

THOSE OTHER BOWLS

Both the Orange and Sugar began in 1935. Miami's game was initially labelled "Orange Blossom." The Sun Bowl was in 1936, the Cotton Bowl followed along in 1937 and the Tangerine Bowl in 1947. Then came the Gator Bowl (1946), Astro-Bluebonnet Bowl (1959), Liberty Bowl (1959), Peach Bowl (1969), and the Fiesta Bowl (1972).

BY ANY OTHER NAME

Harlan "Dusty" Hall was writing for the Pasadena *Star-News* when he was sort of loaned to the Tournament of Roses Association to assist with flackery for the 1922 game. He decided on the name "Rose Bowl" because the shape of the new 57,000-seat stadium in Pasadena would be similar to the Yale Bowl.

The stadium, first used in the 1923 game, was built for only $272,198.26 and financed

An 1897 version of a Tournament of Roses parade float. The only sports activity in Pasadena that day consisted of bicycle racing, both pro and amateur.

The first game played in the new Rose Bowl stadium. In this 1923 contest USC defeated Pen State, 14-3.

by selling seat subscriptions. The first game in the new stadium began nearly one hour late. Not because of dedication ceremonies but due to the tardiness of the Penn State team—caught in a traffic jam. The Nittany Lions should have stayed in traffic; USC beat them, 14–3.

NUMERO UNO TIME

Researchers of the Citizens Savings Athletic Foundation reported in 1977 that more college national champions had up to that time played in the Rose Bowl than in all other major bowls combined. The Pasadena total: twenty. The others: fifteen, including Pitt at the Sugar in '77.

The Rose's national champs were Michigan in 1902; Harvard, 1920; California, 1921; Notre Dame, 1925; Alabama, 1926; Alabama and Stanford, 1927; Georgia Tech, 1929; USC, 1931 and '33; California, 1938; Stanford, 1941; Michigan, 1949; Ohio State, 1955; Washington, 1961; USC, 1963; Michigan State, 1966; USC, 1968; Ohio State, 1969; USC, 1973.

There were some years in which the potential national champion stumbled to a lesser club in Pasadena. For further information, contact a veteran coach in Columbus, Ohio.

STATION BREAK

The first Rose Bowl game broadcast coast-to-coast was in 1927. Graham McNamee reported over National Broadcasting Corporation (NBC) network of fifteen stations and apparently was enchanted by his booth's-eye view of the San Gabriel Mountains, which on one occasion he romantically acknowledged by saying, ". . . the purple shadows of the majestic Sierra Nevada creep slowly downward as dusk approaches." No, the game had not been moved to Lake Tahoe.

McNamee aired the Bowl through 1930 and was followed by Howard Planey, Don Wilson, Don Thompson, Ken Carpenter, Bill Stern, Harry Wismer, Bob Considine, Mel Allen and Red Barber—all doing either play-by-play or color, or both. Wilson and Carpenter would ultimately become announcing foils for radio variety show stars Jack Benny and Bing Crosby, respectively. Except for the games of 1949–51, when the Columbia Broadcasting System (CBS) handled the radio coverage, the Rose Bowl has been in the broadcast hands of NBC.

The first nationwide telecast from Pasadena was at the 1952 game, with Mel Allen in charge. Working with him through the 1963 game were the likes of Jack Brickhouse, Tom Harmon, Dick Danehe, Sammy Balter, Lee Giroux, Chick Hearn, Braven Dyer and Bill Symes. Lindsey Nelson anchored the next four Bowl broadcasts, with the help of Symes, Rod Belcher, Ray Scott and Terry Brennan. Then came big NBC gun, Curt Gowdy, in 1968. His sidekicks would include Paul Christman, Kyle Rote, Al DeRogatis, and Don Meredith.

An array of voices emanating from the purple shadows of some swell mountain range.

HOWDY, MARSHAL

A Rose record you will not find in statistical summaries was set on January 1, 1977, by Leonard Slye and Frances Smith, a.k.a. Roy Rogers and Dale Evans. They had made thirty-five movies together, reared eight children and had celebrated their twenty-ninth wedding anniversary on New Year's Eve to serve as Rose Parade Grand Marshal. Their horses, Trigger and Buttermilk, long had become museum pieces, so Roy and Dale rode in a gold-plated, $115,000 Stutz d'Italia. In fact, Roy and Dale were the first husband-wife Marshal. In most previous years, only one person got the nod.

The selection of a Marshal was a haphazard affair in the early years. C. C. Reynolds was the first fellow selected, in 1902. Then six years passed without a Grand Marshal. The parade's founders, Dr. Holder and Dr. Rowland, shared the honor in 1910. M. S. Pashgian looked so marvelous in his tailored riding habit and stovepipe hat, he was given the title in 1915. The 1928 Marshal was a fellow who had been a Civil War drummer boy, John McDonald.

Then in 1930 an Association official decided the Marshal should be "some celebrity that the world wants to see." And the first celebrity was San Francisco Mayor "Sunny Jim" Rolph. His appearance initiated a number of firsts in Rose Marshaldom.

Screen star Mary Pickford became the first female Grand Marshal in 1933. Harold Lloyd was the first comedian Marshal, 1935. Actor Leo Carillo, who would ride in the parade for thirty years, was the big guy in 1938. The next year Pasadena saw the first juvenile Marshal, lovely little Shirley Temple. And she was followed in 1940 by the first wooden juvenile Marshal, a funny lad named Charlie McCarthy and his ventriloquist, Edgar Bergen.

There weren't any parades in the World War II years but there were still honorary Marshals: the first bandleader, Kay Kayser; the first governor, California's Earl Warren; the first living football legend, Amos Alonzo Stagg; the first former President, Herbert Hoover.

Three men who lived in the White House would be on the list of Marshals through 1977: Hoover, Dwight D. Eisenhower (in 1951, when because of a military assignment he had to be replaced at the parade by a wounded veteran of the Korean War, and in 1964), and Richard M. Nixon (1953 and 1960). Only Nixon, Eisenhower, Warren and comedian, Bob Hope, were twice named as Marshal.

Other firsts in the Marshal category include: first golfer, Arnold Palmer, 1965; first foreigner, Thailand foreign minister, Thanat Khoman, 1967; first moon landers, the Apollo 12 astronauts, 1970; first individual black, home run hero, Henry Aaron, 1975.

The 1952 Marshal holds the record for most persons serving in that category at one time. The honor in that parade went to seven winners of the Medal of Honor.

THE THRONE ROOM

The succession of queens comes easier in the monarchies of Europe than in the bowl-principality of Pasadena. Being named Rose Queen lacks the over-all hoopla, perhaps, of becoming Miss America, but to the young womanhood in the San Gabriel Valley it's nonetheless a big deal.

The Rose Queen is picked in late October, after a lengthy selection process. Contenders must be between the ages of seventeen and twenty-one, be a full-time student in the area, carry at least a C average and be unmarried. Plenty of sweet young things meet the criteria; in 1976, there were 695 initial contestants. In judging sessions, the field is continually trimmed by one-third until the semi-final round is reached and the covey pared to twenty-six. Out of this batch come the seven finalists—one of whom will be Queen and the others members of her court. They all get outfits from I. Magnin's and coifs at the House of Harmon (both Pasadena businesses). Between the time of their selection and New Year's Day, they appear on television (*The Lawrence Welk Show,* for example), at balls, receptions and parties and, of course, on a float at the parade.

Grand Marshal Shirley Temple gets her ribbon from Tournament of Roses Association president Lathrop Leishman. She was the first moppet Grand Marshal.

During her reign, the Queen and her Court are not permitted to give any commercial endorsements. Not even for the House of Harmon.

The first Queen (in 1905) lived in less festive luxury than her well-celebrated successors. Hallie Woods not only had to sew her own gown but helped decorate the float on which she rode. She had been selected, as were all Queens in the early years, in voting by students of Pasadena High.

In 1911 the Tournament of Roses Association beefed up its membership by tempting newcomers with a vote for Queen. Then in 1930 the selection system was changed to its current form: an open competition in area schools.

There was not always a Queen in the early years. The royalty motif seemed rather whimsical. For instance, in 1913 there were co-Queens—one of them a man. A clear first.

Other regal firsts: Joan Woodbury, 1907, was the first married Queen. She was a thirty-five-year-old society matron. May Sutton Bundy, 1908, was the first tennis star Queen. May McAvoy, of "Jazz Singer" fame, was the first movie star Queen, in 1924. A Miss America, Fay Lamphier, became Queen in 1926. The first and, history records, only queen to dress as the Statue of Liberty on parade day was Harriet Sterling, in 1928.

By New Year's Day of 1977, only seven of the previous Queens were deceased.

NAME THAT THEME

The theme of the Rose Parade is determined early in the year by the Association president. His selection is made from suggestions submitted by plain folk. The 1977 parade theme, "The Good Life," was suggested by three post-card-writing folks, but Mrs. Pamela Rubel of Altadena, California, had her card picked in a drawing and thus was treated to a luncheon, the parade and the game. She had initially submitted thirty theme names, her favorite being "The Good Things in Life," which she later abbreviated. She said her husband showed no interest in her theme contest victory until he learned there would be free game tickets.

Actually, a theme was one of the last components for the New Year's Day festivities. There was none until 1918, when "Patriotism" was heralded on the notion there was a war on. "Victory Tournament" quite logically followed at the 1919 parade. Then there was no theme again until 1927. For most of the next forty years, the word "flowers" appeared in the theme, including "Poems in Flowers" (1929), "Victory, Unity and Peace in Flowers" (1946), "Famous Books in Flowers" (1954) and "Headlines in Flowers" (1965).

Other spheres of interest celebrated in themes have been the world (four times), the seven seas (once), the movies (once), childhood (twice) and dreams-daydreams (twice). Never, however, a nightmare.

BUY MY FLOWERS, MISTER?

Once there is a theme, the floatation waltz begins. The bulk of the some sixty floats you see on television every New Year's Day are commissioned by cities and commercial enterprises (the International House of Pancakes, for example). Planning and design begins in the Spring. Floats can cost—depending on a variety of estimates—anywhere from $7,000 to $50,000, the average expenditure running about $20,000. Depending on inflation, this is enough to send a lovely young thing flowers every day of her life.

The maximum dimensions of floats are sixteen feet high, eighteen feet wide and fifty feet long. All you see on each float are the fresh flowers (as many as 350,000 per float), but underneath all those blooms is a truck chassis rebuilt with a heavy motor, an extra large radiator, spare water tank and telephone, or a stripped-down automobile, or jeep. There are two drivers and an observer, who is really a communications man concealed in the front of the float. He relays instructions from parade committeemen to the drivers —slow down, stop, move along. Stuff like that. In case a float breaks down during the long parade, two repair trucks are standing by on side streets. Organization.

From the early designs, a metal or wooden frame is placed over the chassis during warehouse construction. The one-inch chicken wire is stretched over the entire length

This 1896 float appears to feature a Robert E. Lee taking his lady stepping. The sweepstakes winner in this parade was the Knights of the Maccabees float.

of the float. Next, an outside skin, either construction paper dipped in paste or a polyvinyl material, is placed over the chicken wire mesh to provide a surface which will hold the flowers. Sometimes, though, flowers are strung on wires rather than pasted on the float.

The actual placement of flowers (leaves, bark, fruit, and seeds, too) doesn't come until about forty-eight hours before parade time. The hardy mums go on first, followed by the usual array of roses, gardenias, orchids—usually, all of them are put in tiny tubes of water which are sunk into the float's skin. One can view the floats in various gathering areas, both before and after the parade.

There are at least five professional float builders working for Rose Parade entrants. These builders sign contracts with wholesale florists and individual growers, starting in May. If times are bad in the domestic flower business, arrangements are made with growers as distant as Australia. Flowers are ordered by the square foot; for example, a standard bundle of mums will cover three square feet on a float.

The laborious task of gluing on the flowers usually falls to youngsters from local church, social and charitable groups. They start the day after Christmas and work like hell.

Also toiling under difficult conditions is the float's main driver, who is secluded somewhere down below all of that flora. He is literally driving in the dark; to make his task easier, a pink line is painted down the center of the parade route. He can glance down and see the line. And, no, he does not wear a flower in his buttonhole.

BANG THE DRUM QUICKLY

The 1977 Rose Parade had twenty-two bands, including the official tournament band, the Pasadena City College Lancers, so designated by the Association in 1930. This band's regular eighty-five members, who practice ninety minutes a day, five days a week, every week of the year, are joined by sixty other musicians (including alumni) on New Year's Day.

"Not only do we practice the music," said band director Ron Hoar before the '77 parade, "but we must also build up our stamina. It's impossible and boring to march around a city block fifty times, so we try to find an unopened freeway to give us more space."

The other regular bands in the parade are from the two Rose Bowl game schools, Marine Corps, McDonald's (the hamburger folk who put together an "All-American High School Band," with two musicians from each state plus the District of Columbia), the Salvation Army and in-state and out-of-state high schools. The Tournament committeemen try to maintain geographic representation in picking the bands. There is judging of Southern California high school bands. There has even been a back-up band, in case one of those selected didn't show.

An invitation to the parade for a high school band is a matter of great moment. The John Marshall High School Band of San Antonio, Texas, had two hundred and ten marchers in the 1977 parade. They raised the money for the trip ($11,000) by playing continuously at a shopping mall for fifty-two hours and two minutes. A record at the time. At the end of the fifty-two hours and two minutes there were no cries of "Encore!"

HORSIES

The 1977 parade had 260 of them, everything from Missouri Mules to Tennessee Walkers. The equestrian units get into the parade by making application to a Tournament committee; each of the committee's ten members reviews a particular breed of horse. Entries are selected based on experience, conformity to breed, and photographs. The horsies need not have a C average at an area high school or college. Tack for the animals must be silver, and costs between $10,000 and $25,000. Not just any horsy can get into the Rose Parade.

MINOR STATS

Arrests connected with New Year's festivities in Pasadena in 1977: 135, compared to 256 in 1976. Most of those pinches were for liquor-related violations.

Disqualified parade floats in 1977: nine. These were for failing to be in their assigned parking spaces in the parade assembly area on time. (Judging begins in the assembly area.)

Float accidents in 1977: Two. A float apparently lost control of its brakes on a slight incline on Colorado Boulevard, went out of control, and struck a horse and a float in front of it. In the other accident, a hit-run float damaged an overhanging traffic signal.

Deaths in 1977: one, male. Heart attack.

Medical calls in 1977: thirty.

Major crimes in 1977: theft of $1,200 worth of equipment, from an ambulance.

Number of vehicles in Pasadena on New Year's Day 1977: 300,000.

THE BALL PARK

First game played in the Rose Bowl stadium was not the Rose Bowl. USC and California met there at the end of the 1922 season.

Seating in the new stadium for the 1923 game was 57,000. Capacity jumped to 76,000 when the south end of the stadium horseshoe was enclosed for the 1929 game. Further enlargements occurred in 1932 (83,677), and in 1949 (100,807), and in 1971 (104,697), when all new seats were installed. The capacity figure includes 359 press box seats.

The Bowl has seventy-seven rows of seats and measures 880 feet from north to south rims and 695 feet from east to west rims. Its circumference around the rim is 2,430 feet; the circumference around the inside at field level is 1,350. The turfed area inside the bowl is 79,156 square feet. The fence around the Bowl is one mile in circumference. Planted between the fence and the Bowl are 3,000 rose bushes of 100 varieties, maintained by the Pasadena Public Works Department.

Questions? Oh, yes. The press box has one slow-moving elevator.

FUTURE SHOCK

According to a Nielsen rating survey, television audiences for the four major bowl games decreased by nearly 10,000,000 homes in 1977. Seventy-one million people had watched the 1976 Rose Bowl game.

"If the trend continues," reported the *New York Times,* "the network fees for the rights to televise the bowl games may be adjusted downwards."

In terms of rights money in 1977, NBC was paying three million dollars to the Rose and two million to the Orange, while CBS handed over one million for the Cotton, and American Broadcasting Company (ABC) one million for the Sugar.

In 1977, the Rose pulled an audience survey "share" of 45, the Cotton 36, the Orange 34 and the Sugar—with the nation's top-rated team and star (Pitt, Tony Dorsett)—only 33.

ALMANAC

Things that happened off the field through the years:
- 1901: First automobiles permitted to enter the parade, but told to stay at the rear "so you don't scare the horses."
- 1903: Navajo Indian group comes from Arizona and makes an unscheduled parade appearance.
- 1908: The City of Redondo Beach, California, enters a parade float in the shape of a whale which spouts perfume twenty-five feet into the air.
- 1912: Well-known pilot C. P. Rogers flies over the parade route and drops rose petals.
- 1913: Tent-pegging becomes a competitive event.
- Also 1913: An elephant races a camel during the Tournament.
- 1915: Final chariot race, Charlton Heston notwithstanding.

- 1916:   Members of the Washington State football team are paid $100 per day to appear in a movie called *Tom Brown of Harvard.*
- Also 1916:   Bathing beauties, in black bloomer suits, in parade for the first time.
- 1925:   First wirephoto picture of a Rose Bowl game is transmitted.
- 1926:   Two women die and two hundred thirty-six people are injured, when a section of a wooden viewing stand for the parade collapses at the southeast corner of the intersection of Madison Avenue and Colorado Boulevard.
- 1929:   Stadium's mortgage is paid off.
- 1934:   Equestrians required to wear Spanish costume.
- 1947:   First television coverage of parade—the roses looking lovely in living black and white.
- 1954:   Ah, living color on the network for the parade.
- 1955:   First float which carries an airplane (Convair XF-92A).
- 1960:   Stately four and one-half acres Wrigley Estate, built in 1914 and purchased by the chewing gum magnate for $195,000, is officially donated to the City of Pasadena as permanent headquarters for the Tournament of Roses Association. (There's a swell Rose Bowl hall of fame on the second floor which visitors can tour between the hours of two and four P.M. between the months of February and September. Actually, you can visit the entire main house, except for working offices, during that period. Lovely place.)
- 1976:   First time a Tournament Grand Marshal ever performed in the Rose Bowl when Kate Smith sang "God Bless America" in the pre-game festivities.

The old Wrigley mansion in Pasadena, headquarters of the Tournament of Roses Association.

JUMP
THE DEAD ONES

Classic sporting events do not change greatly over the years. They're updated, of course, but only to a point. Horses still run on the first Saturday in May at Churchill Downs. Nine men attempt to score more runs than nine other men at World Series time. Two men with boxing gloves hear a bell, walk into a squared ring, and flail for a mythic crown. The brickyard at Indy remains the brickyard. Continuum. Except for football, and most especially except for the Rose Bowl, which has not always been played on January first nor, for that matter, always in Pasadena.

The first game, on January 1, 1902, was played eleven men to the side. Okay so far. The teams were Michigan and Stanford. Both would be back, often. And, oh yes, there was a traffic jam, what with all the tallyhos and farm wagons and foot traffic and those new-fangled automobiles. The narrow road was clogged, the single gate into the game wasn't a place for a self-respecting sardine. It was your basic Southern California snarl, but not a freeway in sight. Now that was a harbinger, and the most graphic Rose Bowl tradition.

And that was all that was the same, because in 1902 the football point system was different, the game wasn't divided into fifteen-minute quarters, and passing was non-existent. If a time machine transported today's football fan into Pasadena on the first day of 1902 and he shouted for "a forward pass," he might very well have been trucked off by the constabulary on charges of speaking in tongues.

Most foreign to the modern fan would have been the timing. In those leisurely days, the game was played in thirty-five-minute halves. Don't let the fact that the 1902 Rose Bowl had halves of thirty-five and twenty-seven minutes confuse you. What happened that day was that Stanford gave up early. Who could blame the lads from that fine institution of higher learning in Northern California? Because they were higher-learned, they knew when to chuck it in. Enough was enough. 49–0 was more than enough. One half would have been plenty.

Contrast that sixty-two minute game with the clocking of the 1976 Rose Bowl by a minister in San Francisco. The actual playing time from snap of the ball to whistle, the cleric reported to columnist Herb Caen, was fifteen minutes, twenty-seven seconds. Thirty-six commercials consumed twenty-two minutes. The pre-game show ran twenty-nine minutes and halftime ceremonies twenty-seven minutes. Exactly one hundred and five minutes were devoted to huddles, times-out, station breaks, first-down measurements, lining up for plays, instant replays and, one might assume, adjustment of dissheveled equipment. The average play took just under six seconds, while the average television commercial lasted thirty seconds. If Tevye, the dairyman, could have compared the 1902 and 1976 Rose Bowls, he would not have rhapsodized about tradition.

His reaction, at least in 1902, might have been similar to that of Pasadena publisher Lon F. Chapin, who noted in his *News*: "Several thousand Dutchmen and Britishers engaged in several years of bloody fighting for the possession of a government and don't get an encore. Twenty-two striplings argue for an hour over the progress along the ground of an inflated hog's hide, and law-abiding citizens bound up and down on the seats of their trousers, while demure maidens hammer plug hats down over the ears of their escorts with their parasols." Shame on the Pasadena Chamber of Commerce which didn't seize Mr. Chapin's built-in slogan: "Make Football, Not War."

Still, a reporter on the *Los Angeles Daily Times* managed to wrap up the game with more facility. "The Michigan backbreakers," he wrote, "made monkeys out of the Stanford footballists."

With eight minutes remaining to be played, Stanford team captain R. S. Fisher said

The 1902 Stanford team, accompanied by a retinue of local ladies, lolling around the grounds of the Huntington Hotel. They were destroyed by Michigan, 49-0.

to Michigan team captain Hugh White, "If you are willing, we are ready to quit." And Captain White, a fine left tackle and humanitarian who did not wish to break any more footballists' backs, said that was fine and dandy with him. The stuff of history.

In the football seasons of 1901 through 1904, the University of Michigan team was undefeated, and tied but once in forty-four games. During that span, the Wolverines outscored their opponents 2,326 to 40. Michigan apparently could move the ball.

These were the so-called "point a minute" teams of Coach Fielding Harris "Hurry-Up" Yost. His left halfback in those years, Willie "Judge" Heston, reached the end zone so frequently (93 touchdowns) he could have led the National Basketball Association (NBA) in scoring.

There is every reason to believe Yost would have been as successful in coaching today as he was at the turn of the century. His moods and methods are no different than dozens of dogmatic gentlemen now coaching on the college and professional levels.

Judge Heston told football historian Allison Danzig about Yost's favorite command to the team: "Use your searchlights and jump the dead ones." Or as those allegedly glib television "color men" tell us today, "Boy, will you look at that second effort by Billy Reppledepplevitch. It's amazing how he can shake off eleven blocks, make the tackle, recover the fumble and still have strength left to go seventy-three yards for the touchdown. Now that's second effort, fans." But it isn't second effort. It's using your searchlights and jumping the dead ones. No wonder demure maidens used their parasols to hammer down the plug hats over the ears of their escorts.

Somebody once asked Ring Lardner if he had ever spoken to Yost. "No, I didn't," said the most artistically underrated writer of our times. "You see, my father taught me never to interrupt."

Yost must have been a veritable football filibuster. And most sure of himself.

"He always talked slowly and seriously," Heston wrote Danzig. "and meant what he said. A dull sense of humor and no use for liquor, made it hard for him to tolerate anywhere or any time. And he was always truthful, and his morals were the best." Heston suggested his coach would have been "a good military general."

If Yost was a single-channeled football genius, if not an obvious bore, he seemed to have the ability to inspire his lads. Just before one of his teams would take the field to begin a game, Yost would tell the players, "Who are they to beat a Michigan team? They're only human."

The nerve of Stanford even showing up on January 1, 1902.

Yost had been the coach at Stanford in 1900. The Cardinals, as they were then called (later, Indians; then, in the early 1970s when campuses did not wish to offend Native Americans, the nickname went back to Cardinals), went undefeated under good old Hurry Up.

"But," said Rose Bowl historian Rube Samuelsen, "Yost was irked by the adoption of a rule, coincidental or not, making it mandatory for Stanford to hire a graduate coach. That cost Yost, who had attended both West Virginia and Lafayette, his job."

So he put together a modest little program at Ann Arbor, zipping through the 1901 season 10–0, utterly destroying all opposition on the chance there were Stanford grads among them. The Wolverines outscored their 1901 foes (Albion, Case, Indiana, Northwestern, Buffalo, Carlisle, Ohio State, Chicago, Beloit, Iowa) by 501–0. The "closest" game on the schedule was a 21–0 squeaker over Ohio State; the crusher, was 128–0 against Buffalo. Yost's clubs in 1901–04 would give up only six touchdowns and two field goals; only two of the enemy touchdowns would come on sustained drives—the other four resulting from Michigan fumbles.

"In 1901," Yost told Grantland Rice thirty-four years later, "we used spinners, reverses, double reverses, laterals, split backs— everything that is in the modern game except the forward pass."

Judge Heston reported similary in 1952. "We used nearly every running play then that is being used today."

Even without the pass, Yost's Michigan must have been exciting, especially the 1901 team. Heston said it was the best he played on while at Ann Arbor. "We should have

The Michigan team that won the first Rose Bowl. Coach "Hurry Up" Yost is in the center of the top row. Halfback Willie Heston, twice an all-America, is at the right in the middle row.

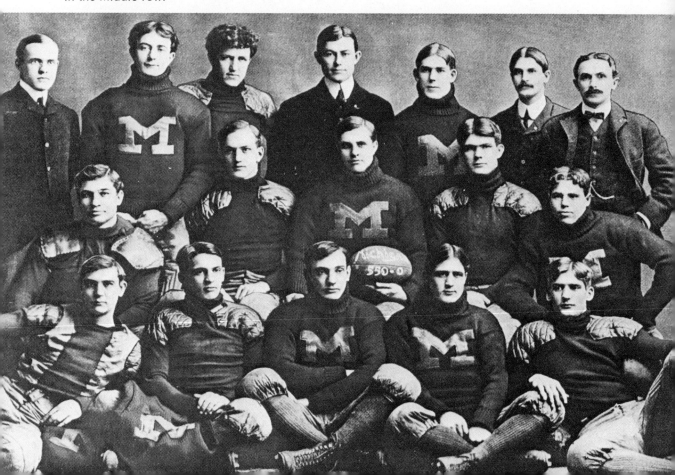

Michigan guard Tug Wilson, identified here, later became Big Ten commissioner.

been fairly good in executing the pass," he said. They were probably good enough to hit grandslam homers, make a hat trick, run a nine-second hundred and pay $2.20 and out, too.

Hurry-Up Yost gave his Wolves fifty plays, undoubtedly many more than Stanford had seen in the 1901 season from the likes of their opponents: the Olympic Club (twice), Reliance Athletic Club (also twice), Nevada, and California. The Cardinals from down on "the farm" in Palo Alto ended the season 3–1–2, outscoring its opposition 34–8. The loss was to Cal.

California, as was Michigan, went undefeated in 1901 and doubtless would have made a more representative foe for the Wolverines, who indicated they would prefer to play the best in the West. But administrators at Berkeley were having no part of this new Rose Bowl thing. Thus, Stanford and thus, the opportunity for Yost to wreak havoc on his former employers. Yost said his 1900 Stanford team "was better than most of the Midwestern elevens of this season, and as good as any team Michigan has met this year. And this year's Stanford material is better than I had last year whether the team's play is or not."

Yost never would have stood for a scoreless tie with Reliance. No sir. Yost and his players never stood, period.

The "hurry up" approbation came from the fact Michigan was as precisely frantic as it was competent. Speed was always Yost's order of the day. When a play ended, Michigan quarterback Boss Weeks would be calling the next play even before enemy tacklers had crawled to their feet, brushed themselves off, and ambled to the line of scrimmage. The Wolverines used quick counts and snaps, and then alternated the counts to draw the opposition offside.

Yost's teams were quick and strong, although not large. Heston, at one hundred ninety pounds, and fullback Neil Snow, an even two hundred (he played end on defense), were the only "big" men on those turn-of-the-century giants.

Only two of the ten teams Michigan played in 1901 managed to creep inside the Wolverine 34 line; four of the opponents did not reach Michigan territory at all. Stanford and its new coach, Charley Fickert, knew what to expect, but showed up in Pasadena on December 20th, anyway.

The Association allotted $3,500 for team travel and lodging expenses, although there was a slight beef by Charles Baird, graduate manager of the Michigan team. The Association had offered two dollars a day for meal money; Baird demanded three so "we can go comfortably and in reasonable style." The folks in Pasadena acceded; you do not offend an unscored-upon team. And to make things easier for Yost, the Michigan Athletic Association plunked over $750 to provide expenses for three substitute players, none of whom would play in the Rose Bowl. Stanford used four reserves, one replacing left guard W. K. Roosevelt, second cousin of the incumbent President. W. K. played fifteen minutes with a broken leg and fractured ribs, before begging off. Bully.

There were seats for only 1,000 at Tournament Park, on the grounds of the Throop Polytechnic Institute, which later became the California Institute of Technology. The day was quite hot and became even more parched by the dust stirred up in the traffic. Tickets were going for fifty cents and two dollars. A few folks in the Association feared the expenses would not be met. But some 8,500 people—more than half the population of Pasadena (then 15,000)—clogged the single entry way at Tournament Park. Many didn't care to stand in line and file through with civility. The one policeman on duty, H. L. Van Schaick, pleaded with the crush to enter single file, and the good folks responded by climbing a fence and overflowing onto the playing field.

In that era, touchdowns counted for 5 points, field goals 5, and points after touchdown 1. Stanford's lone hope was the field goal-kicking ability of large left tackle Bill Traeger, who would later become sheriff of Los Angeles County. The only problem was, could Stanford get Traeger within field goal range?

Michigan, meanwhile, had all of those plays and all of those fine backs: Weeks at quarter, Heston and Al Herrnstein at the halves and the massive Snow at full. Well,

Michigan fullback Neil Snow who was named Player of the Game after a record five touchdown runs.

in the early minutes Stanford somehow managed to stop Michigan from scoring. Cardinal linemen contained the Wolves for twenty-three minutes. In one play, Stanford end G. H. Clark swiped the ball from Michigan end Curt Redden and nearly broke it for a touchdown. Clark did get 17 yards, however—all the way to his own 29. Traeger would have two shots at field goals, from 40 and 45 yards out: both were unsuccessful.

A 21-yard run by Judge Heston put the ball on Stanford's 8. Soon Snow, who would score a record five touchdowns and be named player of the game (MVP), drove the middle for the first points in Rose Bowl history. A 20-yard field goal by Ev Sweeley and a 35-yard punt return by Redden made it 17–0 at the half. If the field hadn't been

Some action at the first Rose Bowl game.

110 yards long, the margin might have been larger. No matter, for in the second half Heston ran rampant, his longest carry going 49 yards down a sideline to set up the game's last score, a 22-yard dash through right tackle by Herrnstein.

Previously, Snow had scored on runs of 6, 2, 17 and 4 yards. Heston managed 170 rushing yards, the team 503 in all. Sweeley's punting was as important to the Michigan victory as all that rushing; he punted almost 900 yards that day and averaged almost 40 yards a kick. Three boomed over 60 yards.

"We left a snowstorm in Michigan, went to California, played eleven men at ninety degrees and beat Stanford 49–0," is the way Yost would put it many years later.

"Michigan certainly gave their California opponents and spectators a touch of the real thing in strenuous living," said the fellow from the *Los Angeles Times*. "Michigan's men formed a collection of superb specimens of all-around physical development . . . calves like piano legs and arms to match—all as hard as rocks."

But all the Wolverines really did was use their searchlights and jump the dead ones.

THE SAILORS
AND THE BEAR

The name looks rather misplaced, for with the passage of time images tend to freeze. The name of George Halas simply does not seem to belong there in the list of Rose Bowl "Players of the Game (MVP)." Yet, after the events on the afternoon of January 1, 1919, he was accorded such an honor. Halas a giant of college football? Halas, the "Papa Bear" pioneer of the professional game, a heroic campus figure?

Well, yes and no. Although the man who is now viewed as a keystone in the development of the NFL did indeed have a brief fling as a collegiate gridder, he did not appear in the Rose Bowl on a college team. Nor—at least in his view—was he MVP. But events occur, and with the years one tends to lose sight of the fact that grand old men of grand old games were once young and significant for reasons having nothing to do with their eventual stature.

Whatever George Stanley Halas was to become, there was a time . . .

One did not know what to expect over the telephone. After all, the man was in his early eighties and the questions concerned events of some sixty years previous. So much had happened since that New Year's Day. So many more important games and titles and events and names.

"He gets so many requests for so many interviews about so many subjects," said the very efficient, cooperative Chicago Bears' publicist. "But we can try."

Halas still was coming into his office first thing every morning: into a football world that had outgrown even him. It must all have seemed so implausible, perhaps like never having been there at all.

The voice was robust, spirited. He had obviously done some research, or had it done for him. He wished to read the starting lineup of the Great Lakes Naval Training Station team which had appeared in, and won, the 1919 Rose Bowl game. He read the names and the schools at which these names had matriculated. There was a sense of pride. "Almost all of these fellows," he said, "were fine players from fine colleges. I guess you could say we had quite a team that year. Quite a team."

George played no organized football until his senior year at the University of Illinois in 1917. He probably was good enough to make the team there as a sophomore, but fractured his jaw; a season later, he had a broken leg. However, he was healthy enough to play baseball in college and carry a batting average in the .350 range. Also in his senior year, he played a little basketball. He entered the Navy immediately after the basketball season ended in 1918; he was, he recalls, four units short of a degree in civil engineering.

What he remembers most about 1918, aside from the events of the football season at Great Lakes, just outside Chicago, was the flu epidemic. "It really seemed to hit the Navy station hard," he said. "I think we even lost a few players but I can't say for sure."

The disease called "Spanish influenza" first struck the Camp Funston cantonment in Fort Riley, Kansas, in March, 1918, and spread with fatal speed through other military installations. Within a few weeks it seemed to be everywhere. Everywhere. Deaths in the military camps averaged one per hour; the ships that weren't port-bound by death and illness among crews were at sea with few fit hands and the stench of death about them. When the troop carrier *Leviathan* reached France, it carried two hundred corpses. Draft calls were stopped when the death toll of servicemen reached seven thousand.

In Pasadena, as elsewhere, schools were closed. Charles H. Prisk, publisher of the Pasadena *Star-News,* suggested in the Autumn of 1918 that the upcoming Rose Bowl game be cancelled. But other civic leaders contended that the epidemic would not spread in an outdoor situation. Not long after the November 11th Armistice, the epidemic vanished as quickly as it had come.

The sailors managed to survive the epidemic and the war. Early on, Halas recalls some high-ranking officer attempting to coach his team of Midwest all-stars. "Every day, he would call us together and give us one or two plays. He made himself sound very important and very knowledgeable about football. But most of us kind of smiled at this kind of 'coaching.' It seemed to us that he had just come from reading about these plays in a book, like he was reciting something from memory. After he'd walk away, we'd go ahead with our practice and do whatever we wanted to anyway. It was really pretty amusing."

Eventually that year, the Sailors got themselves a coach who seemed truly to know something about football, one Lieutenant Clarence J. McReavy. "Fine man," said Halas. "A good coach, too. But he had so many other assignments at Great Lakes that he didn't always have enough time to spend with the team. At least not as much time as he wanted to. So a couple of us would work out plays and run the practices."

The Sailors were loaded with first-rate football minds. Halas, of course, would end up coaching the Chicago Bears to championships. Charley Bachman, the Great Lakes center, one day would be head coach at Michigan State. Jimmy Conzelman would bring an NFL title some thirty years later to the Chicago (eventually St. Louis) Cardinals. And Paddy Driscoll, nicknamed "The Wasp" (for reasons unrelated to White Anglo-Saxon Protestantism) would serve for many seasons as a Halas assistant in Chicago. Driscoll was the Sailors quarterback and, as far as Halas was concerned, the fellow who should have been MVP in the 1919 Rose Bowl.

There must have been a clubby atmosphere on that quickie wartime team, because after the armistice it seemed that everyone was following everyone around. In the regular 1919 season, when the professionals first felt their oats, Halas played on a team called the Hammond Pros with three Great Lakes teammates, guards Jerry Jones and Emmett Keefe, both of whom had attended Notre Dame, and tackle-kicker Hugh Blacklock.

Then in 1920, with a pro outfit called the Decatur Staleys, Halas, Jones, Keefe, and Blacklock were joined by old Sailor buddies, Driscoll and Conzelman. (Trivia fans will recall that latter-day baseball manager Charley Dressen was on that 1920 Decatur team, too.)

By 1921 Halas, Jones and Blacklock were still together—on the Chicago Staleys. Then in 1922, when the team was the Bears, only Halas and Blacklock still wore the same uniform. Blacklock, in fact, stayed with George for three more seasons before moving to the good old Brooklyn Lions in 1926.

The Sailors of 1918 were not a jerry-built ball club. "Most of us had arrived at Great Lakes early in the year, so there was plenty of time for organization and daily practice. Most of us had a great deal of experience," recalled Halas. "I remember we played a tough schedule, but ended up having quite a good season. We beat some Big Ten teams that year that were pretty good, so we had nothing to be ashamed about."

Great Lakes went undefeated in eight games, played a scoreless tie with Driscoll's old mates from Northwestern and tied Notre Dame 7–7. The Sailors outscored their 1918 opponents 138–27; seven points of the Sailor total came in remarkable fashion against the U.S. Naval Academy in a game played early in the Fall at Annapolis.

Navy led Great Lakes 6–0 late in the game and was on the verge of going in for a wrap-up touchdown from the 10. But the Middies' Bill Ingram fumbled, and the Sailors' Harry Eilson, who would someday be the mayor of Springfield, Illinois, recovered and began a long trek toward the Navy goal. The field appeared open for future Mayor Eilson. But as he passed the Navy bench, a Middie reserve named Billy Saunders arose, zipped onto the field and tackled Harry. Referee Harry R. Heneage (Dartmouth) did not whistle the play dead. Eilson's teammates unpeeled Saunders, so the touchdown run could be completed. That's one version.

Football historian Rube Samuelson reported "The officials decided to give the ball to Great Lakes after penalizing Navy half the distance to the goal. But Captain Edward Walter Eberle (superintendent at Annapolis) came down onto the field on the double (and said), 'I don't care what the rules are. I'm running things at the Academy and I say that's a Great Lakes touchdown'."

Halas chuckles when reminded about the play. With good reason. After the TD, however it came, George's glue-like buddy Blacklock, the kicking pride of the old Michigan Aggies, plopped home the extra point for a 7–6 Great Lakes victory.

With somewhat more ease, the Sailors that year also defeated a team called Radio, and more recognizable institutions such as Illinois, Iowa, Rutgers and Purdue—all, but Rutgers, by shutouts.

The Tournament of Roses folks had no difficulty determining which was the best service team East of the Rockies. They were rather confused, however, about who was the pride of the Western military football establishment.

In the 1918 Rose Bowl game, the Marines from Mare Island in Vallejo in Northern California had wiped up the Army lads from Camp Lewis in Washington, 19–7. The Marines were buoyed in that contest by three players who had appeared in Oregon uniforms in the 1917 Bowl. But by the 1919 game, the Mare Island cast was different, although its record still was unblemished. The Marines had been 5–0 in the 1917 season and 10–0 including playoffs, in 1918. Their second-year club was peopled by some fine players from Washington State's 1916 Rose Bowl team. W. H. "Lone Star" Dietz, coached both the WSU and Marine bowlers in 1916 and 1919 but was not the first to run two different clubs in Pasadena. Hugo Bezdek coached Pennsylvania in the 1917 game and Mare Island in 1918, and would return on January 1, 1923, to direct yet a third Rose Bowl entry, Penn State.

All this esoterica aside, the Mare Island Marines were somewhat handicapped coming into the 1919 New Year's classic. They had to survive an elimination series to reach Pasadena. This hardly seemed fair since Mare Island was so dominating (and unscored upon) during the regular season. In the elimination playoff round, which also included teams from Mather Field, San Diego Submarine Base, Rockwell Field, San Pedro Submarine Base, and Balboa Park Navy, the Marines were still dominating, albeit inclined to give up points. Lone Star's lads romped past Mather 32–14 and Balboa Park 12–7. In that latter game, on Christmas Day, 1918, a few Marines were injured, and, furthermore, Mare Island's team captain, Dick Hanley, was abed with pneumonia by New Year's Day.

Still, Halas recalls that the Sailors had a great deal of respect for the Marines. "Any team that goes through its regular season without giving up a point and winning all its games has to be feared. And frankly, when the Rose Bowl game started I was a little scared because Mare Island had such a great reputation."

The Sailors arrived in Pasadena ten days before the game, after an uneventful railroad trip. But Halas remembers the first few days in the West. "I kept getting headaches," he said. "And so did a few other fellows on our team. I don't know if it was the hot weather—you know, the change of climate—or what. But those damned headaches just wouldn't go away for nearly a week."

As a patriotic gesture, the Tournament of Roses committee gave free seats to about

10,000 servicemen; another 15,000 paid. And Paddy Driscoll, the Naval "Wasp," gave the latter group its money's worth.

He, as they say, "did it all" in the 17–0 Great Lakes victory. The Sailor quarterback, Driscoll, punted for 260 yards (a 43.3 average), returned kicks for 115 yards, rushed for 34, passed for 77 (including a touchdown), drop-kicked a 30-yard field goal, and caught a pass that set up a second quarter touchdown to give the Sailors a 10–0 lead.

Driscoll's scoring pass was a 32-yarder to Halas. "It was a play we'd used all season," said the receiver. "I was completely in the clear . . . We had a fast team and that helped us in the Rose Bowl on punt coverage and kick return plays. I had pretty good speed myself. The only reason I didn't go out for the track team when I was at Illinois was because I was playing football, basketball, and baseball, and needed a rest sometime."

Halas' big play in Pasadena was not his touchdown reception. The maneuver that doubtless earned him MVP distinction was a 72-yard pass interception runback in the fourth quarter.

"On defense," said Halas, "I had a way of dropping back four or five yards from my end position whenever I could see a pass play coming. And that's what happened this

George Halas, in 1937, instructing his Chicago Bears. Named Player of the Game in the 1919 Rose Bowl, he still holds the game record for the longest non-scoring pass interception return (77 yards). It was set in the Great Lakes' 17-0 victory over the Mare Island Marines.

time." He picked off the ball on the Sailors' 20 and rambled all the way to the Mare Island 3, before Jim Blewett nailed him from behind.

"I should have scored a touchdown with that interception," Halas insists now. "And that play taught me something: from then on, anytime I'd get within the 5, I'd dive for the end zone. You can't take touchdowns for granted. No sir."

Halas still maintains that Driscoll was "so outstanding all day long" that Paddy deserved the MVP nod. "I'll never understand, I'll never know why they picked me."

True, Driscoll's field goal had given the Sailors a 3–0 edge in the first quarter, after his punting had put the Marines in a hole. True, too, Driscoll's pass reception set up the 10–0 touchdown in the second quarter. And of course he passed to Halas for the final score.

But Halas impressed the proper people. Wrote Rose Bowl historian Maxwell Stiles, "The Great Lakes right end was one of the most superb players ever seen in the Pasadena gridiron classic. His work in getting down under punts and dropping the safety man in his tracks has never been exceeded."

There was one punt in the game, though, that eluded Halas down the years. The Rose Bowl record listings show a 72-yard punt in the 1919 game by a Great Lakes player named E.J. Abrahamson.

"Well," said Halas, "I remember all the fine punting Paddy did that day. But a 72-yard punt? No, I don't recall that one.

"Abrahamson? I don't recall an Abrahamson."

So much has happened. So many games.

STURDY SONS
AND GAMBLERS

When the Tournament of Roses football committee announced somewhat tardily on December 2, 1921, the identity of the Eastern foe it had selected to face the University of California's alleged "Wonder Team" in the holiday game a month later, San Francisco sports editor Jack James applied acid to typewriter and observed, "All I know about Washington and Jefferson is that they're both dead."

The citizens of Washington, Pennsylvania, who knew a bit more about Washington and Jefferson than James, did, however, share his surprise over the college's selection to a game of by-now growing national import. This surprise was reflected in a special testimonial booklet, bound in rich red leather, published by the community early in 1922. The text was *"A Testimonial to the Players, Coaches, Management of W&J College."* In it, editor A.C. Hamilton pointed out with a cheery, archaic touch, "When W&J was first approached . . . regarding a trip to California, Red and Black authorities scarcely could credit the truth of the development. When the long journey finally was started on December 24, it seemed almost impossible to realize that the gridiron representatives of an institution that boasts of a few less than five hundred students was on its way to the Tournament of Roses to uphold Eastern football prestige . . . The team, regardless of the odds against them and ignoring the poor esteem in which they were held by their opponents and the latter's supporters, went into the contest with a determination and a courage that have never been surpassed by a football team anywhere." Hamilton called them "the Pennsylvania gridiron pilgrims . . . sturdy sons." They were gamblers, too.

Thunderstorms on a Summer Saturday had driven Ralph Vince off the Canterbury Country Club golf course and into the men's grill at the suburban Cleveland club. He is seventy-six years old in July, 1976, the senior partner of a law firm with thirty-six attorneys and a former Cuyohoga County municipal judge. He's quite familiar with the 1922 Rose Bowl, having been the right guard for those Pennsylvania gridiron pilgrims.

Vince played high school football in Martin's Ferry, Ohio, and matriculated at W&J "because, very frankly, I had no money and I didn't know whether someday I'd have to walk home from college. Washington and Jefferson was only twenty-five miles away. Not too far away to walk." Vince's father worked in the coal mines and mills of that corner of Ohio. "That was the kind of background most of us had in those days," he said. "We were a pretty tight-knit group. I wouldn't say there wasn't a little bickering, but as a whole we all got along. We thought we could handle ourselves on the football field. When we got out to California and heard that everybody was betting on California, most of us players went ahead and bet everything we had on ourselves. We had waited until almost the day of the game because we were hoping to get twenty-one points. But as game time neared and we couldn't get the twenty-one, most of us went ahead and took fourteen. I don't think the coach knew we were betting on ourselves. Not that we were cocky, but we felt pretty good about ourselves. We felt we could handle most any situation."

Upon graduation, these pilgrims (the team's actual nickname was, what else, Presidents) might have succeeded grandly as professional gamblers.

The situation the Presidents had to handle in Pasadena was named the University of California Golden Bears, a team that during the 1920 and 1921 seasons had a record of 18–0, outscoring its opponents 822–47. One of those victories was a 28–0 demolition of favored Ohio State, in the 1921 Pasadena game. The "wonder team" sobriquet seemed appropriate, and its coach, Andy Smith, was, at least in statistical terms, a

University of California coach Andy Smith, producer of the so-called "Wonder Teams." His team played a scoreless tie with underdog Washington and Jefferson, in the 1922 Rose Bowl.

non-pareil. In the years 1920–24 his teams were 44–0–4, one of those ties occurring against the good old Red and Black from little Washington, Pennsylvania.

Lee Cranmer, one of Smith's guards in that superlative era, said of his coach, "Andy knew football so thoroughly and his rival coaches so completely that in his blackboard talks and lectures before any specific game he would tell us just what to expect. He never missed."

One of those rivals, Dr. John W. Wilce, coach of the 1921 Rose Bowl game loser, Ohio State, paid homage to Smith some thirty years later. "Andy brought to a rugby-steeped West Coast, then relatively backward in football, a brilliance of all-around coaching know-how, which, combined with the great Coast material, left an indelible record in the total annals of football," wrote Wilce.

"Our 1920 team was the best," said Cranmer. "It had the fire and inspiration of youth . . . the most wonderful collective team spirit that ever existed on a football field. We were all for one and one for all while we were playing football. The difference between our 1920 and 1921 teams was that, in 1920 we knew we were good, that we had the stuff, and we were out to demonstrate it. And we listened to everything Andy would tell us. In 1921, we knew we were good, and pretty darn good—so good we sometimes felt we knew about everything there was to know of football, so Andy had his troubles."

Not long before the 1921 Pasadena win over OSU, Coach Smith was as sanguine as Cranmer and the other players. In selecting his All-Coast team, Smith named his entire first string. "We have no weak cog," he said. "I doubt if California could be improved by substituting a man from any other Coast team."

Most definitely beyond substitution was Smith's classic end, Brick Muller, whom Buckeye coach Wilce deified as "a football immortal."

"A young giant," Grantland Rice dubbed the 6′2″, 215-pound Muller,—an end who could pass with great distance and accuracy and was a sprinter and Olympic high jumper, besides. But he earned his fame throwing the football. "It is probably true," wrote Joe Williams of the *New York Post* in 1930, "that Muller could throw a football farther and with a flatter trajectory than any other player the game has ever seen." Berkeley's strapping redhead was an obvious choice on the all-time, all-America team selected by *Collier's* magazine in 1946.

"The best man I ever saw put on a football suit," said Gloomy Gus Henderson, coach at USC in the Twenties. "If Walter Camp had seen the 1921 Rose Bowl, he would have picked Muller for *both* ends. On defense he often played eight yards back of the line, yet was so fast he always tackled the ball carrier before he crossed the line of scrimmage. He is head and shoulders over any player in the United States and is one of the best tacklers I have ever seen. And he has no peer as a pass receiver."

Yet it was Muller's fate before the meeting with W&J in the 1922 game to come down with a bad case of carbuncles and boils. He did play, but with less than gargantuan distinction. No matter, for Muller had already enjoyed his share of Pasadena history on a single play in the second quarter of the 1921 meeting with Ohio State. The

California end Brick Muller,
the West's first all-America.

Buckeyes were 8–5 favorites, but trailed 7–0 as Cal kept driving. The Bears were on State's 37 when Muller did his thing. Rube Samuelsen characterized the next play as "one of the most debated in football history." Well, interesting anyway.

Immediately after the preceding play, Cal fullback Archie Nisbet pretended to be hurt. "The spot where the big fullback lay prone," wrote Samuelsen, "was the center of a makeshift California line, mapped strictly according to plan. It had been secretly rehearsed time and again in practice. Helping to build the surprise factor, Muller purposely strayed out of position in backfield territory, while Latham, the center, stood at the end of the line where Muller belonged. Then, without warning and before time could be taken out, Nisbet leaped to his feet, centered the ball, and passed it back to halfback Pesky Sprott."

Meanwhile, end Brodie Stephens "ran lickety-split down field."

Sprott lateraled deep in the backfield to Muller. Standing on his own 47, Brick prepared to throw long.

State's all-America halfback Pete Stinchcomb, a safety on defense, "was taking in the drama as an unperturbed onlooker," witnessed Samuelsen. "As Stephens sped by, Pete quipped, as though the Bear end was acting plain silly: 'Just where do you think you're going?'

"Stephens had better than a casual idea because, a few yards beyond, he turned for a look. The timing was perfect. Muller had let fly a rousing, low-trajectory pass—53 yards—straight into Stephens' arms on the goal line! . . . . After the game, when asked why he didn't cover Stephens more closely, Pete replied sadly, 'I simply didn't believe anybody could throw the ball that far.' "

The Buckeyes were down 14–0 and finished. As was, until the 1947 game, the Big Ten Conference, which had no interest in further embarrassment at the hands of those Western upstarts. By the time the Big Ten had contracted for an annual meeting with the Coast champ, the embarrassment was ready to be fitted on the other foot.

Now, with the mighty Buckeyes and the dazed Big Ten summarily dismissed, the "wonder team" was, in late fall of 1921, curious about the identity of its next Pasadena victim.

Yale was initially considered—until it lost to Harvard in "The Game" of 1921. Other possible Cal foes were Iowa, Cornell, Lafayette, Penn State, and little Centre College down in Danville, Kentucky.

Centre's Praying Colonels, now celebrated for upsetting Harvard, chose instead to play a holiday game in San Diego, which had tentative thoughts of upstaging Pasadena.

For one reason or another, the possibilities eliminated themselves. Thus, the pilgrims from Pennsylvania.

"We finished undefeated that season," said Vince as the rain kept socking the windows of the Canterbury men's grill, "and then we got an invitation to play up at the University of Detroit, which also was unbeaten. But our Detroit alumni didn't want us to go up there because they thought Detroit had a bunch of pros and were too tough and would beat us. I guess, though, the school needed money, and Detroit had offered a good guarantee. So we went up there and played them. Now, just before that game, we were told we had an invitation to go to the Rose Bowl—but in order to go we had to win the Detroit game. We were somewhat skeptical of the California rumor. We thought it was a ruse to get us to play well. In any event, it worked. We beat Detroit 14–2. They gained only 21 yards against us. Then we found out the invitation to California was valid."

When folks on the West Coast heard W&J was coming they were incredulous. Sports writers called the Presidents' eleven "Willie and Jake," and needling names such as that.

W&J sent out a sixteen-man squad; only eleven of them played. Among the starters was a black quarterback, Charles West—quite a rarity then. He didn't start every regular season game but played frequently as the Presidents went 10–0, outscoring their foes 222–33 and numbering among their victims such Eastern "names" as Carnegie Tech, Syracuse, Pittsburgh and West Virginia. From one opponent, Bethany, West endured racial abuse.

"He was a fine gentleman," said Vince of his black teammate. "But some of the other teams gave him a hard time. If I recall correctly, Bethany had imported two or three Southerners, from Texas, because in those days, you know, they did a good job of proselytizing just as they do today. In that Bethany game they were abusing West something awful. They kept yelling, 'Send the boogie through here; send him into the line.' All that kinda stuff. Now in this particular game he didn't touch the ball for about a quarter and a half. And we were in a scoreless tie. But then when we gave him the ball for the first time, he ran seventy yards for a touchdown. I don't know," and Vince laughed, "whether he ran that fast or that far out of fright or what. Bethany was bounced 14–0. If I recall, the rest of us were pretty protective of him, treated him like anybody else. He played poker with us and everything. And we thought very well of him."

However, the most highly considered President, at least by the outside football world, was the captain and tackle, Russell F. Stein, who later became an All-America. "While he may or may not be the greatest in the country," wrote Frank F. O'Neill in the *New York Sun* early in 1922, "it is certain there are few men of greater value to their respective teams. It is safe to say that few teams ever had a more versatile player. Although listed as a tackle, the leader of the Presidents is a four-position man. He plays offensive end and halfback as well as tackle, and roves at will behind the line on defense. His fierce tackling and remarkable skill as a diagnostician render him doubly valuable . . . Stein is gifted with a football brain."

But Vince said that he and many of his teammates held Stein in somewhat less esteem. "I think if you were able to talk to the other ten fellas you'd find out we didn't think he was anywhere near as good (as his publicity) and wasn't qualified as an

---

All-America. He was not the leader nor the best player on our team. If you check the records of that Rose Bowl, you'll find that the only two first downs made by California in the game were made running through our left tackle, Stein. Then he was offside on our touchdown run. And he missed four field goal attempts. Let me add this: I was just one of the players. I was not one of the stars. I played every minute of every game (at guard), but I was not a star. So it's not me against Stein. No jealousy. But I want it known that we did have some great players on that team: Hal Erickson was a great halfback; Chet Weiderquist, who played tackle alongside of me, was terrific; Joe Basista was a great linebacker; Wayne Brenkert, a halfback, was a good runner and good passer."

(In mid-1976, seven of the eleven W&J bowl game starters were still alive, and Vince, who had become a trustee of the college, was planning a reunion gathering in Pasadena —"we have 'em every five years." Erickson and Stein, who had become sheriff of Trumbull County, Ohio, had passed away by that time. This was true, too, for their coach, the interesting Greasy Neale, who came to W&J via a football career at West Virginia Wesleyan and the outfield of the Cincinnati Reds, and who, in the mid-1940s, would coach the Philadelphia Eagles into a professional football championship. In 1921, though, Neale was merely a rookie college coach and seen as no match whatsoever for Cal's Andy Smith.)

"I can remember the first day Greasy became our coach," said Vince. "We opened practice on September first and he didn't show up until September tenth because he'd been playing baseball. Well, that first day he came in we could have killed him because he almost killed us. It was the most brutal practice, and we had thought we were in pretty good shape. But Greasy was a great conditioner, a great strategist, a great motivator. He was lousy, though, on fundamentals, but he had a good line coach on fundamentals."

While the Golden Bears were working out in Pasadena, Neale and his Presidents were still entrained westward. Greasy was in no rush. "He had the idea," said Vince, "that Ohio State had gone out there too early the previous year and that the California weather had sapped their strength. So we didn't arrive until the Friday night before the Monday game." (The actual date of the 1922 Rose Bowl was January 2; when New Year's Day falls on a Sunday the game always is switched to January 2. Trivia fans might be able to win bets on such minutiae.) "Greasy put us through only two light workouts; he said he didn't want us to be sapped by the heat. And the fact that we played the whole game with only eleven men proved his point. And not only that. You'll find out the two California first downs came just before the end of the first half. They had no first downs in the second half. The point is, we didn't get any weaker as the game went along."

Not in the rain they didn't. For several days before the game, in fact for much of December, 1921, Pasadena was pelted by rain. Many of Cal's practice sessions were washed out. Wet field or dry, the Bears were expected to prevail effortlessly. As one California sports writer noted, "The score will depend upon the condition of the field

Monday. On a dry field California would have defeated Stanford this season close to 100 to 0 (the actual score was 42–7). The Bears travel best on firm footing. They showed in the Oregon game, however, that they can play in the rain (39–0). So let 'er come. When you have a fighter like Dempsey or a football team like California, it doesn't really matter how good the other fellows are, does it?"

Vince recalls that the rain stopped by parade time. "I remember we were privileged to witness the parade for a little while," he said. "It wasn't raining then and it didn't rain the rest of the day."

During the storm the night before the game, some of the old football types, including the legendary Walter Eckersall, plus some writers, among them columnist Warren Brown, got together for a bull session in a suite in the Hotel Green. Cal coach Smith walked over from the Hotel Maryland to join them.

At one point, Brown remembers, Smith stuck his head out the window of the hotel suite, brushed off the dampness and said, to no one in particular, "We'll kick. The score will be nothing to nothing."

Judge Vince said Neale was a superstitious leader of men, "just like a lot of athletes are. He always wanted to have his team on the field first. And we did get there first that day. But then when California came out, Muller went down to the other end of the field and started throwing the ball 67 yards." (Brick astonished the Buckeyes with a similar display in pre-game exertions a year earlier.) "I think Muller was doing that for psychological effect," said the old W&J guard. "I don't know whether we were too dumb or too cocky or what. But remember, we just couldn't be intimidated."

Vince said the field "wasn't as bad as people made it out to be. It was muddy, certainly, but it wasn't impossible." Samuelsen suggests the tormented turf "was close to [a] quagmire," an apparently accurate appraisal when one considers that the athletes are so busy playing the game they have only minimal perception of the conditions. (Another example was an Indiana-Wisconsin game played in a Godawful blizzard in Madison in the early 1950s. Spectators could barely see the ghost-like forms on the field. Afterwards, several Indiana players said they'd never had so much fun in their lives —"the snow was no trouble at all.")

Added to Neale's bent for superstition was his penchant for calling the plays from the bench.

"Greasy wore a light-colored, broad-brimmed hat, and a cream-colored polo coat, so we could identify him easily on the sidelines," said Vince. "Herb Kopf, an end, would look over at Greasy from the huddle to get signals. Then once in a while, so it wouldn't be too obvious, somebody else would look. But there were no defensive signals coming from the bench. In those days it wasn't the sophisticated game it is now. It was pretty much of a set defense, and, God bless you, you better take care of your own territory."

The Golden Bears knew what was going on but didn't have Charlie Dressen, or anyone else, around to help them steal signs.

Neale's lads were as puckish as they were deceptive. "Greasy introduced something new to Western gridirons," adjudged Samuelsen. "Heckling, the barbed insult, any distracting caper—something that had been a part of baseball strategy for years."

For example, Stein asked Cal halfback Don Nichols—as the Bears were setting for a play—if he had an uncle in Pittsburgh. The signals were being called as Nichols tried to remember if he indeed did have an uncle, or perhaps even a cousin, in Pittsburgh. He told Stein he didn't, all the while losing track of the game.

When Muller entered in the second quarter—"apparently the idea was," surmised Vince, "that he was going to demoralize us"—the Presidents heckled him supremely.

"We thought we'd kid him a little bit," Vince glows. "Because we weren't going to let him intimidate us. No, sir. So most of us wiped our muddy hands on him as soon as he got on the field. You know how a thing like that goes: one guy starts it and everybody follows."

In his book, *Bowl Game Thrills,* Joseph Bell provides this possibly part-fictive account of the Muller muddying: "As Brick moved to his end position to await the signals, Stein stood up opposite him, stuck out his hand and said, 'So this is the great Brick Muller. I want you to know that we are deeply impressed. May I introduce myself. My name is Russ Stein.'

"Muller, who had been watching the [earlier] byplay from the sidelines, was expecting something like this, but, even expecting it, he was taken aback. He hesitated, then grudgingly put out his hand. Russ looked down at his own proffered hand and said, 'My, oh my, but my hand is dirty. Excuse me a moment.'

"With elaborate politeness, he wiped his muddy hands on Muller's clean jersey, then shook Muller's hand warmly. Kopf took his lead from Stein. . . . One by one the other W&J players followed suit . . . When they finished, Muller's spotless white uniform was as black as their own. Muller, too bewildered at first to break away, and then too angry, put up with the charade to the end."

Until Muller's second-quarter arrival, the Presidents had dominated the game. "Washington and Jefferson flashed a superior brand of football at the start," recounted the *New York Times.* "The Presidents received the kickoff at their 25-yard line and marched straight down the field to the California 35 without relinquishing the ball."

Halfback Wayne Brenkert, a wispy lad out of Detroit, then swept end, reversed his field and went in for the TD. Nice 35-yard run. But Stein had jumped offside, which negated the only touchdown threat of the entire first quarter, first half, and game.

"The first thing I thought about when Wayne got in the end zone was that he might have stepped out of bounds. But then it turned out Russ was offside," reflected Vince gloomily.

The game quickly evolved into a punting battle, with Cal's Archie Nisbet usually booting on first down. The "wonder team" was being a cautious team against the obviously competent fourteen-point underdogs. W&J moved the ball but, as the man from the *Times* reported, "seemed to lack the punch" to take it in.

In the second half, the Presidents fumbled early. Cal moved to the W&J 28—its deepest penetration. But then the Bears fumbled. And so it went. Stein kept missing field goals, Cal kept punting.

"California was wholly on the defensive, except for a period near the close of the fourth quarter," said the *Times*. "The Bears' forwards rushed Brenkert so fast on his punt that the ball went almost straight up in the air and out of bounds on the W&J 22-yard line. It looked as if a break that might win for California had come and the California rooters, with a mighty roar, called for a touchdown. California then essayed a forward pass (Muller to Toomey) in a desperate effort to snatch the victory. Toomey caught the ball back of his scrimmage line, but as he seized it he was tackled so hard by two W&J men, who hurled him back five yards, that the ball fell from his arms. Erickson picked it up and ran to his 22 and California's only chance was lost."

Playing a scoreless tie is never having to say you're sorry. But all-time All-America Walter Eckersall of Chicago, the game's field judge, said the Bears used "poor judgment" in not trying field goals in the final seconds of the first half and in those dying moments of the game. "California should have known it could not penetrate its opponent's strong defense," said Eckersall, who also pointed out that one of Stein's field goal attempts, from the 45, was "a desperate chance."

The Presidents had won a moral victory, not to mention their bets, but, in the eyes of Vince, "thought we should have won. I don't mean we were robbed by the call back of that touchdown run, but we thought we had the better team and that we outplayed them. Whether we did have the better team or not, I don't know, because California did have a helluva ball club."

Southern Cal coach "Gloomy" Gus Henderson allowed as how W&J "played the best brand of football of any of the Eastern teams that have been seen in action in the annual New Year's Day tussle." Gloomy Gus had his date wrong but his assessment right.

"The wet field handicapped Smith's men," said Henderson, "and made his difficult plays and passing impossible. On a dry field the story might have been different, yet I think Erickson would still be of All-America caliber on a dry field, and W&J's tackling would have been just as effective. My hat is off to a coach who can bring his team three thousand miles and put up such a wonderful brand of football without using a single substitution."

"We set four records that day that still stand," said Vince. "Cal didn't complete a pass, had only two first downs, gained just 49 yards, and we played with only eleven men. Those are records, sir."

When Neale's team returned to Washington, Pennsylvania, "we were received by a big crowd that had a big dinner for us," said Vince. "It was a big event for a little town and a small school." He didn't have to worry about ever having to walk back to Martin's Ferry.

OF HORSEMEN
AND MULES

If you want celebrities, welcome to the 1925 Rose Bowl, a veritable month-long guest list for Johnny Carson, a sixty-minute Hall of Fame, a boggling stroll down memory lane. The great Scorekeeper in the sky would be so busy recording their names that He would, in fact, truly not care whether they won or lost—or even how they played the game.

They merit slow rolling off the typewriter. Singly. No commas.

Ernie Nevers. Knute Rockne. Glenn "Pop" Warner. The Four Horsemen: Harry Stuhldreher. Don Miller. Jim Crowley. Elmer Layden. *Those* Four Horsemen. Then, Adam Walsh. Walter Eckersall. Even Walter Camp, the All-America maker. And, the least-sung unsung hero of sports history, one Harold Anderson, a Stanford student who figured out how to clear the Rose Bowl parking lot of 20,000 automobiles within two hours (it had taken until midnight after previous games) by the brilliant method of using chalk lines to mark all exits.

Everybody seemed to be there except Jim Thorpe and The Gipper, O.J. and Archie Griffin, Woody Hayes and Red Grange.

The '25 game was, when you get right down to it, not the eleventh Rose Bowl but the first Super Bowl.

Ernie Nevers would have been the right person to tell the story of this game, because even though his Stanford team had been beaten by the Irish and the Horsemen 27–10, Ernie appeared to most onlookers the star of the contest. But he died the week he was to have granted the interview.

"Perhaps his most courageous performance," memorialized the obit writer for the *San Francisco Chronicle,* "came against Notre Dame's Four Horsemen in the Rose

Bowl on January 1, 1925. Although casts had been removed from two broken ankles only ten days earlier, he carried the ball 34 times for 114 yards against Knute Rockne's great team. He was the Stanford offense. But his team couldn't match the Horsemen. He also played the whole game on defense. Nevers' creed was: If you go, go all the way."

Ernie, who stalwartly never made a big deal out of his sports successes (if you'd ask specific questions, you'd get specific answers), once said that his coach, Pop Warner, "told me I was going to start in that Rose Bowl game. So that was that. They'd made an aluminum cast for one of my broken ankles. They used tape and an inner tube of an automobile stretched from my foot to the knee. Ten days before the game the cast came off, and I played."

"No one," wrote Walter Eckersall for the *Chicago Tribune,* "not even Coach Warner, expected Ernie to play through the entire game."

"What a game Nevers played," enthused Rockne.

"No one on the field today performed more brilliantly than Nevers," reported the *Associated Press.* "Except on the one occasion when he was halted on the eight-inch line, the Notre Dame line was unable to stop his terrific smashes that carried the force of every ounce of his two hundred pounds."

Stanford star Ernie Nevers, left, and his famous coach, Glenn S. "Pop" Warner. They were humbled by Notre Dame in the 1925 game, 27-10.

Pop Warner had coached Jim Thorpe at Carlisle, and Warner testified Ernie Nevers was "a better player than Thorpe because he always tries to do his best."

Ernie came from Minnesota with his blond Nordic brawn to play football at Santa Rosa High School, in California. The team was new and its coach a novice, so Ernie diagrammed the plays. Switched from line to fullback, he moved over to Stanford. Later he played for the Duluth Eskimos, the Chicago Cardinals of the NFL and the St. Louis Browns of the American baseball League, for whom he pitched, giving up two of Babe Ruth's sixty home runs in 1927.

Bob Reynolds, the fine Stanford tackle of the mid-1930s who played every minute of three consecutive Rose Bowl games, remembered that Ernie "was our backfield coach in my sophomore season. I recall a few guys on our team saying, 'He doesn't look so big. He doesn't look so tough.' And I guess Ernie must have been in his early thirties then. He would show our punters how to punt, and time after time after time he'd punt it 60 yards with ease. And our punters were struggling to come within a country mile of him. After that, we were a bit more respectful toward him.

"Our whole team went to see him play in an all-star game in Kezar Stadium, in San Francisco, one year. I think it was his team against a Red Grange team. Ernie kicked off, did all the passing, kicked all the extra points, did all the punting, and played fullback on offense and linebacker on defense. His club won before a packed house. All of us to a man said to ourselves: now we know why he was one of the greatest football players to come out of anywhere.

"He also was one of the most self-effacing men I've ever seen. And always a gentleman. He would never get personal. One of the greatest guys I ever met."

Nevers.

Adam Walsh, Knute Rockne's classic center, called his coach "about as close to the perfect man as anyone I have ever known." Walsh said that in 1968, and, presumably, with the wisdom of years, was discerning of people.

The morning after Rockne's plane went down in Kansas in the Spring of 1931, John Kieran of the *New York Times* suggested Rockne "was far bigger" than football. "He was a national figure. He appealed to the imagination of the country. He was a leader and a builder. He was a clear thinker and a fine speaker. He had the salt of keen wit. He was an inspiring force."

Pop Warner termed Rockne "the greatest football coach of all time." That eminence was reached via Norway, Chicago and South Bend. Knute Kenneth Rockne's father was a carriage builder who brought his five-year-old son with him from Voss, Norway, when he displayed his wares at the World's Fair, in Chicago, in the 1890s. Knute grew up in a neighborhood of Irish and Scandinavian immigrants and played sandlot football. His idol was Eckersall, a prep hero on the other side of town. Rockne would sneak into the University of Chicago stadium to watch Eckersall play for Amos Alonzo Stagg. But his early bent was more toward middle distance track than football.

Rockne didn't reach Notre Dame until he was in his early twenties; he had to work for four years after high school, arriving in South Bend, he recalled, "with a suitcase and a thousand dollars. I'd hardly seen more than two trees at one time anywhere, so the first impression on me was the sylvan beauty of the campus . . . but I felt the strangeness of being a lone Norse Protestant—if the word must be used—an invader of a Catholic stronghold. There were 400 undergraduates, in 1910, physical training was compulsory, and a fellow wasn't thought much of unless he went out to try and make his dormitory football team."

Song, story, and movie have seemingly established Rockne as the man who (1) introduced football to Notre Dame and (2) invented the forward pass, with the help of Irish teammate Gus Dorais. But, as the *New York Sun*'s George Trevor advised, "Football was a year old at South Bend when Rockne was born in 1888" and "the forward pass, incorporated into American football in 1906, was old stuff by the time Dorais began pitching to Rockne in 1913. . . . If Eastern football authorities had never heard of Notre Dame before the Irish exploded that barrage of passes against Army in 1913, it was because the smug Brahmins of the Atlantic coastal sectors never bothered to look beyond the Allegheny Mountain barrier."

Today's smug Easterners are thus informed nothing ever changes.

Rockne, a brilliant student of chemistry and the classics, became an assistant coach after graduation. He was head coach from 1918 until his death, at forty-three, in the Kansas plane crash.

"When Rock first took charge of Notre Dame football," wrote Kieran, in 1931, "the team had no such financial resources as it has now. He had to be coach, trainer, rubber, ticket taker, baggage master and financial secretary. He did everything, and this included blowing up the footballs with which the boys played. . . . The boys worshipped Rock. To those who didn't know him personally, these things should be testimony to his fine character. Year after year, great squads of boys passed through his hands and went out into the world. All of them were convinced Rock was a great leader, a great man, and a great friend. They were, and are, ready to fight for that proposition at any time, and in any place."

Rockne was, said Kieran's colleague on the *Times,* Allison Danzig, "erudite and cultured, intense and emphatic."

And always, in his own mind, a bit out of place. "A lone Norwegian, always mistakenly dubbed a Swede, had difficulties among so many Hibernians," Rockne wrote in *Collier's,* in 1930. "But these were largely dissipated when, blushing furiously, I was called on to talk at a football rally and having heard somebody call somebody else just a dumb Irishman, I had the good fortune to remark: 'There's only one thing dumber than a dumb Irishman.' Before the bricks could fly, I explained: 'A smart Swede.' "

Rockne.

Grantland Rice believed Rockne "came along at a time when football coaching was at its peak in both class and color. . . . I have no intention of trying to tell you that Rockne was the greatest coach of all time. Rock, of course, was *one* of the greatest—

Knute Rockne lectures his team on the practice field at South Bend.

but I doubt if there was anyone good enough to wear the undisputed crown. Pop Warner wasn't far away. The great inventor of plays, including the single and double-wing attacks, for thirty years at Stanford, Warner was always the coach to beat."

"Warner was not the magnetic, vibrant personality that was Knute Rockne," wrote Allison Danzig, "but he was a dominant, forceful leader of men . . . contemplative, deliberative, a tinkerer who worked on car engines—dismantling them and then putting them back together again. He was one of the two most fertile and original minds football has known—the other being Amos Alonzo Stagg. Warner was preeminently a creator, and his fame is secure as one of the trailblazers who led football out of the wilderness of massed, close-order, push-and-pull play and into the open game of speed, deception and brains that is so much more worthy a pastime for college youth. His was one of the more intelligent and visionary minds that helped to bring about the evolution of football from a mere physical test of unimaginative brute strength to a contest of skill, in which the college youth was given the chance to show that there was something underneath his long hair, besides a skull."

Warner, they all said, put finesse and mobility into the game with his single and double wings. No more was the game a series of center plunges. Warner spewed out reverses, fakes, spinners, flankers, and unbalanced lines.

And Pop was as protean as Rockne. Warner had lettered in football, baseball, boxing and track at Cornell. He sold his own watercolors (mostly landscapes). He took a degree in law; but his entire adult life was spent in coaching college football—Cornell, Georgia, Carlisle, Pittsburgh, Stanford, and Temple. His best team, he said, was the 1916 Pitt club. Warner, the aloof, somber tactician, coached from 1895 to 1939. Forever. He had three Rose Bowl teams (Stanford in 1925 and 1927–28) and was 1–1–1 in Pasadena. The team that lost to Notre Dame was the most historic. January 1, 1925, wrote Danzig, "is a date that should be encircled in red in football history. On that day the double wingback formation was used exclusively for the first time by a Warner team." But then, ten years later, in three different post-season games, the Warner system was used by the *losers* of the Rose and Sugar Bowls, and the East-West Game. The skulls under the long hair were finding new ways.

Warner.

"Outlined against a blue-gray October sky, the Four Horsemen rode again. In dramatic lore they are known as Famine, Pestilence, Destruction, and Death. These are only aliases. Their real names are Stuhldreher, Miller, Crowley and Layden." Grantland Rice was big on aliases, in 1924.

Rockne said the evolution of his Horsemen "is the story of an accident. How it came to pass that four young men so eminently qualified by temperament, physique, and instinctive pacing to complement one another perfectly and thus produce the best

Notre Dame's Four Horsemen. From the left, Don Miller, Elmer Layden, Jim Crowley, and Harry Stuhldreher.

coordinated and most picturesque backfield in the recent history of football—how that came about is one of the inscrutable achievements of coincidence, of which I know nothing save that it's a rather satisfying mouthful of words."

- QB—Harry Stuhldreher of Massillon, Ohio, 145 pounds.
- HB—Don Miller of Defiance, Ohio, 160.
- HB—Jimmy Crowley of Green Bay, Wisconsin, 160.
- FB—Elmer Layden of Davenport, Iowa, 162.

Rockne had seen them in freshman practice, in 1921. The coach believed the sleepy-eyed Crowley "looked as though he were built to be a tester in an alarm clock factory." Miller appeared "half puzzled by everything going on," said Rock. He found Stuhldreher's only assets to be "a sharp, handsome face, and a clear, commanding voice," while Layden "ran quite as often into the hands of tackles as through slits in the line."

The coach's appraisal: "Not so hot. This freshman bunch could be whipped into a combination of average players. Not much more."

Stuhldreher seemed, to Rockne, to have the most promise; Layden the most speed and kicking ability; Crowley the most humor; Miller the best bloodlines, for his brother was a 1909 Irish football hero named "Red."

In their sophomore season, the Horsemen saw service because Rockne had lost all but one of his veteran backs via graduation. So Harry played a little quarterback, Crowley and Layden a little left half, and Miller a great deal of right half.

Crowley became a regular in 1922 after a fine game against Purdue, and all four performed well in a victory over Georgia Tech. The veteran was injured, and all four started against Carnegie Tech. "These boys," wrote Rockne in *Collier's,* "surprised the football fans of Pittsburgh with their perfect timing, as they functioned for the first time as a unit backfield."

The rest, as they say, is the Apocalypse. In their three seasons, the Four Horsemen lost only two of thirty games (both to Nebraska in 1922–23). All had great moments individually in collegiate play. All ultimately became coaches. Layden and Crowley eventually became commissioners of two different professional leagues. Miller turned to the law and survived the others.

Rice gave them quite a ride. Without the aliases there would have been less distinction for people named simply Stuhldreher, Miller, Crowley, and Layden.

The Four Horsemen had their seven Mules—the alias of the Notre Dame line. The middle mule, the center, the team captain was all-America Adam Walsh, who, in 1922, had been told by a hot dog vendor in South Bend that he was too light to make the grade on the line and should try out for another position. Well, Walsh did play high school ball in Hollywood at only 132 pounds. Because his father had injured his sternum while playing at Duke, Walsh nearly was refused family permission to become a footballer. He had his cap set for Stanford, a yearly loan of three thousand dollars was promised by the school, but the Walshes were Irish-born and wanted Adam to attend a Catholic college. So he went East to play for "the Swede." He grew up to 195 pounds—perhaps from eating hot dogs.

Rockne once suggested Walsh was his "gamest" player, citing Adam's sixty minutes of play in the celebrated 1924 Army game. "I thought because he had five broken bones in his two hands that he would last ten minutes," said Rock.

Danzig called the Irish center "Apollo-like." Also business-like. Walsh and the Horsemen oversaw the program concession in the 1924 season and netted $1500 apiece. Pasadena spending money. Walsh was making the prodigal's return. Not only was Eckersall, the head linesman, watching him, but in the press box was Walter Camp; in the stands was Adam's father, who had not seen him play college ball previously, and on the field, in Stanford uniforms, several old teammates from Hollywood High.

Walsh. Eckersall. Camp. And outside making chalk marks in the parking lot, Harold Anderson.

Stanford was not a popular choice for the 1925 Bowl. There was heavy political pressure in Los Angeles for an invitation to USC. California and Stanford also had fine clubs but were tangling with the Trojans over an eligibility matter. Further, USC's Gloomy Gus Henderson was a Rockne buddy; so a match-up against Notre Dame was deemed fitting. But late in the 1924 season, USC lost to Cal, 7–0, and then to tiny St. Mary's, 14–0. The Irish opponent emerged from Stanford and Cal's annual "Big Game," which Stanford won, in effect, by tying 20–20 with two fourth-quarter TDs. The last came at the final gun. The latest of Andy Smith's "wonder teams" had been too confident because Stanford had played the game without the injured Nevers and another first-string back. But, the Indians would go to Pasadena for the holiday. Stanford's president was rather reluctant about his lads meeting the Irish on New Year's, for he felt Notre Dame was scholastically inferior. When Rockne heard the criticism, he nearly called off the game. Then a neatly planted wire service story (the work of a Rose Bowl publicist) talked about the law studies of the Four Horsemen, and Rock was soothed.

The Irish came slowly West. "We spent two weeks getting from South Bend to Pasadena," Jim Crowley recalled thirty-five years later. "Rockne got very irritable because he felt the players gorged themselves out of condition. We went by bus by way of New Orleans, Houston and Tucson, and everywhere we stopped people feted us. I remember at Houston we stuffed ourselves so much on oysters we couldn't move. Finally we got to Tucson, which was a cow town then. The Rock made us stay there a week. But he told us to be careful about reaching for a handkerchief or billfold in our pockets. He said somebody might interpret it as a draw, and we might get shot." Erudition.

Nevers had both ankles so heavily taped it was amazing his blood circulated. But Ernie was intent on playing; this would be his last game for Stanford, and then, too, he wanted a look at the Four Horsemen and Mules. Joseph N. Bell says that one day during the 1924 season, Ernie looked at that fabled publicity photo of the Four Horsemen in football togs on horses and told a teammate, "I'd like to play those guys someday, with or without the horses."

He had to wait a while, though, for Rockne opened the Bowl with his so-called "shock troops," a group of competent irregulars used much in the manner of a scouting party. Sub quarterback Eddie Scharer had been instructed "to call plays which I knew wouldn't work. . . . After two or three plays we would always be right where we started and forced to kick. The sportswriters never caught on either."

Apparently not, even though Rock had been employing this method consistently. The Associated Press account of the game reported, "The start was inauspicious for the Easterners. Coach Knute Rockne sent in his second-string men to open the game, but Stanford shoved them steadily down the field. . . ."

The Irish shock troops, playing with manifested conservatism, were showing Rockne the posture of Stanford on both offense and defense. And his first stringers on the sideline could observe the enemy in action without having to bash heads with them for a few minutes—much in the manner of a detective seeing his case on a stage, and then walking up and solving it.

But when the detectives did finally walk on stage this day, they played a little Keystone Kops first. In the initial Four Horsemen series, Miller fumbled, with Stanford tackle Charley Johnston recovering on the Irish 17.

Eckersall was covering the game for the *Chicago Tribune,* in addition to officiating. Or, maybe he had a ghost writer (or a typewriter and Western Union messenger on the sidelines). Anyway, he picks up the action after the fumble: "Nevers and Murray Cuddeback made 7 yards in three plays and then the latter dropped back to the visitors' 17 and, with quarterback Fred Solomon holding the ball, made a beautiful place kick. The strength of Stanford was seen as early as this score was made, and it was apparent Notre Dame was in for a busy afternoon." After the kickoff, the Irish got down to busy-ness. "Swift parries by Layden and Crowley, mixed with Stuhldreher's passes and bewildering plays, brought the Irish to Stanford's 9," wrote Rube Samuelsen, for years sports editor of the *Pasadena Star-News.* "Here the men of "Pop" Warner dug in and wrested the ball from Notre Dame on their own 10. But the exultation which swept over the Stanford crowd was short-lived. As Cuddeback attempted to kick out of danger, the ball squirted off his foot and out of bounds on Stanford's 32. It was the Irish opportunists' turn to cash in on a break."

Mistakes would be common in this game, and would turn it; Notre Dame was clearly more opportunistic than Stanford. Layden especially.

Crowley carried off tackle for thirteen yards, then Miller and Layden ran for a first down to the 7 as the first quarter ended. Ended, too, was Irish tackle Joe Bach's day; he was gone with broken ribs.

When play resumed, Crowley got four and Layden went in. It was 6–3 Notre Dame after Crowley's extra point attempt was blocked.

After an exchange of punts, including a 72 yarder by Layden, Nevers went to work

Notre Dame right halfback "Sleepy Jim" Crowley picks up yardage.

rushing. Stanford found itself on the Irish 31—fourth and six. "Then," said Rockne, "they called for this dangerous pass out into the flat zone."

Nevers was aiming for end Ted Shipkey, but Layden reached the ball first, batted it forward, caught it and ran down the sidelines to score. How far? Eckersall reported 85 yards; Samuelsen said 78; the Associated Press called it 70; Joe Hendrickson, in his book *The Tournament of Roses,* said 60. Even sports writing can provide a good object lesson in historiography.

Anyhow, it was a long touchdown run, with the pained Nevers not quite able to catch up with the thin, quick Layden. And the Irish led, 13–3, after Sleepy Jim's kick.

Here came Ernie again. Mostly on his rushes, Stanford moved to the Notre Dame 10. There sub end Jim Kelly fumbled, Walsh recovered, and the half expired. Walsh never could get over Ernie's durability. "Nevers was tremendous," the Notre Dame captain said forty-three years later. "He gained enough ground that day to win ten ball games. But it was between the 20 yard lines. I was black and blue for ten days from contact with him."

Crowley recalled that Rockne was not particularly inspirational in the locker room that day. But all seemed to be going well.

In the third period, Stanford's safety, Solomon, fumbled another of Layden's long, crashing punts deep in Indian territory. Ed Hunsinger, the Irish end who had blocked so well on Layden's touchdown sprint of undetermined length, picked up the fumble

---

on the Stanford 20 and, abetted by Crowley's drop kick, gave Notre Dame a 20–3 lead.

Writers used to wonder what the Four Horsemen "could do with a kicking game," said Rockne. "As if in direct response they put one on in the Rose Bowl. The entire team had wilted in the heat. The boys were unable to move. They had to rely on Layden's punting, not their usual game." But it was sufficient.

•

The kickoff, an aborted Stanford drive—again featuring Nevers (who also had been making three-fourths of the tackles on defense)—and an Irish mistake. Inside his 25, Stuhldreher passed. To Nevers! And Stanford now had the ball on the Notre Dame 29. Ernie and all-America end Jim Lawson, the Indian captain, in a series of rushes carried to the Notre Dame 3 (Eckersall), or 7 (Samuelsen) or 8 (AP). Probably, taking a consensus of other accounts, it was the 7. The Irish looked for another rush, which is why Ed Walker threw to Ted Shipkey over the right side and in the end zone. It was now, 20–10, and into the fourth quarter.

Again, Stuhldreher made a mistake, this time a pass attempt from inside his 30. "A tactical error," said Rockne. "We were ahead, yet Stuhldreher passed straight into the hands of a Stanford player. The fact is that Stuhldreher had hurt his foot, badly. We didn't know until the game was over that he had a broken bone and was suffering agony throughout the game.

"Even this circumstance, of course, could not excuse passing on second down with his team leading. But Hunsinger, our right end, had told Harry in a huddle that the Stanford halfback who should be covering him did not follow him deep into the scoring zone on our plays. Knowing this, Harry opened up on second down and called for a forward pass from himself to Hunsinger. Sure enough, on the play Hunsinger got clear away from the Stanford defensive halfback, who failed to follow him deep enough. He was clear in the open, ready to race for a touchdown on receipt of the ball. A 45 yard pass would have done the trick, and a 45 yard pass straight to the target was easy enough for Stuhldreher. But not this time.

"As the plucky little quarterback squared himself to shoot, bringing down the foot with the broken bone to take his stance," explained Rockne, "excruciating pain shot through him, so that instead of his usual vigorous throw the ball sailed a feeble 20 yards."

Stanford center George Baker intercepted and returned to the Notre Dame 31. Pop Warner had used the end-around with some success earlier in the game, so now Shipkey carried to the 26 to begin a drive that would, if successful, bring Stanford within three points.

Nevers drove to 18 on the next play and, in three more carries, to the 6. Crowley told the Irish that Nevers would continue to carry. And Ernie did. It now was third down on the 1, and Nevers cracked only a half yard out of the Notre Dame Mules. On fourth down the future Eskimo again slapped at the middle. Eckersall raised his arms in the end zone, but the referee signalled that Stanford was stopped about half a foot short of the goal line.

Layden punted out of there in a hurry, then with less than a minute to play again intercepted a Nevers' flat pass and again went for a TD—either 70, 60 or 35 yards, depending on whether you believe Samuelsen, Eckersall or AP. (Hendrickson also called it 70. He works for Samuelsen's old paper.)

Crowley kicked the point after, which created the final 27–10 score.

Pop Warner blamed his team's errors for the loss. "They earned only six points," he said. The Stanford coach pointed to the statistical battle: Stanford had outgained the Irish by 119 yards and made ten more first downs. "I think I had the better team," said Pop.

For several days after the game, as Chicago columnist Warren Brown observed in his memoirs, the nation's newspapers "were filled with Warner's new plan for keeping track of good deeds in a football game by giving credit for first downs and yardage gained.

"If Rockne had heard about this before, he made no mention of it. On the train back home, Rockne read a lengthy account of Warner's plan. When the train reached Ogden, Utah, a wire service writer came on board to ask Rockne if he had anything to say about the Warner plan."

In Brown's recollection, the Notre Dame coach said, "Sure I do, but I'll not say it until they start giving baseball victories to the teams that have the most men left on base."

Warner may have had the plan. Rockne had the Four Horsemen—big factors in the 1925 Rose Bowl win.

WRONG-WAY RIEGELS

There have been many great individual triumphs in the Rose Bowl. Yet, the most famous incident in the seventy-five years since the game began involves the failure of one man. It was that long-ago afternoon when Roy Riegels picked up a loose football and didn't stop running until he had reached the goal line. The wrong goal line. In that unfortunate span of about ten seconds, Riegels cost his school a Rose Bowl victory, made himself a legend among bumblers, and guaranteed that there would be little peace the rest of his life.

On the morning of January 1, 1929, Roy Max Riegels, a quiet, soft-spoken young man of twenty with all-American blond, blue-eyed looks and an All-Coast reputation as a center, stepped off a bus with his University of California teammates for their first look at the Rose Bowl. Riegels would later leave the stadium, branded, as Wrong-Way Riegels, a name he is forced to live with nearly a half-century later.

Of all the bonehead plays in history, perhaps Riegels' is the most famous. Fred Merkle neglected to touch second base, and it cost the New York Giants a pennant. Fred Snodgrass dropped a fly ball and Heinie Zimmerman chased the winning run across home plate to decide separate World Series. There are young people in this country who've never heard of Merkle, Snodgrass or Zimmerman, but who know the name Wrong-Way Riegels. They are not sure who he is or what he did, whether he is dead or alive, but they've heard the name, and know that it represents something off-course, or turned-around.

"Kids who were in the womb twenty years after I made the run know about it," said Riegels, very much alive at age sixty-nine in 1977 in Woodland, California, twenty miles northwest of Sacramento. Riegels, whose hair now is white and thinning, sits at his desk at Roy Riegels Chemicals, a fertilizer business he has owned since 1956. Woodland (population 25,500) is an agricultural area in the Sacramento Valley, and Riegels has four full-time salesmen and thirty trucks to service the farmers. He also owns a plant in Robbins, seventeen miles away. "Business is ten times better than when we started," he said. "I don't spend much time in the office. I'm out with the farmers. That's where you make your sales."

Two years had passed since he was last interviewed about his misdirected run, giving him hope that, perhaps at last, interest had finally died. Died down maybe, but not died. In truth, he knows that there is no real escape. "Every so often the phone rings," he said, "and a reporter will be calling from somewhere. They seem to track me down. I think to myself, 'Here we go again.' But at least you're known."

Known as an oddity. Wherever Riegels goes, whether registering at a hotel or signing a gas receipt, he immediately recognizes what the other person is thinking. "Are you *the* Wrong-Way Riegels?" The question blurts out. Riegels always answers softly, "Yes," and smiles. "You have to go along with it," he reasoned a long time ago, "whether it's meant in a deleterious manner or as a joke or what. If you show it, you're playing into someone's hands. I just go ahead and take it." Riegels said the insults, and there have been insults, never once forced him to lose his temper and retaliate. "I've never hit anyone, but there were times I wanted to kick some people in the butt. However, most people aren't critical. What I did was just an oddity, not the first and certainly not the last."

Riegels' run led to a safety and the eventual margin by which Georgia Tech defeated California, 8–7.

Benny Lom, a California tailback, chased and caught Riegels just before he stepped into the Tech end zone. "The thing that has saved Roy all these years is his personality. He always has had an even disposition and can throw things off very well, like rain off a roof," said Lom, seventy-one, who now owns four women's stores in and around Oakland and lives in San Francisco. "Roy is a very compassionate person. When some kind of adversity happens to an athlete, Roy sits down and writes him a letter. You couldn't find a more honorable or conscientious person than Roy Riegels. He has all the qualities you'd want your son to have."

One of the athletes to whom Riegels has written is Jim Marshall. On October 25, 1964, in San Francisco, Marshall, a defensive end for the Minnesota Vikings, grabbed a 49er fumble and raced 60 yards into his own end zone, giving the 49ers a safety and two points. Finally realizing what he had done, Marshall grabbed his helmet with both hands and bent over, while 49er play-by-play announcer Lon Simmons screamed into his microphone, "Jim Marshall has pulled a Wrong-Way Riegels here today." The Vikings managed to win the game, 27–22, but the phone began ringing continuously at the Riegels' home.

At the time, Riegels was at a convention in Coronado, near San Diego, but the news media caught up to him. "I think I'll write Marshall and tell him, 'Welcome to the club,' " said Riegels at the time. He did write Marshall, in a somewhat more serious vein. "I told him not to let this bother him, that he'll receive a lot of kidding for the rest of his life, and he'll just have to learn to take it and laugh with the crowd."

Jim Marshall hasn't had to live down, or even live with, his error, partly because he became a valuable member of Minnesota's outstanding defense, played in several Super Bowls, and set a NFL record for consecutive games by a defensive player. Marshall also was spared by the fact that he was an imitator, not an originator. No one refers to him as Wrong-Way Marshall. It isn't euphonious either, not like Wrong-Way Riegels. No, Marshall will not have to bear the blame, shame, or the name. This remains the burden, as it always will, of the fertilizer man from Woodland.

Times were good on the first day of 1929. There was a Model A in most garages in the Los Angeles area. The 71,104 who filled the Rose Bowl that day were largely prosperous, at least comfortable, and unaware that in eleven months many of them would be wiped out financially. But this was still the Roaring Twenties to the Rose Bowl fans, and few football teams in the country could roar like Georgia Tech.

The Yellowjackets were 9–0, having scored 213 points to only 40 for the opposition. Among their victories was an impressive 13–0 defeat of Knute Rockne and Notre Dame. Georgia Tech, under coach Bill Alexander, was in every sense of the word a powerhouse. California, on the other hand, hadn't nearly the same luster. The Golden Bears finished the regular season 6–1–2, having tied USC, 0–0, and Stanford, 13–13, while losing 12–0 to the Olympic Club of San Francisco, a club composed of graduated college stars. Clarence "Nibs" Price's Bears actually were the second choice from the

California coach Clarence "Nibs" Price.

West Coast by the Rose Bowl. USC declined the first bid because of a dispute with Tournament of Roses officials. California was made a two-point favorite over Georgia Tech only because West Coast sportswriters had established the odds.

Roy Riegels was about average size for the college football players of his era at six feet, 170 pounds. He was a junior and had been voted All-Coast for the first of two straight seasons. No one held such promise for him when he arrived on the Berkeley campus from neighboring Oakland. "I wasn't romanced by any coach when I came to Cal, but there wasn't any recruiting back then. I just turned out for the team," Riegels recalled. He worked his way up to starting center on the freshman team, but was fourth string behind Andy Miller, Herm Eichmeyer and Fat Glasgow when he reported to the varsity the next fall. But Riegels was starting by the opening game and there would be no getting him out of the lineup the next three years. "I missed one minute of playing time as a sophomore, three minutes as a junior, and five quarters as a senior, because of a bad knee," he said. "I was a 'rover' on defense. I would play either in the line or drop back on passing situations. I was very quick and blocked a lot of punts in college. I can't remember the exact number."

"Roy was one of Cal's great centers," said Lom, a triple-threat tailback in the Bears' single wing. "When he centered the ball, he'd lay it in there so softly you could catch it with one hand. In three years, he never centered a bad snap. He was a smart player with a good sense of timing."

Not only was there no recruiting in the Twenties, there was hardly any scouting. "We didn't know much about Georgia Tech except that they were competing for the national championship," said Riegels. "I believe we got some help from schools that had played them. We knew they liked to run a lot of wide stuff. Game plan? We didn't talk about game plans back then. We just went out and smacked them."

California's players weren't as large as Georgia Tech's, but the Bears were fast, experienced and flashy. Lom broke loose for 25 yards on a fake punt after the opening kickoff. But the drive ended when several Tech players smothered Stan Barr on a fake field goal pass attempt at their 34. The 'Jackets also had a flare for showmanship. On their opening series, the quarterback, Bob Durant, crouched with his back to the line, tail-to-tail with center Peter Pund, facing the Tech backfield. Durant would take the snap and then pitch out or hand off, namely to Stumpy Thomason, a dangerous outside runner.

California seemed bent on self-destruction from the beginning, with a helping hand from referee Herb Dana, the best known football official of that period. Lom threw a 40-yard pass to Barr, standing by himself on the Tech goal line, but he dropped it. Thomason fumbled in the second quarter, and the ball jumped out of the pile like a deer in a thicket. Lom scooped it up and ran 60 yards for an apparent touchdown. Only Dana, thinking the ball still was in Thomason's clutches somewhere in the mass of bodies, blew the play dead at the spot. He later admitted it was a quick whistle.

So instead of a two-touchdown California lead, it was a scoreless game when Thomason took another pitch at his 20 and broke around end for 15 yards. California end and captain, Irv Phillips, hit him with a vicious tackle, jarring the ball loose. Riegels saw the ball pop free and grabbed it on the bounce at the 34. He eluded two Tech players along the sidelines, then, unaccountably, turned and started back towards his own end zone. Pretty soon there was nothing but daylight as Riegels streaked for what he thought was a certain touchdown. Fast for a lineman, he could see the 5-yard stripes flash under his feet. No one was even near him, except for one figure out of the corner of his right eye.

It was Benny Lom. "I could hear him shouting at me when I got about 30 yards from the goal," said Riegels, "although I couldn't make out what he was saying." So Riegels shifted the football from his right to left arm and kept running. But the faster Lom caught up at the 15 and grabbed his right arm. "Benny shouted at me, 'Stop, you're going the wrong way.' I thought, 'What's wrong with him?' " It wasn't until they reached the Tech one-yard line that—photos of the famous run sequence show—Lom (No. 28) was able to bring Riegels (No. 11) to a halt and turn him around. They had barely taken more than a step or two upfield when they were swept under a wave of Tech tacklers, knocking them back to the 1.

"I'm sure that Benny would have caught me sooner, except that he was using all his breath to shout at me," said Riegels. "When I realized what I had done, I thought, 'This couldn't be true.' " The full impact of what he had done would not register until following the game. After the bodies unpiled, Riegels hadn't time to hide. He went right back to work at center, in hopes of getting California better field position and preventing himself from becoming a goat. But his fears turned into a nightmare.

The football of the flapper period was played without hashmarks. Wherever the football came to rest, that's where the next play started. Riegels was tackled about a yard from the sidelines. In those days, teams often punted on first down, and this is what Lom intended to do in order to get Georgia Tech away from his goal line. There was only room between Riegels and the sidelines for one blocker and Tech, seeing this, wisely overloaded on that side. Riegels' snap was perfect, but Lom hadn't a chance. Tech tackle Vance Maree came pouring through the short side of Cal's line to block the punt, which rolled out of the end zone for a safety. "He (Maree) came like a bat out of hell," remembered Lom. "I kicked with my right foot, and that's where we had to have protection. But because there was only one man next to Roy, the ball was blocked even before I could get my foot up."

Various explanations were offered after the game as to why Riegels whirled and went the opposite direction. Riegels was quoted at the time: "It was a terrible boner. I don't know how it happened. I can't even think of a decent alibi. I just bounced out with the ball, saw a pair of goalposts, and headed for them. I'm almost broken-hearted that it cost my team a victory."

Price, the Cal coach, said, "Roy had been hurt just before that run and that's why we took him out of the game not long afterwards."

Photo sequence showing the "wrong way" run of California center Roy Riegels. He recovers a Georgia Tech fumble (1) and then suddenly spins the wrong way (3) —toward his own goal line 65 yards distant. Teammate Benny Lom (No. 28) turned him around at the one-yard line.

Roy "Wrong Way" Riegels.

Andy Kerr, coach of Washington and Jefferson, observed, "A Georgia Tech man hit Riegels about the head in the general melee, and I am convinced the blow turned him in the wrong direction."

Victor G. Sidler, Associated Press sportswriter, reported, "The consensus was that Riegels, who was opposing Peter Pund, Georgia Tech's All-America center, had taken a ferocious beating on the Tech line plays, and simply was befuddled momentarily, and was more or less groggy when he picked up the ball."

Joseph N. Bell's book *Bowl Game Thrills,* offered still another theory: "Thomason pushed him (Riegels) as hard as he could along the sidelines, hoping to shove him out of bounds. The push spun Riegels, and he danced along the sidelines for an instant, partly off-balance, striving desperately to keep his footing and stay inbounds at the same time. For an instant he teetered precariously, then regained his stride, cut away from the sidelines and headed downfield."

The *New York Times'* account was that Riegels saw the "Tech men spring up in front of him and in eluding them, he cut back across the field. He turned to escape and in doing so apparently became confused and started towards his own goal."

Nearly five decades later, Riegels continues to renounce all conjecture that he was either groggy or confused. "I was never dazed. I was only dizzy once the whole time I was in college, and that was when I was kicked in the stomach, but it wasn't in the Rose Bowl," he said. "I started for the (Tech) goal, dodged a few people, then turned around automatically. There was nothing going through my mind except that I wanted to make a touchdown. It happened so quickly. I was right. I was so sure I was doing the right thing. The play was wrong, but I was right."

Bob Randolph was a backup fullback to Father Lumpkin for Georgia Tech that day. "I was warming up on the sidelines, getting ready to go into the game, when the play happened right in front of me. I saw it better than anyone else," said Randolph, seventy-one, and now a beer distributor in Atlanta. "The ball hit the ground and bounced right into Riegels' arms. He just circled and took off. Everyone was chasing him, even the Tech players. We were all confused."

Tech led 2–0 at halftime, and another Lom punt block, this one by end Tom Jones at the California 9, made it 8–0 not long after. Although the Bears stopped the 'Jackets at the 1-foot line, Lom had to punt again, this time successfully to his 45. An aroused Tech scored in two plays, Warner Mizell's 30-yard scamper around end and Thomason's 15-yard burst off tackle, where he reversed his field and outran the Bears into the end zone. The point after touchdown failed.

Meanwhile, California continued to play hari-kari. Quarterback Harold Breakenridge fumbled the ball away in the third quarter. Phillips, on an end reverse, stopped and threw a 40-yard pass to reserve quarterback Lee Eisan, who stumbled and fell just as he was about to make the catch deep in Tech territory. The same thing happened to Lee Rice on a perfect pass from Lom, with a clear field ahead. Eisan then caught a pass from Lom and fumbled, Tech recovering. Riegels also missed a chance for a touchdown when he blocked a punt, but couldn't pick it up before it bounced out at the Tech 29. As final proof that it wasn't California's day, Lom punted the football—and it burst! It traveled five yards, then flopped on the ground. Lom was allowed to punt again.

The Bears finally crossed the Tech goal with a minute and a half left to play following a 98 yard drive. Lom connected with Phillips and Eisan on long passes before passing to Phillips for the touchdown. Barr's kick made it 8–7, and that's how the game ended. California outgained Tech, 248 yards to 185, and had more first downs, 11–5.

"It was a heckuva way to lose a game, missing all those opportunities," said Lom, voted player of the game. "But the proof is in the pudding. Tech won, and that's what counts. Everyone on our team felt tremendous sympathy for Roy. He was a pretty dejected player after his run, but he came back and played a heckuva game. Peter Pund was an All-America, but I'll tell you this, Roy outplayed Peter Pund."

On January 2, 1929, a newspaperman wrote, "Roy Riegels will never forget his faux pas, nor will he be allowed to forget it." Although no one is quite sure who coined the expression Wrong-Way Riegels, it wasn't long afterward that he began hearing the name. Hearing, hearing, hearing.

Riegels had one more season left, and his California teammates elected him team captain, as a senior. He became, in Price's opinion, "the best lineman on the Coast." Riegels blocked a punt against USC and recovered for a touchdown, in a 15–7 California victory. The Bears repeated as Pacific Coast Conference co-champions, but lost their final game to Stanford, 21–6, and didn't make the Rose Bowl. However, in three years with Riegels as their center, the Bears had a 20–6–3 record.

Riegels coached at his alma mater for one year before becoming a high school teacher at $1,600 a year. He both taught and coached on the high school and junior college levels, and was head coach at McClellan Air Field, near Sacramento, for two years during World War II. He switched from teaching to the chemical field and moved to Woodland in 1956, the same year he started his own business. Riegels has four children, two daughters living near his first wife in Vermont, and two sons. There are six grandchildren, and Riegels would much rather baby-sit than watch a football game. The oldest son Dave, went out for freshman football at Stanford, but "was too small," according to his father, and now is a lawyer in Sacramento. Youngest son Dick, rowed on the freshman crew at California, which started the jokes flying again. Here was the son of Wrong-Way Riegels competing in a sport where you face the wrong way, rowing with your back to the finish line. Dick competed just the one year, but his father said it was because of his study load. He's now an architect in Alaska.

"Right after we got through playing football at Cal, there was the depression and then the war," said Lom. "Everyone was working hard and you didn't get to see much of your friends. I hadn't seen Roy for about fifteen years, when one day I get a phone call and it's him. I picked him up and brought him back to my place for cocktails. I

1929 Player of the
Game Benny Lom.

had this phonograph album of Graham McNamee describing Roy's run and I played it for him. We laughed about it. Then Roy looked at me and said, 'Benny, do you remember when you grabbed my arm at their 15?' I said I did. 'Well, you know what I thought you were trying to do? I thought you wanted me to give you the ball so you could score the touchdown'."

"I suppose I could suffer over what happened long ago, but I'm not the kind who suffers. I guess I could hide from it too, but I'm not about to hide," Riegels says now. "I've been successful in Woodland, and people have treated me as a person. When I taught school, they treated me like a regular person. I've always worked hard to do the best I can. The way I see it, if I hadn't been trying, I wouldn't have been on that football field in the first place. What happened then is just one of those things in life you have to accept."

WRONG-WAY RIEGELS

"BIG APPLE" POWER

They called him "Horse," although "Iron Horse" would have been more accurate, except there already was an "Iron Horse" on another coast in another sport. In a modest sense, though, Bob Reynolds was to the history of the Rose Bowl what Lou Gehrig was to the game of baseball in the Thirties. Reynolds did something no other Pasadena performer accomplished before, or since, and no other athlete is likely ever to turn the Reynolds' trick because of the nature of the sport in its growing dependence on specialization.

What the Horse did was play in every single minute of three consecutive Rose Bowl games, the contests of 1934–36, only one of which, the last, was won by Reynolds' Stanford "Vow Boys."

The first of those three games falls into the "legendary" class for three reasons: it was a classic upset, doubtless the biggest upset in Rose Bowl history; it was played under conditions which Noah would have found insulting; it involved an underdog from the sidewalks of New York and thus benefitted from all of the big-name media attention accruing to the involvement of a New York team in any major sporting activity.

In other words, this team, Columbia, this game, the 1934 Rose Bowl, this stunner of an upset, 7–0, and this game-breaker of a play, "KF 79," were all elements of Holy Writ-like literature by the biggest jock journalists of the day. The marvelous John Kieran lyricized; Bill Corum romanticized; and, ultimately, Red Smith eulogized.

All good stuff. All, in the slippage of time, quite charming. But in the memory of Horse Reynolds, as he chats during a busy noontime in a crowded Los Angeles restaurant, the drama of Pasadena in 1934 becomes more of a minor embarrassment than a football landmark. There were, in his life, other Rose Bowl games and, in the season following the Columbia folly, a much, much better Stanford team. And way down the list of his recollections, still quite vivid, is the "Iron Horse" skein. From his point of view, the labor in those 180 Rose Bowl minutes was no big deal.

"It wasn't much thought of for some time for some years," he says. "I know I never thought about it after the games. I knew I was awful tired. But nothing much was ever made of it for seven, eight, nine years later, not until a writer picked it up and said that this guy played all the way and nobody's ever done that. But it doesn't mean a helluva lot. Really, it doesn't.

"Today's football player couldn't have done it because of the way the game is played now (1976). And I couldn't have done it either in this era. The game's too fast. Most players are not trained these days to play both ways, but even if they did get the training, the tempo of football has speeded up so much that I don't think it would be physically possible. Still, I think football is a better game now. It's more exciting. It's faster. All you have to do is compare how many plays are run now with the number of plays in my day. Not only do you have two platoons shuffling in and out of the game, and somebody always resting, but you also have your damned specialty teams now. To go both ways today, you'd have to be as good as a man coming on the field for defense, a man coming on the field for offense and, additionally, you'd have to be as good as you had to be in a given situation—on a specialty team. In other words, if a punt was kicked down there, you'd have to give a burst of speed."

In 1961, Bob Reynolds was in New York for a Football Hall of Fame luncheon. He was placed at the same table as the gentleman who coached Columbia in the 1934 game, Lou Little. "After the luncheon was over," said Reynolds, "we sat there, Lou and I, for two hours, until about four in the afternoon, just talking. Everybody else who'd been at the banquet had cleared out. And we just talked—about football and life in general. And of course we replayed that game. Little was made a hero because of that game. And he was generous enough and kind enough to admit it."

Little's coaching philosophy, which today would be considered naive and/or heretical, can be boiled down to one of his comments during his nearly thirty years at Columbia: "I want men who will knock the other fellow's brains out, then help him up and brush him off."

Stanley Woodward, who was to become sports editor of the *New York Herald Tribune,* reminisced in *Paper Tiger* about spending time at Columbia's Baker Field watching Little at work.

"I had followed the career of the coach since I was in high school," wrote Woodward, "when he played for Worcester Academy. His wanderings then led him to Vermont, where he played for a year or two; Trinity College of Hartford, where he skipped before football started; University of Pennsylvania, where he played for a couple of years; United States Army, in which he was a combat infantry captain; the Frankfort Yellow

Jackets, where he coached and played right tackle; Georgetown, where he coached, and finally, Columbia.

"Lou's football team operated in mortal terror of their roaring boss. He was a strange kind of coach. He made himself heard all over Baker Field, but when trouble came to one of his players, he was kind and considerate. He insisted that his players dress neatly, shave every day, and get a haircut once every two weeks."

One of Little's players in the 1933 season was a sophomore halfback from Jersey City named Al Barabas, who recently summoned his recollections of the coach. "I had the impression then that he was as good as any coach around," said Barabas. "He was a very, very hard taskmaster. A disciplinarian. Nobody got away with any shenanigans on the field or even off the field. And he had that strict dress code for us when we traveled. We couldn't possibly appear in a public place, especially a restaurant, without being clean shaven and neatly dressed, with a tie. Little insisted on that.

"He always had a personal interest in you while you were in school. I used to marvel at the fact that he knew how you were doing in your grades in each subject. If he thought you weren't performing up to your potential in the classroom, you got a call from him: 'What are you doing with a C minus in this course? How come?' Even in situations where a person had all passing grades but you had too many C's, he'd call you in and ask you if you needed any help. I'm sure partially he did it because he didn't want to lose the player through ineligibility, but I think basically he did it because he just didn't think it was right for one of his players to be on the edge, on the verge of flunking."

Columnist Red Smith, writing in the *New York Herald Tribune* not long before Little's retirement at Columbia in 1957, noted that Little had been referred to as "Columbia's best teacher.... Sports writers and alumni, as a rule, rank football coaches according to the number of games their teams win, which is a meaningless criterion," said Smith. "A far more accurate measure would be provided if one could count the hundreds of young men from Columbia and other colleges, amateurs and professionals, and boys who never played any game, former proteges of Lou Little and strangers to him, who have written or called on him over the years seeking his help in the business of living."

There was the instance, Smith added, of one of Little's athletes "pulling off his padded playsuit after the final game of his senior year. He would never play college football again. Showered and dressed for the street, he walked over to offer his hand to the coach. 'Thank you, Mr. Little,' he said, 'for teaching me so much more than football.' "

Another Columbia football player, in similar last-game circumstances, said to Little, "Thank you for everything you've done for us."

The coach's response: "I never did anything for you boys. You did everything for me."

Little, said Smith, "always tried to teach his guys to think for themselves." Which is sort of what happened in Pasadena in the mud on January 1, 1934.

"If it had been a typical, good weather day," said Bob Reynolds, "the result might have been different. Or it might not have been. I don't know."

"I was an all-state high school tackle in Oklahoma and nearly went to Princeton or Northwestern because of friends of the family. But my father had another close friend who'd been on the Stanford track team in 1916–17 and was still a great Stanford booster. A friend of mine and I got in an old jalopy and were on our way to Arizona to work a placer mine. But we had a few extra days, so we drove first to California to meet some Stanford people recommended by my father's friend. And while I was there, I also met Pop Warner—but he was on his way to coach at Temple. His contract had another year to run, but some of the alumni at Stanford weren't happy with him," Reynolds continued. "He was such a proud guy, he decided t'hell with it, if you don't like what I do, I'm gonna leave. As long as I was at Stanford, I thought I'd take the aptitude test to see if I could pass it. And I did. Meanwhile, I'd also applied for, and was admitted to, USC. I was accepted at Princeton, too. But I really wanted to go West. Maybe, I figured, they wouldn't take to Okies at Princeton. I always got razzed at Stanford about being an Okie. Guess I had quite a Southwestern drawl.

"Then I got the nickname Horse because some of my friends put a horse in my room in the Stanford dormitory. On the third floor. It was a miracle how they got it up there. But it was all done in a friendly way. You know, we couldn't live in the damn room for three months afterwards because the horse—well, actually it was a pony—had been in there long enough to leave his mark. So we all had to move out of there.

"I didn't have a scholarship. My father was able to pay for my first year. Then the depression fell very hard on him, so I made up the money by taking out tuition notes. Some of the kids today aren't paying back those college loans. I'm a regent at the University of California, and the amount of those loans today is staggering. The kids want to borrow the money, but they don't want to pay it back. But back then it was something different to me—a sense of responsibility to pay back the notes."

Responsibility was Barabas' task at Columbia in those years, too. Al was the youngest of eight brothers, all of whom were athletes and several of whom had won college scholarships. One of the brothers, Steve, had played for Little at Georgetown.

"Both my parents were immigrants," said Barabas. "They helped all of us financially as best they could—which was very little. I'd played high school football in Jersey City, then got the scholarship to Columbia. While I was there, I waited on tables; generally I had a couple of jobs. I'd work for two hours a day in the cafeteria—wash dishes or bus tables—and get my meals that way. And then for spending money, I had a two-hour job which paid five dollars a week. And that was a reasonable amount of money in the early Thirties. You certainly could maintain yourself on five dollars a week."

On both campuses the athletes seemed to have an understated sense of commitment. The Stanford Vow Boys nickname stemmed from a varsity game-loss to Southern Cal in 1932. It was a humiliating loss, and two days later a "vow" was made as the Stanford freshman team dressed for practice.

"Suddenly," wrote Julie Fiedler in *Touchdown* magazine, "quarterback Frank Alustiza delivered an impromptu speech and concluded, 'They will never do that to us. We'll *never* lose to USC.' When halfback Bones Hamilton shouted, 'Let's make that a vow,' the entire team cheered in agreement."

And the Vow Boys never did lose to SC. Five of them would become All-America, including Reynolds, Hamilton and halfback Bobby Grayson, whom Ernie Nevers termed "the best back I've ever seen, and I've seen a lot of good backs."

"There was great rapport," said Horse Reynolds. "Oh, you might say there were rivalries from the standpoint not of personality clashes per se but because writers would give publicity to a certain few, like Hamilton or Grayson. But those clashes were minor. We had a great bond of camaraderie, and it has existed through the years. I think there were about nine of us who started in all three Bowl games, and seven of us are still around. We're one of the few clubs that has periodic reunions. That bond still exists."

Those Stanford clubs were sandwiched between the coaching reigns of the brilliant Warner and the innovative Clark Shaughnessy, and were directed by Claude "Tiny" Thornhill. "He did a great job," said Reynolds. "He wasn't as strict or as distant as Warner. 'Tiny' would kid everybody. He made us into a friendly, cohesive group."

In the three Vow Boy years, Thornhill had a 25–4–2 record, including twenty shutouts. Stanford surrendered just ninety-nine points in those thirty-one games.

In the 1933 season, Stanford was 8–1–1 and outscored its opponents 131–36. Particularly because the team had broken SC's three-year winning streak, the young Indians from Palo Alto were clearly the Coast's best.

But the selection of a Rose Bowl foe became one of those typical early-years dilemmas. There seemed to be a surfeit of Eastern riches that year.

"We certainly weren't expecting Columbia," said Reynolds. "Princeton was great then, and Minnesota had a powerhouse."

"Army had a great team that year," wrote John Kieran. "So did Duke. Columbia started with a fine squad and great prospects, but overconfidence gave Lou Little's Lions a terrific setback. In an early season game against Princeton, which had a corking team that year, too, Columbia fumbled the opening kickoff, was thrown backward in haste by the joyous Tigers, and took a lopsided beating, 20–0. So Columbia was crossed off the list.

"Princeton swept on to one triumph after another, and could have had the Rose Bowl bid on a silver platter, but the old 'Big Three' of Yale, Harvard, and Princeton had an agreement against taking part in such post-season festivities. (Harvard had defeated Oregon 7–6 in the 1920 Rose Bowl.) Duke went along undefeated to the last game. Army marched over all rivals up to the final game against Notre Dame, beating Yale, Harvard, Illinois, and other good teams en route. Only 13 points had been scored against Army in all those games. Stanford and the football fans of the Coast would have been delighted to entertain the Army football team—the whole corps of Cadets, for that matter—in the Rose Bowl."

But on the final Saturday of the 1933 season, Notre Dame beat the Army and Georgia Tech blanked Duke.

After Stanford's selection, and following the finale dumpings of Army and Duke, Columbia was given another look. The Lions had, after all, lost only that early Princeton game and gone on to defeat a strong Navy—finishing 7–1 and scoring 172 points to its opponents' mere 45. And 20 of those were by Princeton.

"The scholastic requirements at Columbia are so high and on a par with Stanford's," said Stanford graduate manager Al Masters, "that we feel honored in meeting the football team of such a great university."

As Columbia's faculty council on athletics pondered the invitation, Kieran teased in the *New York Times:*

> "The eastern Coach, with all his staff,
> Was standing in the hall.
> The Rose Bowl bid was in, and they
> Were waiting for the call.
> The faculty was huddling and
> The Dean still held the ball.
>
> "If twenty men we used against
> Eleven on their side,
> Do you suppose, the Head Coach said,
> That Stanford could be tied?
> I doubt it! groaned an aide-de-camp,
> And broke right down and cried.
>
> "If all our men wore armor plate
> With rivets at the seam,
> We still might save the lives of all
> The players on our team,
> The Head Coach said. But that seemed just
> A hopeful eastern dream.
>
> "There rose a wailing, warning voice
> The coaching staff amid:
> From fire and from pestilence
> Please keep the East safe hid,
> From famine and from slaughter and
>   From Bowl of Roses bid!"

"The next day," wrote Stanley Woodward, "the Columbia committee, comprising faculty members and graduates, met at the University and accepted the invitation. Among those who were hanging around the lobby waiting for the decision was Al Barabas. No other football player was there. The interest of Barabas was prophetic. . . ."

At Stanford, Masters received a wire saying, "Why didn't you pick Slippery Rock? Columbia belongs in the same bracket."

In Little's office in New York, a passerby chided, "Aren't you interested in the physical welfare of your boys?"

"I'm still hale and hearty, and I went to the Rose Bowl with Penn in 1917," said Little. "We lost (to Oregon, 14–0) but we saved our lives."

The Columbia faculty council accepted the bid, and Little scurried to round up his athletes, who had pretty much disbanded at season's end.

The puckish Kieran jibed again:

> "What! You still insist on playing? Woe is me! I'll take the ball,
> And if you survive the massacre, my dying words recall
> **Moriturus te saluto!** For Columbia I roar!
> And tell them to remember me but please forget the score."

The East was covered with snow that December. Little's fellows worked indoors before entraining for the coast. Their trip would take nearly two weeks. En route they paused for practices on high school fields in St. Louis, Dallas, El Paso, and Tucson. One myth suggest KF 79 was honed on the playing fields of Tucson. "This secret weapon had been in Columbia's arsenal all season," wrote Joseph Bell, "but it had been seldom used. So in Tucson, Little and his captain and quarterback, Cliff Montgomery, polished and burnished this weapon."

Kieran suggests Stanford took the matchup lightly: "The hardest part of their preparation for the great day was posing for pictures and giving autographs," he wrote. Reynolds, however, demurs.

"The fact we were going to play Columbia and not Princeton or some other great team did not lessen our enthusiasm or preparation. What did put a damper on the whole thing," said the Stanford tackle, "was this awful storm that blew into Southern California. It was a miserable damn thing. There were a lot of drownings in that storm."

Appropriately, the theme of the Rose parade that year was "Tales of the Seven Seas." The parade's grand marshal was Admiral William Sims, who barely made it ashore in time to join former President (and Stanford alumnus) Herbert Hoover on the reviewing stand.

"The ex-President spurned an umbrella provided him," wrote Joe Hendrickson, "and sat in a green slicker, rain dripping from his hat, as the floats sloshed down the parade route. Four bands failed to show. Some bands rode in buses." And most of them were playing "It Ain't Gonna Rain No More." One report has the local fire department pumping two million gallons out of the Rose Bowl before the game began.

At the previous game, played on January 2, 1933, because New Year's Day fell on a Sunday, the crowd watching USC crush Pitt 35–0 numbered 74,874, less than 1,000 under the record attendance set in 1932. But now, on this torrential New Year's of 1934, only about 35,000 squished into the stands. Scalpers took a beating. "One Pasadena hotel," reported Samuelsen, "offered four dollar seats, the top price, for fifty cents."

Until just a few hours before kickoff, there was doubt if the game would be played at all. "The field was under water the day before," said Horse Reynolds. "All but the very apex of it. They had a bunch of fire engines there trying to drain the water out, and we were told we wouldn't know until about eleven in the morning on game day if we'd play."

Pasadena had caught twelve inches of water in the big storm. The pumps on the city's fire department trucks worked nearly a full day to drain the field. By game time, the playing field itself had been cleared of water, although as Reynolds recalls the track along the sidelines was your basic quagmire.

"The weather kind of jostled our thinking a bit," said Horse. "Because I don't care who you are—what kind of an athlete—you prepare mentally if you know you're going to be in the ring, or on the field, at two o'clock. So I think we were in somewhat of a state of indecision there. But that's not an excuse. Nor is it intended to be. Columbia just wasn't that good, especially their defense. And they were not a large team (Stanford's weight advantage averaged about twenty pounds a man). We clearly should have beaten them. Clearly. That was the truth of the matter."

The Indians were heavily favored by whoever was making book that year; four to one, or three touchdowns. Size was the factor essentially. When confronted with the physical difference, Barabas, told a pre-game interviewer, "The seat of a big guy's britches can get just as hot as a little fellow's, if you sit down on them often enough."

Barabas was not so much of a little guy, though; second heaviest on his team. He played at 187 and was 5–10. "Good size even today for a halfback," he said recently. There is a tone of ease and confidence in his voice now as he discusses the "underdog" role of the Lions in 1934.

"We fully expected to win," he says. "I think that's a common feeling among football players. If you're a perennial doormat in your own league and everybody's beaten the hell out of you, then I guess you get that losers' complex after a while. But we had a good team that year and we knew it. We'd beaten some formidable opponents."

Little enlisted some coaching help in the weeks before the game. His temporary brain trust included such worthies as ex-Four Horseman Jim Crowley, then coaching at Fordham; Jock Sutherland of Pitt; Hunk Anderson of Notre Dame; Bert Bell of Penn and, later, the NFL commissioner. Then there was Chick Meehan—"a prominent coach at NYU and then Manhattan College," in Barabas' memory. "During the holidays in 1933, Meehan assembled a group of his own football players on a voluntary basis, of course, and told them that Little needed a squad to practice against. He asked his guys if they'd be willing to come over and be sitting ducks. They did, and so we had some pretty good scrimmages against Manhattan College, in preparation for the Rose Bowl."

In addition to all of this extra coaching guidance, Little also had living inspiration: one of the Columbia assistant coaches was Herb Kopf, who knew all about being a Rose Bowl underdog. Kopf was the starting left end when Washington and Jefferson had played that heroic scoreless tie with California in Pasadena in 1922. "The very presence of Kopf on Columbia's bench," wrote Bob Foote of the *Pasadena Star-News,* "as a living reminder of what could be done in the face of everybody's disbelief, was invaluable."

Maybe. But the major value that day lay in KF 79.

"I remember," said Reynolds, "they called that play some glamorous name. Columbia made great capital out of the whole thing, probably to give the New York writers something to talk about. It was their privilege."

The play which enchanted the writers was one of the spinner series developed by Little for his single-wing Lions. On KF 79 the line was unbalanced, strong to the right, with only a guard as an end on the weak (left) side.

That's the simple part of this play. It was the alignment of the Lion backfield that ended up being described in 237 different ways. The play, however, was rather elementary.

"We used it in the regular season," said Barabas. "And we always called it KF 79. There was a reason for that name, because our backs were the K (for kicking) back, the F (for faking) back, the L (for leading) back and the T (for tackle) back. And the 79 just indicated how the ball was passed.

"On KF 79 the ball went straight to our K back, Montgomery. I was the F back, Ed Brominski the T back and Bill Nevel the L back."

Montgomery, about a half dozen yards behind the center, would take a direct snap from center, spin halfway around and then hand the ball to Barabas, who'd been positioned a couple of yards to his right rear, for a sprint around left end. While Barabas was running in a stealthy, don't let 'em see I've got the ball manner, Montgomery was to keep spinning and fake handing off to Brominski, who'd come over from the right flank. Brominski would of course pretend he was carrying the ball through left tackle. And Montgomery meanwhile was faking a line buck. The other back, Nevel, merely swung to the left from his position just behind the right side of the line and took out the left defensive end.

In theory, it was a fine double fake. In practice, there could be any one of three ball carriers on the play: Montgomery could fake twice and keep the ball himself; he could fake the handoff to Barabas and then give the ball to Brominski; he could slip it to Barabas and then, along with Brominski, carry out the fake.

"When we practiced, we always practiced that particular play more than any of the others," said Barabas. "I don't recall that we did it in Tucson when we stopped there during the train trip West as much as we did it back home in Baker Field. I remember a couple of sessions where Little would run the damn play fifty times in a row."

In the first quarter, which was scoreless, all three variations of the series were used. The one in which Barabas carried picked up good yardage; Al was stopped at the Stanford 12 by Indian safety man Buck Van Dellen. It appeared that all of the other Stanford defenders had been fooled by Montgomery's faking. Unfortunately, Columbia fumbled on the next play, so KF 79 was momentarily detained from destiny.

The first period did not go at all according to preconception. "Right from the start, the radio listeners back in the East knew that fun was afoot," wrote Kieran. "The altogether too self-satisfied Stanford stalwarts were unceremoniously jolted by the underrated Easterners. Those Stanford adherents and California neighbors who had turned out to watch a triumphal parade put on by their heroes sat back open-mouthed, eyes wide in absolute horror. Could such things be? Every time Columbia made a gain, which was frequently, the radio announcers spoke of it tentatively as though it were something they probably would have to take back later on. And, to tell the truth, that was also the feeling of the listeners back home in the East. What was going on seemed to be too good to last."

"When we started the game," said Horse Reynolds, "we figured that the conditions were so miserable on the field that if we could score a touchdown and kick the extra point we could do no worse than a tie. It would be the kind of lead you could almost sit on. We were a young club, and that day we played like a frustrated, anxious ball club. And I guess our youth and our anxiety led to all of our fumbling. We kept losing the ball inside their 10. And that was completely frustrating, just like being one run behind in a baseball game, having the bases loaded and nobody out, and not being able to get in a damned run."

The run most damned by Stanford came early in the second quarter. Following a Stanford punt, Columbia began a drive from its own 43. After a penalty and a Montgomery pass to end Red Matal, the Lions reached the Stanford 17. First down, and the ball to Barabas.

"He was not that impressive," said Reynolds. "Columbia had a good end named Owen McDowell, and Montgomery was a good ballplayer. Oh, maybe Barabas was good, too. But we outweighed them and outmanned them and outplayed them. Heck."

On the first down play Barabas fumbled, but recovered for a loss of about half a yard. On the next play, Montgomery called for KF 79.

"When the play was called in that situation," wrote Red Smith, "McDowell said (in the huddle) to Larry Pinckney, the short-side guard, 'This time you cross over and take my man, the right half. I'll go get the safety man.' " And it worked out.

"What they did," Reynolds recalled, "was make a fake over to the right side of their line. And that sucked in our right end, so Barabas went right by. Hamilton, our halfback, was a fine defensive player and tackler, but he just took one step the wrong

Al Barabas of Columbia in the end zone after scoring the game's only touchdown, on the famed KF-79 play against Stanford.

way and Barabas had the edge on him. On what was really a slant play, Barabas went 17 yards into the end zone. That was it."

It sure was. McDowell, as promised, knocked safety Van Dellen out of the play. Barabas went in untouched by a Stanford hand. After Newell Wilder's kick, Columbia had all the points that would be scored this gray day.

"I think there was a gnawing anxiety about that one touchdown of theirs standing up," said Reynolds. "It was such a miserable damned day, every time you'd hit the turf you'd just sop up water. And it was too miserable to pass. It was such a sloppy field, you just couldn't keep your footing. We were frightfully let down. It was completely frustrating for us. All those fumbles of ours."

"I never thought that day that the one touchdown of ours would stand up," said Barabas. "I was fully confident we could score again, or maybe a couple of times more. And Stanford ran so well against us I didn't think 7 points would be the final result. I honestly figured we had to score again to win it."

The final statistics were intriguing: Stanford, at game's end, led in net yardage, 258–107, and in first downs, 16–5. The Indians' Grayson, who along with three other Vow Boys (Reynolds, Hamilton, and guard Bill Corbus) would be elected to the National Football Foundation Hall of Fame, rushed that day for 152 yards, 45 more than the entire Columbia attack.

A man from the *New York Times* reflected, "The game reminded many old time Rose Bowl veterans of the 1925 contest, in which Knute Rockne's Four Horsemen triumphed over Stanford. The Indians made all the ground that day, and Notre Dame made most of the points. Curiously alike, too, were Ernie Nevers, the great fullback of 1925, and Bobby Grayson, Stanford's latest line cracker. Grayson, using the same churning foot motion that Nevers made famous, banged his way over center, raced through tackle and rushed around end."

"Oh, Grayson was all the backs you've ever seen on this day," romanticized Bill Corum in the *New York Journal-American*. "Dazzlingly fast even in the slippery going, he was all but unstoppable. All but . . . but not quite. For when he finally laid it all on the line three yards from home on a heart-stopping lunge, it was Al Ciampa, a bespectacled, studious-looking, 165-pounder from Brockton, Massachusetts, High School, who picked him up and hurled him back as if he were a babe in arms. Let me try and set the picture for you." Okay, Bill.

"It was the third period. The big scoreboard, its white letters and numerals standing out in sharp relief against the gray of the day, told an amazing story. Back of the 'S' there was a zero. On the other side was the 'C' with its tantalizing 7. Through fleeting sunshine and shadows and gusty windblown spatters of rain, the middleweight Lions had held their heavyweight foes in check.

"As one Columbia rooter had said 'The game seemed all wrong. Every time Stanford sent in a replacement, he seemed larger than the man he relieved, and every time a substitute trotted out from the Columbia bench, he seemed smaller.'

"But here it was the third period, and the clock was beginning to play for Columbia. Stanford was starting to put the pressure on. 'Enough of this,' the young giants in the scarlet jerseys must have been saying to themselves. 'This has gone far enough!'

"It was Stanford's ball three yards from the last stripe, and Grayson was galloping. (On first down) Grayson hurled himself forward, and something hit him amidships. I think it was a chunk of a kid named Steve Dzambe and two or three more in the Blue and White. But no great matter.

"That was only one down. Three more downs to go. Give it to Grayson again! So they gave it to Grayson, and once more those driving, powerful legs of his threshed as he spun and charged. And, once more, those kids with their bellies on the ground came up with the crash and, once more, Grayson stopped as though a bullet had felled him.

"So now it was third down, and they must try deception . . . or what passed for deception. They pulled the reverse, Grayson to Hamilton, and this time Mr. Hamilton went down in a smother of clawing Lions and the ball was still that same three yards from home. Bad, yes. But not cause for alarm. There was one more down and Bobby wouldn't fail.

"He slanted off tackle like a rocket, but Ciampa also leaped with the snap of the ball. Ciampa's head bored into his chest and, wonder of wonders, it was Grayson who was lifted off his feet and dropped back with a sickening thud."

Grayson actually fumbled on the play and, Corum continued, "the ball seesawed idly toward the goal line. There was a moment of agony among the small band of Columbia rooters (including a few from the Hollywood community, one of whom had presented Little a pet lion at the train station), and then once more Barabas filled the hero's role. He lunged, and gathered the ball into his arms."

"You know," Barabas said thirty-two years later, "I got damn close to as much satisfaction out of that fumble recovery as I did out of the touchdown run."

Little had his quiet satisfaction, too. "He wasn't a very excitable man, true," said Barabas. "But as I recall after the game, he had a grin from ear to ear in the dressing room. He was greatly pleased about the result. Greatly pleased."

"I resent all of this talk about us being lucky," said the Columbia coach after the game. "Our first eleven was darn good, something that West Coast fans didn't appreciate. As good as Stanford's, in fact."

"To be honest with you," Bob Horse Reynolds would someday apologize, "Columbia was the weakest of the three clubs we played in the Rose Bowl. In terms of manpower, I mean. On a round-robin basis, both Alabama and Southern Methodist—the other Rose Bowl clubs we played—would have beaten Columbia. And we would have, too. But heck, that's not to take anything away from Columbia. They were good enough to win on that day and in those conditions. So that made them an awful good ball club."

Lou Little had been the starting right tackle on the University of Pennsylvania team, in the 1917 Rose Bowl. En route home to Philadelphia from that game, the eventual Columbia coach fretted about being unprepared for upcoming examinations. He decided to feign illness, according to Kieran, and reported to the Penn infirmary for removal of his tonsils on the assumption he could buy a week's time for study. But as he was being wheeled to the operating room, Little had second thoughts. As he battled the anesthesiologist, the operating table on which he lay began rolling across the floor. Several orderlies were required to subdue him; however, the tonsilectomy was completed, and Little passed the exams.

And now, after the winning effort in 1934, Little, newspaperman Woodward, and a couple of other gentlemen headed to a Beverly Hills party. "It was a wing-ding for the Columbia team," wrote Woodward. "We found the house and as we got out of the car Little saw one of his players, a third-string fullback, sitting in the window with a highball in his hand.

" 'Wait driver,' Little said. 'I'm going back to the hotel. I won't go anywhere where my players are drinking.'

"That's the way it was all the way back across the continent," continued Woodward. "We stopped at Denver, then Chicago for an alumni banquet. Little kept strict reins on the players and lectured them daily on the need for getting right back to work on their studies when the team reached New York. I can almost guarantee that Columbia had less fun winning the Rose Bowl championship than any previous or subsequent winner."

Woodward should have asked Barabas.

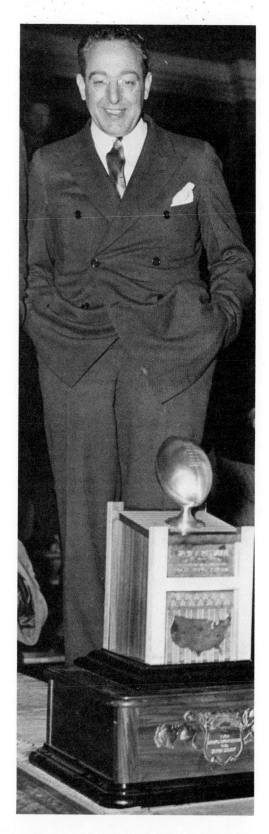

Columbia's coach Lou Little, whose
team upset Stanford 7-0. Here he beams
at the Rose Bowl victory trophy.

At least two newspapermen of the day dipped into the Holy Bible in order to capsulize the game. Its essence, they found, was in the line: "Barrabas he was a robber." The spelling, they decided, was close enough. And Al Barabas became "the thief in the night" for his spinner series bootleg.

"For a long, long time," he said, "everybody I'd run into would instantly recognize my name. But in the years just after that game, it was tough living up to my reputation. I was flattered, certainly, but don't forget that I was the only sophomore on that team. And that reputation became a burden for me in my final two seasons at Columbia. In my junior year, I hurt my knee pretty badly after the third game and didn't play the rest of the year. And in my senior year, we had a mediocre season." In that last year, "the thief in the night" was named team captain.

In his meetings with Columbia alumni and in private conversations with them, Barabas finds himself "constantly rehashing that game. I guess my name is still pretty widely recognized. Not only because of the game. Maybe because it's an uncommon name, too. Just seems that people still remember me." (And the play. *New York Times'* sportswriter Leonard Koppett, as soon as he moved to California, bought personalized license plates reading KF 79.)

"Have I embellished that game over the years? No, not really," says Barabas. "But you know, after so many years, when you're talking about something, for instance about famous World Series games—Mickey Owen's passed ball game or Don Larsen's perfect game, and I saw them both—you begin to wonder, 'Now, was I actually there at those games or do I think I was there because I've read and heard so much about them?' And maybe at this late stage I'm reading things into that Rose Bowl game that didn't occur. I don't know. I've never doubted that it all happened to me, that I was the guy. But little aspects of it have become more vague with time. Some people will come up to me and say, 'Do you remember this particular thing happening?' And sometimes I don't remember. I just take their word for it because they were there. But oftentimes, they're wrong, too."

After the game of January 1, 1934, Al Barabas never again returned to the Rose Bowl. "The Horse," however, would be back. More thieves in the night were lurking.

SAVE YOUR CONFEDERATE MONEY

The South got a chance to rise again in the Rose Bowl game of 1926, an event which spawned a couple of movie stars named Brown and Brix-Bennett. Starting with that thrilling encounter, football teams from Dixie would be appearing in thirteen of the next twenty-one Rose Bowls, invasions ended only by the contract between the Big Ten and Pacific Conference.

Six teams from Gritsville made Pasadena appearances in those two decades, with Alabama the most frequent visitor. The Crimson Tide came West a half dozen times and concluded its Rose sniffing with an exemplary 4–1–1 record. Georgia Tech and Georgia each made a single, victorious appearance; Tulane lost in its lone Pasadena outing; Duke and Tennessee went Bowling twice and lost twice. The final Southern tally in the Rose Bowl is 6–6–1. What all those schools did was follow the essential sports maxim of playing .500 ball on the road.

And to think that when a Bowl representative was sent East late in 1925 to seek a foe for Washington he initially shrugged off 'Bama by saying he'd "never heard of them as a football team. I can't take a chance on mixing a lemon with a rose," he said. Well, the mix was made for the 1926 Bowl, and it turned out to be champagne.

Stanford's Bob Reynolds wasn't unfamiliar with the exploits of Alabama's Johnny Mack Brown as Bob and his "Vow Boy" playmates prepared to meet the Tide in the 1935 Rose Bowl. But by this time, Brown was more fabled as a cowboy movie star than a football player who had shared star-of-the-game accolades in the 1926 Rose affair. Brown and Bill Boyd (the "Hopalong Cassidy" who did not play for Woody Hayes) and Tom Mix were the celluloid forerunners of Roy Rogers and Gene Autry. The cowboy movie star was distinct, unique Americana from the pioneer days of the film industry until the 1950s, when the advent of television brought financial setbacks to the movie studios which had been cranking out the low-budget, "B" Western adventures.

Somehow, television never spawned another Johnny Mack Brown. Heroism on horseback was too diminished by the small screen. By the 1960s and '70s cops and private eyes and Bionic folk had become the bigshots of good guy-ism. To the hip generation, the name Johnny Mack Brown would doubtless conjur visions of an unknown country-western singer who recorded on an obscure label.

But in Bob Reynolds' day, the horse and rider were worshipped by every young man attuned to the times.

The 'Bama club Reynolds and Stanford faced in 1935 was in many ways as fascinating, colorful and potent as Johnny Mack's bunch who came to Pasadena in 1926. The 1935 Tide had Howell and Hutson; a decade earlier it was Brown and Hubert—old "full steam-ahead" Pooley Hubert.

In 1951, wire service electors would rank the 1926 Alabama-Washington Rose Bowl game as one of the ten "greatest" football contests ever played. The game must have been a thriller; yet, most written reports don't do it justice. Perhaps one had to be there.

Washington, led by all-America halfback George Wilson, who starred when the Huskies tied Navy in Pasadena two years earlier, was a heavy favorite against the Tide. Probably, this was because bettors knew little about undefeated 'Bama (9–0, with only one touchdown scored against it all season). Washington was 10–0 and had averaged nearly forty-six points a game. In their 1925 season opener, the Huskies devoured Willamette 108–0. But hadn't the Tide crunched Union 53–0?

"We were nothing but little country boys when we started, then Coach Wallace Wade made something out of us," Brown recalled. And George Wilson, said Johnny Mack, "is only one guy, isn't he?"

Yes. And nearly enough to turn the tide against the Tide. The 1926 Rose Bowl ended up a battle between Wilson and Alabama.

There was, too, that encounter of future movie stars. The Huskies had a reserve tackle named Herman Brix, who would go on to win a silver medal in the shot put at the 1928 Olympics and then, still using his own name, play the title role in *The New Adventures of Tarzan* in 1935. As Bruce Bennett, Herman appeared in some eighty feature films. Brix-Bennett made his first film in 1931, but Johnny Mack Brown's movie career began in 1928, less than two years after his Rose Bowl heroics. Johnny Mack was first cast in a comedy but, because of his ruggedly handsome features, quickly moved into Westerns, where he stayed for nearly two decades.

George Wilson wasn't a movie star. He was barely fit long enough to be a star in the 1926 Rose Bowl. Wilson played in only three of the four quarters, having been rendered unconscious by three 'Bama tacklers late in the second quarter and forced to sit out in the third.

Washington tackle Herman Brix, a. k. a. Bruce Bennett in uniform, and "out of uniform" playing the title role in *The New Adventures of Tarzan*.

Alabama left halfback Johnny Mack Brown, named Player of the Game in the Tide's 20-19 victory over Washington in the 1926 game. He entered the movies in 1928. Here he is in *70,000 Witnesses*.

In the first quarter, Wilson intercepted a pass, returned it 38 yards to the 'Bama 47 and then carried most of the way as the Huskies went ahead 6–0.

In the second quarter, George tore off a 36 yard run to the Tide 20, and then threw a TD pass from there to Johnny Cole. It was 12–0 Washington at the half.

But with George hearing birdies in the third period, the Tide went to work. Quickly, devastatingly, fatally. In less than seven minutes, 'Bama scored three touchdowns.

Their first score came in a five-play, 41-yard drive. Quarterback Pooley Hubert, told at halftime by Coach Wade to "run yourself all you want," carried all five times for gains of 26, 10, 1, 3, and 1, and a TD. Now it was 12–7.

Moments later, 'Bama right halfback Grant Gillis heaved a 59-yard touchdown pass to left halfback Brown. The Tide finally had the lead, 14–12.

Soon thereafter, following a Husky fumble near midfield, Hubert tossed for 30 yards and a touchdown to Johnny Mack, described by one participant as having "the sweetest pair of elusive feet I have ever seen." It was 20–12, Alabama.

Wilson returned in the fourth quarter to run and pass Washington in an 88-yard touchdown drive and a 20–19 finale. While George was in the Husky lineup, Washington gained 300 yards; while he was sidelined, the Husky offensive output netted only 14 yards.

A thriller, yes. Not to mention a fruitful entrance exam into the Rose Bowl for the South.

When 'Bama, sans Johnny Mack Brown and Pooley Hubert and all but two of their starters from the 1926 Bowl, returned for the 1927 holiday game against Stanford, Pasadena had a sellout but less than a repeat thriller. Stanford, totally dominated the game yet could carry only a 7–0 lead into the final two minutes. A blocked punt gave 'Bama the ball on the Indian 14, and Wade sent in injured half-back Jimmy Johnson, who'd been out the first fifty-eight minutes with a dislocated shoulder.

The Tide needed five plays to move the 14 yards; Johnson carried from the couple-of-inches line for the TD. A conversion would mean a deadlocked Bowl. The onus was on 'Bama placekicker Herschel "Rosy" Caldwell, but the Tide had made plans to ease Rosy's burden. Coach Wade had worked out a tricky maneuver, just in case a clutch kick would be necessary. The Tide signal caller began to chant the signal, then stood up and said, "Signals checked." This message was to be ignored by 'Bama center Gordon Holmes, but not, of course, by the Stanford defenders, who had to assume there'd be a lingering pause.

Rosy's kick was good as not one Indian rushed. Stanford coach Pop Warner must have loved that one. As must have the facile Graham McNamee, announcing, via NBC, the first national radio hookup attempted.

Another interesting feature of that 1927 Rose Bowl was Pop Warner's use of a zone pass defense. ('Bama was only one-for-one in the air.) When the pros began playing the ball instead of the man on pass defense in the 1960s, it was as though the tactic were revolutionary. And so, for the record, it must be noted that Pete Rozelle did not invent the zone defense against passing. Of course, Pop Warner didn't beat Alabama with the zone either.

Alabama made one more visit to Pasadena prior to its meeting with the Vow Boys. That game came in 1931, against Washington State, a team branded as the Red Devils (nee Cougars) after going 9–0 in the 1930 season. But 'Bama's Wade also had a 9–0 club at Tuscaloosa, although he lacked the big names who would emerge into pro ball from the Washington State lineup: center Mel Hein and right tackle "Turk" Edwards.

The Cougars had been to Pasadena only once before, stopping Brown 14–0 in the renewal Bowl of 1916. And after this '31 visit, Washington State hasn't returned again. That's your basic football drought.

Cougar/Red Devil Coach Orin E. "Babe" Hollingbery complained that his players ate too many oranges on the grounds of the Huntington Hotel in the days before the game, and were thus a bit acidic for their appearance against the Tide. Whatever, Alabama scored three touchdowns in the second quarter and won 24–0, thanks to the running of MVP Johnny Monk Campbell, and the punting and passing of Jimmy "Hurry" Cain.

Never again did anybody call the Cougars the Red Devils. Or the Oranges. And Wallace Wade was still undefeated at Pasadena—as a coach. Wade played for that Brown team beaten by the Cougars in '16. Soon, he moved East, to Duke. He didn't have a club in the Rose Bowl again until 1939. But Alabama, under Frank Thomas, returned in '35 for a memorable meeting with Bob Reynolds and the Vow Boys. The Tide didn't have an Al Barabas to haunt the kids from Palo Alto. Nope. All they had were Howell and Hutson. And an obscure end named Paul Bryant.

By the 1970s, nobody called him Paul anymore. "Bear" was good enough. He had eventually returned to Alabama to coach its football teams into a succession of conference titles, national acclaim, and every Bowl game known to man—except the Rose, from which he was shut out because of that Pacific-Big Ten agreement.

But Bryant carries fond memories of his visit to that one Arroyo Seco game in 1935. Bear clearly remembers the fellow he faced across the line in that Rose Bowl—our old friend Horse Reynolds.

Reynolds says he doesn't recall Stanford having scouted Alabama to any great extent before the Rose matchup. "And they were the best team we played in our three Bowls as far as I'm concerned," said Horse. "Going into that game, we didn't know how good Don Hutson was. What we didn't know, what we weren't told to look for, was the speed of Hutson and the potential throwing ability of Dixie Howell. They had some fine ballplayers up and down their whole lineup. Fine personnel. And Bear Bryant was a damned fine end."

Bryant chuckles about his own abilities in those days. "I was just a very ordinary member of the team," he says. "We had some great players, but I certainly wasn't. . . . It was just a great thrill to me going out to the Rose Bowl. I mean, heck, it was a lifetime ambition. I was on cloud nine all the time just by being in the lineup. I was fortunate just to be around and to get a chance to play . . . the records show that . . . that game was just about the biggest thing that ever happened in my life."

Reynolds was one of the biggest things that ever happened to the Bear too. "I guarantee you, I scouted *him*," laughs Bryant.

"I knew I was going to have to play right in front of him that day. A few days before the game, Hutson was at a luncheon and got to meet some of the Stanford players—Moscrip and Grayson and Reynolds. Afterwards, Don came and told me—we were roommates—that I had no reason to be scared to death thinking about playing against those guys. Don said, 'Don't worry, Reynolds looks just like Schoolboy Rowe (at that time a pitcher for the Detroit Tigers).' Well, when I got onto the field and looked over and saw Reynolds warming up, I got frightened all over again. Sure he looked like Schoolboy Rowe, except sixty pounds bigger. 'Horse' and a guy named Williams at Georgia Tech were about the toughest I ever had to play against on the line. I never did block Reynolds in the Rose Bowl game, I'm sure. I held him a couple times, though." And the "Bear" giggles.

Hutson and Howell were no laughing matter at all to Stanford in that game. Individually they were destructive. In tandem as a passing combination, they were superb.

Bryant first saw Don Hutson in high school football in Arkansas. Bryant played at Fordyce, Hutson at Pine Bluff. "He had class and greatness written all over him even then," says Bryant. "Our high school wasn't scheduled to play one day, so I had a chance to go over and see his team play North Little Rock. And 'Hut' caught five touchdown passes. I had known of his abilities but I sure got to know them a little better that day. We've had many great players here at Alabama, but he was the greatest in my opinion. He always practiced a great deal, and of course he had great hands. I heard him talk once when he was playing with the pros in Green Bay about how important he thought that timing was. 'Hut' would just run. He had three speeds. He looked like he was going fast all the time, but he'd turn it on a little faster and then a little faster still. He would run under the ball. He'd just outrun the ball. He had that great timing. He'd never reach for the ball. Many times you see a young man get his arms up and reach for the ball too soon—a player like me or somebody. But 'Hut' would always get there at the last instant, and with his great hands and great timing would make the catch. In my opinion, he's probably the greatest player there ever was really. He could do everything."

They called Hutson the "Alabama Antelope." In the pros he weighed 195, and could run the hundred in 9.8.

"Don caught passes that lesser men would have merely waved at," wrote Robert Smith in *The Illustrated History of Professional Football.* "He caught them over his head, at his knees, just off the grass, at the absolute end of his straining fingertips. In one game Hutson, closely covered at the goal line, sped straight at the goal posts, grabbed one post as he was going by, swung around in a vicious pivot that left the defensive man running top speed away from him, and then reached back with his free hand to snake a pass out of the air for a touchdown."

" 'Hut' would always beat you some way—end-around, or he'd catch a pass. He'd always do it some way," said Bryant.

Grantland Rice put Hutson on his all-America team in 1934. But he omitted Howell. "As long as I live," said Rice after watching Dixie rise in the '35 Rose Bowl, "I'll be sorry I overlooked him."

Howell's given name was Millard. He was named MVP at Pasadena that day, and was eventually elected to the National Collegiate Football Hall of Fame. Howell died of cancer in March, 1971, two months after his induction into the Alabama Hall of Fame.

Frank Thomas' Alabama team swept crushingly through its 1934 schedule. They emerged 9–0, and outscored their opponents, who in those days included such as Howard and Sewanee, 287–32.

"I had great respect for Coach Thomas, and still do," says Bryant. "I didn't know much what he was doing then. Now I look back and think that, first of all, he had a great football mind. His planning was always well thought out. But the thing I think he did best was getting you mentally ready with the help of his assistants. Then on the day of the game, he didn't miss a bet. He ran a game better than anyone I've ever known. He was prepared. He'd adjust. He'd do the right thing at the right time."

Stanford did the right thing much of the time in 1934. It finished 9–0–1 (a 7–7 tie with Santa Clara) and ran up 211 points to its opponents' 14. Coach "Tiny" Thornhill developed a sound defense "formulated over a period of time by Pop Warner and with some variations from Howard Jones, Greasy Neale, and some other Eastern coaches," recalled tackle Reynolds.

"Thornhill gave our defense some damned silly name called 'Butterfly Accordion' —you know, romantic, just like that KF-79," continued Reynolds. "The theory of it was this: Because the two principal offenses of the time were the Notre Dame and the Warner, you knew that the only way they could work was if an offensive end could handle a defensive tackle by himself, or at least check off the tackle with a brush block or something like that. If you could contain the tackle, this gave you a great advantage on end sweeps. You made a good many long runs in those days by containing the tackle, blocking the defensive end, and taking out the linebacker and defensive halfbacks. If you could generate this kind of blocking, your offense could go. So what Tiny had us do to counter this kind of offensive blocking was to play a couple yards off the line so the offensive guy couldn't knock you down.

"Against Alabama, our defensive line was sitting back and we weren't rushing the passer. We were set to stop their running game because we just didn't realize how good a passing attack they had. With us sitting back like that, Howell had all darned day to throw. And we weren't aware of Hutson's speed. What he did to us that day, he went on to do for eleven years against the best defensive backs in all of professional football. What this Hutson guy could do was just fantastic. He'd lope down the field, turn on a burst, and be ready for a pass from Howell, who had all that time to throw. I got the feeling the pass patterns were pretty much left up to Hutson. He'd see where he could make a cut and break open. And Howell was hitting him because he had all damned day to do it.

"We tried to modify our defense in the second half, but by then it was too late," said Reynolds.

In fact, too darned late.

Stanford, despite its humbling by Columbia the previous year, had to be considered a slight favorite over 'Bama. After all, these were still the "Vow Boys."

"We were very much aware they were a fine football team," says Bryant. "But we had a team that was raring to go all the time. Our people back here were all fired up and keyed up to play a good game. And the only good game you play is a win. . . . We all had one thing in common: We wanted to win. And I guess that as a team we may have surprised Stanford."

O. B. Keeler of the Atlanta *Journal* suggested that 'Bama coach Thomas and his assistants, Red Drew and Hank Crisp, would keep their passing game under wraps early, and would catch the Stanford defense napping, and then open up. Which was rather the way it all turned out.

Stanford scored in the first quarter on the running of Bobby Grayson, "Bones" Hamilton (who on defense would become a victim of Hutson's speed and moves) and "Buck" Van Dellen. Grayson climaxed a drive of 29 yards, which started after a 'Bama fumble, by scoring from the 1. The Indians led, 7–0.

Now it was the second quarter. And it was time for halfback Howell and end Hutson to go into action. Moving from the Stanford 45 after a punt exchange, Howell hit Hutson for 17, then a halfback, Angelich (as Hutson decoyed defensive back Hamilton) for 12. Next, Dixie threw to Paul Bryant for 15. ("My catch was really pretty incidental," he chuckles.) Howell carried in, but Riley Smith missed the conversion, and Stanford still was ahead, 7–6.

At one moment in that first half, the "Bear" not only found himself basking in a rainbow but appeared to have discovered the pot of gold, too.

"After one play near their sideline, I found a bunch of money," says the "Bear." "A handful of quarters and half dollars, and so forth. It may have been small change, but it wasn't small to me at the time. I mean, very few of us had money in those days. I know I didn't have any. Most of us on the team had jobs with our scholarships. I cleaned up the washroom in the gym, and in the dorm. Some of us we lived in the gym. I got board-and-room for that work—more than I deserved, really. Can't remember where Howell worked, but 'Hut' had a job in the mess hall. And that worked out fine for me: He didn't drink milk, so he was always swapping me his milk in exchange for my dessert."

Oh, yes. The small change.

"Well, we were on defense, and I thought that after the next play I was going to run over to our bench and put this money away. So I held it in my hand. On the next play —they were on our 35 or 40—this great blond back of theirs, Grayson, runs a sweep

Stanford fullback Bobby Grayson (No. 22) carried against Alabama in the 1935 game.

toward me. I think it was the only tackle I made the entire game, and when I made the tackle I lost my money."

On their first series of plays after their initial TD, the Crimson Tide rolled again. Howell to Hutson for 25. Howell to Bryant for 18. To Hutson for 5. Then a 22-yard field goal by Smith, who was quarterback-blocking back-play caller, to put 'Bama up 9–7.

Within moments it was 16–7. Howell ran 67 yards for a score. Many years later, the 1935 Rose Bowl Queen told Pasadena *Star-News* columnist Joe Hendrickson "one of her most distinct memories was of Dixie waving his hand at the Stanford bench as he ran down the field" for that touchdown.

Howell soon got a rest. But not Stanford. Still in the second quarter, Joe Riley, Dixie's replacement, combined with Hutson for a 60-yard TD pass, and it was 22–7 'Bama.

By halftime, the Tide had connected on eight of nine passes. "We decided during the half to exert more pressure on Howell. Rush him," said Reynolds. "And secondly, we had to open up the game and get some points. Which we did. But we never could overcome that second quarter of theirs."

Stanford did score in the third period as Van Dellen rushed in from the 12. But the fourth quarter was Howell-Hutson time again. Their touchdown pass covered 59 yards. That made it 29–13—the final score.

Howell had a personal game total of 341 yards: 107 rushing, 74 in punt returns, 160 passing. He completed nine of twelve passes, five to Hutson for 110 yards. Hutson caught six in all for 164 yards, a reception record for the Rose Bowl which still stands.

Albama stars Millard "Dixie" Howell (left) and Don Hutson practice their speed-reading in Pasadena the day after their 29-13 victory over Stanford's "Vow Boys."

Said Stanford captain Hamilton after the game, "I couldn't recognize Hutson if I met him face to face because I spent all afternoon chasing him. The rear view, I will never forget."

And Grantland Rice wrote, "Dixie Howell, the human howitzer from Hartford, Alabama, blasted the Rose Bowl dreams of Stanford with one of the greatest all-around exhibitions that football has ever known." That against the best Stanford team Bob Reynolds felt he'd ever played on.

He'd see Hutson again—in the pros—but Bob had another Rose Bowl game to play first: in 1936 against Southern Methodist, which was 12–0 and the only team from Texas ever to play in Pasadena.

"All of the Stanford seniors hated to have our Christmas vacation interrupted again," said Reynolds. "But then we had second thoughts. The fact is we wanted very much to have an invitation to the Rose Bowl and fought like hell to get it. We beat a tough Cal club in the 'Big Game' (13–0). If we'd lost, they would have gone to Pasadena. Finally we realized, 'Hell, let's go. Let's get ready and win.'"

Which, finally, the Indians did. They got a first quarter TD in front of those nine special trainloads of SMU fans as quarterback Bill Paulman culminated a 42-yard drive by sneaking in from the 1. And that was the only scoring of the day. The "Vow Boys," who had bet $1,200 on themselves, at last had a 7–0 New Year's present. "We took no chances with our defense in that one," said Reynolds. "We had everybody on their ends, and everybody on the line. And our ends and our line just ran their all-America halfback Bobby Wilson ragged." Wilson gained only 21 yards, as Stanford defensive end Keith Topping spent the afternoon on Wilson's back. (Earlier in the season, Topping was nearly expelled for over-aggressive pranksterism.)

Stanford all-America tackle Bob Reynolds, the only player ever to play every minute in three consecutive Rose Bowls, 1934, '35, and '36.

"If the truth be known," Reynolds said thirty years later, "Bobby Wilson was probably a better passer than Howell. At least we finally proved we were good enough to win a Rose Bowl."

"Horse" also proved he was quite good enough to play with the pros. He spent two years with the Detroit Lions, playing for $185 a game—ten bucks more than Hutson was getting from the Green Bay Packers. Don remained with the Packers for eleven seasons and scored 101 touchdowns. In 1951, AP selected Hutson on its all-time, all-America team.

Reynolds' Lions played the Packers four times in Bob's two Detroit seasons, and split with them. Then Reynolds split from football. "I wanted to go into my dad's oil business because I'd once pushed tools for him. But his business was still lousy at that time," said the "Horse."

"Dick Richards, the Lion owner, knew I wasn't going into coaching. He owned a radio station in Beverly Hills and offered me a job there as a time salesman. But he also wanted me to stay with the team and be captain at $4,000 a year, about four times what I had been making as a player. I just decided t'hell with football and went out to the radio station."

Eventually, in partnership with cowboy film star Gene Autry, Reynolds owned a string of West Coast radio stations and the California Angels baseball team. And always he would remain a Stanford man. How could it be otherwise, after giving the school all of those minutes in all of those Rose Bowls?

"27" VS. "OSKIE WOW WOW"

Howard Harding Jones was described in 1931 by the *New York Times'* Allison Danzig as "the most under-recognized coach, from a national standpoint, the game has had in many years. It seems incomprehensible that Jones should have received so little attention as has been accorded him."

Ten years later, Howard Jones was dead. By then proper attention had been paid him. He took USC teams to five Rose Bowls (1930, '32, '33, '39, '40) and won them all. At Pasadena, Jones' teams—the first three of which were labeled "Thundering Herds"—took on four of the nation's most distinguished football coaches, and beat them all. Jones claimed two victories over the celebrated Jock Sutherland, Pitt (both stompings), plus one each from Bernie Bierman, then of Tulane and later of Minnesota glory, Wallace Wade, Duke, and Tennessee's stolid General Bob Neyland.

The 1939 Bowl victory was secured in uncharacteristic fashion for a Jones team. It was put together with a Hollywood-like, final-moment flurry of passes by the fourth-string Trojan quarterback, Doyle Nave, who overcame a 3–0 Duke lead. This was not Howard Jones football, and not, as was later revealed, even his strategy.

"He preferred to win with his system," one of his USC quarterbacks, Ambrose Schindler, pointed out recently. "It was a matter of coaching technique coming down to the wire. He liked a highly contested game. He didn't like runaways. That is to say, he liked to win by seeing that his techniques prevailed, and that his methods were superior. He did not believe in taking unnecessary risks. He didn't believe in gambling. He was basically conservative but not to the point where he wasn't mentally ahead of things. I consider him a genius."

Schindler should know for after his Jones days, he played for, and coached with, Amos Alonzo Stagg.

"I was so wrapped up in Howard Jones' mentality while I was playing at USC, I felt as if I almost lived with him. He was the best defensive coach I've ever seen. Even today with multiple offenses, he would still be one of the best minds in figuring a defense. Regardless of the situation, he would have adapted," Schindler said.

Jones coached some thirty-five years in all. He played end at Yale at the same time his brother, Tad, was quarterbacking his way to all-America honors with the Eli. Howard's early coaching success came at his alma mater, and in those days he built a growing rivalry with another renowned coach, "Pop" Warner. In fact, their personal competition began in 1908, when Jones ran Syracuse and Warner was at Carlisle. By 1909, Howard was back at Yale; that year's team, in fact, was, according to Danzig, Jones' favorite.

Jones' student Schindler is amused today by the history of the Jones-Warner competition for the role of ranking football genius. "When I began coaching in the Forties," says Schindler, "the single wing was called 'Warner B' and the double wing the 'Warner A'—even that late in football time. And I hadn't heard those designations used before, so I'd ask other coaches what the dickens a 'Warner B' was. They'd tell me, 'You've been running it for four years at USC, so you must know.' And I'd say, 'That's a Howard Jones single wing.'

"He was just such a genius at football. He believed in knowing the opponent by having them well-scouted. That way his team could properly set up a defense for them. And by controlling them, his team could beat them with their own selected offensive patterns.

"Howard Jones believed in a well-disciplined team. His players had to do it his way. His teams trained very well. He was very thorough.

"He used a two-team competition on his squad; great rivalry, but harmonious in another sense. A major belief of his was proper execution: get your shoulder in the right place and block your man. Move your man out of the way correctly.

"And that single-wing offense of ours was really something," says ex-quarterback Schindler with a soft, nostalgic smile. "Today, people look at that and say, 'Three yards and a cloud of dust.' However, it was a very sophisticaed system. The quarterback had a selection of five plays through a given hole. We had a selection of how to open the hole, how to run pulling guards and tackles through there, how to double team or not double team, how to angle-block on linebackers, and how to pick up defensive half-backs. So it was very sophisticated."

"Running to daylight is a new development, I guess. We didn't do that. We ran to a hole. If the hole wasn't there, we ran into where the hole was supposed to be anyway. We had to prove that it wasn't the running back's mistake for that hole not being opened. If we ran someplace else, the coach would say, 'Well, you ran wrong. That's why the hole didn't work.' So we had to know why the hole wasn't working.

"Howard Jones believed in running directly at the other team's best lineman. Jones would pick their all-America and concentrate the attack on him to prove to his own

USC coach Howard Jones coached the Trojans in five Rose Bowls: 1930, '32, '33, '39, and '40 and won them all. The only other coach to win five Rose Bowl games is USC's John McKay.

men that you had to beat their best man, and that when you did, you had the game. He had us do that against everybody. His players had to feel they could dominate the other team. And we almost always did.

"But you know, when he brought out this approach to us for the first time—this notion of whipping their best man—I thought it was illogical. But we were scared to death of Howard Jones, so of course we believed in doing what he wanted. And of course, it usually proved to be the right way to do things. We would get that all-America of theirs with double-teaming, or whatever it took. We'd whip him, and prove to the rest of his team that we could go on them. And then you'd see that other team losing confidence. Howard Jones was saying to that other team: 'We're not going to turn tail and run away from anybody!' That was our coach. He never said a team was too good for us."

In the 1930 Rose Bowl a USC team which had lost two games went up against Sutherland's undefeated Pitt, a team with no less than four All-Americas. This Panther team was being described as one of the greatest in the history of Eastern football. And the Trojans, particularly "Racehorse" Russ Saunders, passed the Panthers to death, 47–14. Jones went to his reserves early.

Two years later at Pasadena, a once-defeated Jones club met 11–0 Tulane and galloped 21–12. Trojan halfback Ernie Pinckert, who had a gala day on both offense and defense in the 1930 game, scored two touchdowns in the third quarter, each on an unorthodox double wingback reverse. Tulane at least came out of the game with an $80,000 share, and used the money to build a men's gymnasium.

Jones had most of his fine linemen back for the 1933 Bowl; this club was undefeated, as was its Pasadena opponent, Sutherland's kids from Pitt. This time USC's victory was even more convincing, 35–0, as the Panthers were introduced to an elusive flash of a back named Cotton Warburton. (This was one of those Monday, January 2, games.) Warburton, who wound up working for Walt Disney, replaced MVP Homer Griffith with SC up 14–0 starting the final period and scooted quickly to a pair of touchdowns.

Jones' clubs bowed to the domination of Stanford's "Vow Boys" in the middle Thirties and did not return to Pasadena until the melodrama of 1939. This was the Doyle Nave Bowl.

In one of the sports humor treasuries he edited, Herman L. Masin talks about Nave entering "the tumultuous Trojan dressing room" after his last-second, game-winning, off-the-bench heroics and asking, "Gee, I wonder if I'll get a letter now?"

"Son," he was told, "you're going to get the whole alphabet."

Jones had a surfeit of quarterbacks in the regular 1938 season. There was the starter, the all-America and one-time Pasadena prep star, Grenny Lansdell. "An easygoing, nonchalant individual," a teammate called him.

The coach first liked Lansdell two years earlier, in a game against Notre Dame. Grenny had been knocked out on a play, but kept going after being revived. After that day, he wore a special padded helmet. "Jones liked his courage in that game," says Schindler, "and decided to keep starting him."

Then there was Mickey Anderson, who played in 1936, but was shifted to wingback in 1937 because of Lansdell's capabilities. Anderson was a fine runner, a clear All-America candidate, and another former Pasadena prepster.

Also, there was Schindler. He hurt his leg during the season, and because Jones was not totally pleased with the condition of the field on New Year's, was held out of the Bowl.

Then there was a fellow named Ollie Day.

And Nave.

"Not to take anything away from Doyle," says Schindler, "but he was not a crushing runner. He just didn't run very well. And you had to be if you wanted to be a quarterback in those days. Lansdell was a big man. Mickey Anderson was quick and hard-running. And I was quite strong in those years. But Doyle was a specialist at throwing the ball. He was one of those types who could thread a needle anyplace. That was his forte. In later years, in a situation where he wouldn't have to run the ball, I'm sure Doyle would have been a very fine T-formation quarterback."

He didn't have to run it at all during his two minutes on the field in the Rose Bowl game of 1939. "What happened with Doyle that afternoon seemed the logical kind of thing to happen," says Schindler.

Storybook logical, that is.

Wade's Duke club had two gridiron geniuses in Eric Tipton, halfback and punter extraordinaire, and fleet George McAfee, who later became a classic pro for George Halas with the Chicago Bears. Wade brought three Alabama clubs to Pasadena and was 2–0–1. Like Jones, he was undefeated in the big one.

Early in the fourth quarter, the Blue Devils parlayed a McAfee punt return and Tipton pass into a 23-yard field goal by Tony Ruffa, to break a scoreless tie.

Grenny Lansdell couldn't move the 8–2 Trojans against 9–0 Duke, and for good reason: The Devils hadn't been scored upon all year. Neither could Mickey Anderson dent the Duke defense. Nor Ollie Day.

The 3–0 lead appeared impregnable, so much so that USC's assistant coaches stationed in the Rose Bowl press box abandoned their perch, with just under three minutes to play, and headed for Jones' side on the field. But one of their juniors, assistant freshman coach Joe Wilensky, remained in the press box to man the phone to the bench.

With slightly more than two minutes remaining, the Trojans acquired the ball on the Duke 34. And Wilensky, who was nothing more than the telephone relay voice for his now-absent coaching superiors, made an impetuous move—discovered years later by Maxwell Stiles of the *Long Beach Press-Telegram*.

The assistants were still working their way down to the field when Wilensky—with Howard Jones listening on the other end—shouted into the telephone, "Yes, yes, I get it. I'll tell him right away."

Short pause. USC's coach, Howard Jones listened attentively.

"The word is to send in Nave and have him throw passes to Krueger."

As Schindler looks back: "I think that move would have met with everybody's approval, including that of Sam Barry, the key assistant coach who left the press box early. When time is running out like it was," says Schindler, who was watching the game from the sidelines in civvies and nursing his bum leg, "it's very hard to march down the field. We'd had trouble running. Footing was very bad. So putting in Doyle at that moment made a lot of sense."

To Howard Jones, too. What the heck. Why not?

"Antelope Al" Krueger was, like Nave, a sub. In practice sessions, they would pair off, as subs are wont to do. They persistently threw "27" patterns.

"I'd played more with our starting end, 'Scrap Iron' Bill Fisk, but I knew that Al Krueger could catch anything," says Schindler. "He had fingers that were like bananas. He could make these fantastic moves. Nobody could teach him how to fake somebody because he didn't know what he was doing to fake anyway. He just did a lot of things, and then he'd find himself open."

The Trojans' "27" pattern had four major variations: a flat pass; a deep throw; a long crossover (down and out); a comeback (buttonhook). There was even a 27 (left end) end around.

Nave and Krueger could execute any of the 27s in their sleep, and probably did. Especially Nave, for he had little exertion in the regular season of 1938, playing only 28½ minutes in USC's ten games. Well, the Rose Bowl would bring his playing time to over half an hour anyway.

Here he was on the Duke 34. First down. On the 27 deep he hit Krueger for 13 yards. First down on the Duke 21. On the 27 deep he hit Krueger for 9 yards. Second down, time scurrying, on the Duke 12.

Nave's third play was a 27 flat to good old "Antelope Al," which Krueger caught behind the line of scrimmage. But the Duke defense dropped him immediately for a 2-yard loss. Third down, 3, on the Duke 14; just about one minute to play.

Another 27. This time the buttonhook. Krueger eluded the tiring Tipton and caught Nave's toss in the end zone.

With only forty-one seconds remaining to be played, Duke had finally been scored against, and lost, 7–3. "We were all right as long as USC didn't show us more than three teams," said Wade. "But when the Trojans came up with fresh and talented fourth-stringers, it was too much. Krueger simply outran our players, while Nave had all day to pass because our linemen were just too tired to rush him."

Signing his autograph is fourth-string SC quarterback Doyle Nave, last minute hero of the 1939 7-3 win over Duke.

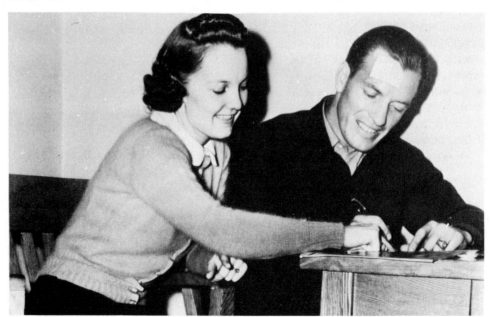

"Many, many more football games will be played in this land before they put on another like that," wrote Henry McLemore.

Nave and Krueger shared MPV honors.

"But, I think that Rose Bowl was a wonderful thing for Doyle," says Schindler. "I'm glad it happened to him. These are the kind of things we should get out of athletics. Those two minutes he had far outshadowed others' performances. That Rose Bowl also became a big factor in his life. It was good for him, business-wise and otherwise.

"It was just phenomenal the way he handled that series of plays. He got some fine blocking from our fullback, Bob Peoples. Bob took out two men at different times. And Doyle had four completed passes in a row. Just fantastic.

"I guess Doyle anticipated this game would probably be a stepping stone to better things for him at USC the next season. Which it was. Had he not had that fantastic day in the Rose Bowl, he might not have played as much as he did in the 1939 season with us."

Nave, too, appeared again in the 1940 Rose Bowl. But he didn't start that game, either. Lansdell did. And Doyle wasn't the hero again. That honor belonged to the fellow they called "Desperate Amby" (a Twenties comic strip), Parks Ambrose Schindler.

"Some great USC people came from my school, San Diego High," says Schindler. There was Russ Saunders, who'd had a great Rose Bowl. And Cotton Warburton. My coach was Hobbs Adams; he'd been captain of the 1926 USC team. He was a tough taskmaster who patterned himself after Howard Jones. So by the time I got to USC, I'd already had two years of that. Through Hobbs Adams I knew the USC system pretty well. In fact, I owe Adams most of the success I've ever had."

Lansdell was Jones' top choice for starting quarterback before the 1939 season began —Nave's heroics of the preceding January notwithstanding. "I think Grenny just shrugged off what had happened to Doyle in the Rose Bowl," says Schindler. "Grenny knew he had his own glory because he started so many, many games. He knew that he almost always got the call over the rest of us, which is something damned good."

In practices leading up to the 1939 season, Schindler worked hard on his passing. "I showed I could throw the ball as well as anybody. And I could run a little better. So Jones finally said that I was to be the regular quarterback. Over Grenny. Which was a big thing.

"I know that Howard Jones could be a ruthless person in a way. That is, unforgiving. A boy could make a mistake, and sometimes the coach didn't give that kid a second chance. But by saying I would be the starting quarterback, he was being magnanimous, in a way, because he knew I had been injured the year before.

"Then once the season got going, I had another injury. I was very agile, and I jumped over a spot where someone was going to tackle me in the open field. I landed awkwardly on a heel and bruised it. Jones thought it was a simple thing, but it was very, very painful and kept me out of a couple of ball games. Jones used to say that I let little things bother me. That just about broke my heart. Then I wasn't his starting quarterback, anymore. Grenny was again.

"I wouldn't say that was punishment. Howard Jones did not punish. But he just refused to give me the opportunity again to start, even though I'm sure he knew I was his type of quarterback. He knew I was well-versed, that I knew his system better than any of our quarterbacks. I always think Jones used me to control a ball game when we got into tight situations. Against Notre Dame that year (USC won, 20–12) he put me in with the score 13–12 to run things, to make sure things were going along according to his way. Later, I had the feeling that he put me in when he really needed the game to be controlled, that I was in a sense his coach on the field, his strength. And that he trusted me—even though I didn't start games. I happened to get lucky and ran 40 yards against Notre Dame, and that iced it a little bit.

"To get over the hill in the 1939 season, we had to beat Oregon State up there. We were slightly ahead at the half, and Jones called me aside and said, 'I'm going to have you control the game and not run up the score.' He knew our superior numbers would dominate the game in the end. He didn't want our team to get fat, by building up a big score. He felt he could trust me. And that's how it turned out again in the 1940 Rose Bowl."

For a change, the Eastern participant in the Pasadena game was selected before the identity of the Coast club was known in late 1939.

"There was some fear that Tennessee would not accept a bid should UCLA be named as the Pacific Coast standard-bearer," reports historian Rube Samuelsen, "because of four Negroes on the Bruins' roster." Among the four were one of UCLA's all-time finest gridders, Kenny Washington, and a young man named Jackie Robinson, who had prepped in Pasadena.

"Fortunately, the doubt proved to be without basis," wrote Samuelsen.

Because USC and UCLA weren't scheduled to play in the game which would decide the West's Rose Bowl entrant until December 9, both teams selected undefeated Tennessee early; the Cotton Bowl also had been seeking the Volunteers.

UCLA had to defeat the Trojans to get to Pasadena—and the Bruins had never beaten USC. Late in the fourth quarter, USC stopped three Bruin plunges from the Trojan 2, with the game scoreless. On fourth down, Kenny Washington threw an incomplete pass. Inexplicably, Robinson was not given the opportunity to try a field goal on that play. The 0–0 tie prevailed, and USC went to Pasadena.

"Robinson was somewhat obscured by Washington's talents at UCLA," says Schindler. "Kenny was a better triple threat. But in later years, watching Robinson's progress, I often thought about having played against someone who was such a great success later. I remember watching him run the basepaths in college. And I remembered how graceful Jackie was in the basketball fast break. He was really a smooth, beautiful athlete."

Tennessee had its share of smooth, beautiful athletes that year, too. And it had a coach who led them to twenty-three consecutive victories by the end of the 1939 season, with a 10–0, unscored-upon record in 1939—General (actually, Major) Robert Neyland. In a dozen years with the Vols, Neyland was 108–12–8. He retired in 1953. Revered.

Herman Hickman, a 310-pounder, a guard in 1929–31 under Neyland, later a coach at Yale, once observed, "If Neyland could score a touchdown against you, he had you beat. If he could score two touchdowns, he had you in a rout. His forte was defense, coupled with an air-tight, flawless kicking game. This meant every phase of the kicking game, both returns and coverages. He made a fetish of pass defense and the return of intercepted passes. Only twenty-five percent of our practices were spent on offense. The practices were short, the lecture periods long. He was a strict disciplinarian."

Neyland, a Texan, had been the Army's heavyweight boxing champion for three years while at West Point as a military science professor and, eventually, an assistant football coach. He was a rather good baseball pitcher, too.

He had a habit of writing maxims on blackboards: "The team that makes the fewer mistakes *WINS.*" "If a break goes against you, don't let down. Turn on *MORE* steam."

"Whenever we returned an intercepted pass, he taught us to give out this blood-curdling cry: 'OSKIE WOW WOW,' " said Hickman. "And he also taught us to gang tackle."

And there was one other thing Hickman remembered about the General. During winning streaks, Neyland told his "Remember the Sparrow" story. It concerned the sparrow who got so fat and happy when all the horses were on the street. But then came the automobiles. And no manure. Neyland's moral: "Don't get it in your neck."

So here was the 1940 Rose Bowl with one coach, Jones, who didn't wish his team to grow fat by running up the score, and the other coach, Neyland, who did not wish his team to grow fat by forgetting sparrows.

The Vols were loaded for this one. There was all-America quarterback George Cafego. A winner. There was guard Bob Suffridge, a two-time all-America; in 1951 the AP selected Suffridge on its all-time all-America team. Naturally, it was at Suffridge whom Jones directed the Trojan running attack.

Lansdell had started at quarterback for USC, but there was little progress. Then Jones opted for Nave and, with the game still scoreless in the second period, for "Desperate Amby."

Schindler returned a punt to the Tennessee 47, and began from there to direct the Trojan offense. His fullback was another sub, Jack Banta. Back during the regular season, in the Oregon State game, when Jones ordered Schindler to control the club and prevent a runaway, Amby had faced momentary, puzzled defiance from Banta.

"We were in the huddle, and I was hurting from two Charley horses," says Schindler. "So even though I had rarely called a fullback run, I told Banta to carry the ball. And he says, 'I've got a Charley horse.' I told him I had two of 'em. Then Jack says, 'For God's sake, throw the ball.'

"I told him, 'I can't.' He said, 'What do you mean, you can't?' I told him Jones didn't want any more scoring." And no one else knew this. They all questioned Jones' system, and that made it hard for me. But also very gratifying."

And now against Tennessee, Schindler called on Banta immediately. Jack picked up 2, Schindler 7, Schindler 6 more.

"Usually in our single wing, the quarterback was about 5 yards in back of the center. But in our system, the quarterback kind of sat differently almost every play. We had lots of options. But we had game plans. We had a labyrinth of plays but against certain teams would throw some out. I believed a lot in running left formation. I'd had so much success with it, I just believed in it," Schindler says.

After picking up a first down at the Vol 32 with that 6-yard run of his, Amby hit halfback Bob Robertson with an 11-yard pass. Then Amby ran for 9 more in a play on which the Vols were called for unnecessary roughness. Now USC had a first down at the Tennessee 3.

"I knew when I came into the game I was on the spot," says Schindler. "It was a very draining situation. I presumed that if I couldn't come up with something, Grenny probably would come back in. Not that I thought of myself as the last hope. To me, this was a job. I knew this was the Rose Bowl.

"Funny. I was just thinking about the bus ride to the game that day. We'd gotten jammed in traffic. It was so frustrating sitting there in traffic. But I didn't expect to play much that day. Howard Jones had picked on me in our Bowl practices and just ridiculed me. I don't know whether he was trying to get me up or what. I don't know to this day; I'd like to find out eventually from somebody.

"So here we're sitting stuck in traffic and I'm thinking to myself that I'd be going into my last game and I wouldn't get to play. I told myself that if I were a sophomore, I'd quit. It was a very, very trying thing. Seemingly, I had no place in Jones' plan for that game."

His place now was 3 yards from a touchdown, something Tennessee had not given up in its last fifteen games. Schindler carried twice, and scored—running through Suffridge after some fine blocking by Captain Joe Shell, a reserve halfback that day. "Joe told me he could handle him," Schindler recalls.

"The big picture that came out of the game showed me with my head up, in a run from the 3. My head was up because I was looking to see where the defense was. I didn't score until the next play, but all the picture captions said I had scored on that run with my head up. I challenged the photographer later, and he said, 'We didn't have our camera ready because you came back and ran that touchdown play so quickly.'"

USC quarterback Ambrose Schindler, named Player of the Game, runs for daylight in the Trojan's 14-0 win over Tennessee.

Ambrose Schindler, who says he was "the smallest man on the field" that day at 5–9½, and 182 pounds, had penetrated the impenetrable. USC, 7–0. And in the third quarter, Grenny Lansdell was once again quarterbacking the Trojans. During that period, the Vols mounted a major threat before fumbling on the USC 15.

Now it was the fourth quarter. Schindler returned and immediately guided the Trojans on an 85-yard scoring drive. USC was now wearing down the outweighed Vols. In fact, the USC subs—led by Amby, Banta and Shell—were grinding it out against Tennessee. In nine plays, Schindler directed the Trojans to the Vol 1-yard line.

"I knew I could probably run it in again," says Schindler. "And normally I would have. We were ahead seven, and in those days we played it so tough that seven points were pretty good.

"I went back into the huddle and, honest to God, I looked around and said, 'We're in the Rose Bowl. Why don't we give these people something to think about.' I was just going to throw a little pass to Al Krueger in the end zone. A 27 flat. I knew it was a sound play, very sound. Howard Jones designed it just for this purpose.

"I looked around at the stands. I was having a great day and knew it. You feel so good, on top of the world doing something you want to do and doing it so well. So in the huddle I said 27 flat.

"When I went to throw, Al wasn't even looking. But I knew that he would catch it. I just threw it up there, and I knew he would turn around and find the ball. I just knew it."

"Antelope Al," under less melodramatic circumstances, had himself another Rose Bowl touchdown reception. Final score: 14–0, USC.

In Navy flier's togs is end "Antelope Al" Krueger, who caught touchdown passes in both 1939 and '40 USC wins.

"I knew my performance didn't have the same impact as Doyle's in the 1939 game," says Schindler, who was named MVP in the 1940 event. "But I think it had an impact on Howard Jones. What pleased me so much was that one of Jones' close personal friends was sitting on the bench—I learned later—and heard that Howard had wanted me to call the 27 flat on that down. The friend told me, 'As you came out of the huddle, Howard started standing up off the bench and looking. He stood and looked at what you were doing and said, "Yes . . . yes . . . that's it . . . that's IT!" '

"After the game, Jones was reluctant to give out bouquets. That was always his way. He didn't believe in boys getting fat-headed. He wasn't reluctant to criticize, though.

"I was in the shower room when he finally came over to me. Howard Jones was the only one who ever called me 'Schindy.' Everybody else called me 'Amby' or 'Banana Nose.' My name is German, but I have this English nose from my mother. Well, whenever the coach was feeling good, he called me 'Schindy.' And that was kinda fun; I knew who was talking to me. So he comes over to me and says, 'Well, Schindy, you won it the way it should be won.' Meaning that it was a hard game and I had marched the team by using his power plays.

"Then he said—referring to the touchdown pass—'You remembered that play.' He repeated that two or three times.

"I live that moment so much in my memory.

"That Rose Bowl game was a wonderful thing," says Schindler, pocketing his notes on Howard Jones. "It was kind of like winning a championship. But that was the way Jones approached the Rose Bowl game. He wanted to get there and do it right."

Ambrose Schindler on occasion runs into folks who remember his Rose Bowl success. "The younger people don't know who I am," he says. "They don't pay too much attention to those old games. But my contemporaries know the name. And it's fun for me, because these people enjoying kibitzing about football in those years.

"I really started realizing how the years have gone by when one time this man of about forty with gray hair came up to me and said, 'I used to climb the fence to watch you play at Southern Cal.'

"And I said, 'Can I be that old?' "

SHAUGHNESSY'S "T"

Frankie Albert's eternally elfin face grins even now when he thinks how Stanford revolutionized college football in 1940. "We played the University of San Francisco in our opening game," he said. "I walked up on our first play, stood directly behind the center and sent Pete Kmetovic in motion. USF didn't know what to do. They had never seen a man under the center, or a man in motion. I just kind of flipped the ball to Kmetovic, that's all I had to do, and he went 40 yards."

And the modern college T-formation was born. A wild hair of an idea from the complex, fathomless mind of Clark Daniel Shaughnessy that would drive defenses berserk and Stanford to the heights of campus football. "We played USF in the second game of a double-header that day, Santa Clara having met Utah in the opener," Albert continued. "Utah's star was Mac Speedie, later a great player with the Cleveland Browns. Mac had showered up after his game and came back onto the field after we got started. He took one look, as he told me years later, and ran back to the locker room, shouting, 'Hey, you guys come out here. There's this crazy formation and these guys are running all over the place. I can't find the football!' "

No wonder. Albert was an unlicensed magician playing quarterback. He could do everything with a football but make it appear. By the time Stanford's opponents learned where it was, the Indians had rolled unbeaten through ten straight teams, including Nebraska, 21–13, in the Rose Bowl.

Shaughnessy changed the college game in the lightning-fast time that it took him to dominate it. One autumn. The T-formation, because of Shaughnessy's success at Stanford, would in the span of approximately twenty years remove the single wing—the dominant offense of the Thirties—from every major college playbook. There are varia-

Stanford T-formation passing star southpaw Frankie Albert.

tions of the T-formation today, such as the I-formation, Wishbone and Veer, but the quarterback still takes the ball directly from the center.

Shaughnessy has been called the Father of the T-formation. A more correct title would be Recreator of the T. The formation dates back to before the turn of the century, when Walter Camp used it at Yale. Princeton and Harvard soon followed. Amos Alonzo Stagg, who played for Camp at Yale, advanced the concept after becoming head coach at the University of Chicago. But in the early 1900s, Glenn "Pop" Warner introduced the single and double wing formations at Carlisle, which a Sac and Fox Indian named Jim Thorpe made famous. In time, football formations, like fashions, lose their flair and are considered outmoded. Warner practically abolished the T with his success at Carlisle, and a decade later Knute Rockne was making the Box formation the offense of the Twenties at Notre Dame.

SHAUGHNESSY'S "T"

On the professional level, the Chicago Bears were having difficulty staying alive after the 1929 stock market crash. George Halas turned his attention from coaching to the business end of the team and brought in Ralph Jones from Lake Forest College. Jones installed the T, but with a man in motion. He stayed as coach for three years (1930–32), winning the NFL championship in his final season before returning to Lake Forest, where his salary was greater than with the Bears. Halas resumed coaching again, and the Bears played for the league championship eight of the next thirteen years, winning five times. Chicago's success with the T had an indelible effect on the NFL and Clark Shaughnessy, the head coach at the University of Chicago.

Shaughnessy played tackle at Minnesota from 1911 to 1913 then immediately upon graduation in 1915, at the age of 23, became the head coach at Tulane, where he shared an apartment with a shoe salesman named Huey P. Long. He later coached at Loyola of New Orleans before winding up at Chicago in the Thirties. His Chicago teams lost by scores like 85–0 to Michigan, and would be long forgotten today except that they produced the first Heisman Trophy winner, Jay Berwanger, in 1936. Shaughnessy regularly attended the Bears' practices, won Halas' favor, and began showing Halas innumerable plays diagrammed on two-foot by two-foot cards. Halas picked the ones that he wanted and threw the others back at Shaughnessy. But a bond was struck between the two men that endured as long as both were alive.

In 1939, the University of Chicago gave up big-time football, and Shaughnessy was without a job. That same year, Stanford had a 1–7–1 record, using the single wing. Claude "Tiny" Thornhill was fired and Shaughnessy hired in his place. Shaughnessy's arrival on the Palo Alto, California, campus was not treated as the "Second Coming." The Indians had averaged exactly six points on offense and had been shut out four times the previous season.

"I remember my first Spring practice under Shaughnessy," said Albert. "The thing that impressed me about the man was that he was so positive. He'd make statements we couldn't believe, coming off a losing team. He'd diagram a fullback counter play on the blackboard. 'Boys,' he'd tell us, 'you're going to make a half-dozen touchdowns off this play.' It seemed crazy to us because we'd barely made a half-dozen touchdowns the whole 1939 season. While we wanted to believe him, we thought he might be over-appraising the present talent."

Shaughnessy was not over-appraising, just re-shaping. At the University of Chicago he wanted to run the T, but had little talent, except for Berwanger. So Shaughnessy was mired in the single wing. But after he assessed the talent on hand at Stanford, he knew he had the right ingredients to concoct a real surprise during the 1940 season.

Although he wouldn't be recognized until that first year at Stanford, Shaughnessy was in every sense of the word a football genius. He knew the intracacies of the game from every angle, breaking it down like an automobile engine and rebuilding it in his mind. Football seldom left his head; he was obsessed with it. He would be having dinner with his wife Mae and their three children, when he would suddenly stop eating and begin diagramming furiously on a napkin some new idea that formed in his head, perhaps leading to a Stanford touchdown, but almost certainly a cold lamb chop.

Once he was pulled off to the side of a highway after a traffic cop noticed his car was swerving. Shaughnessy wasn't drunk. He didn't drink anything stronger than buttermilk. He had been diagramming plays on a windshield fogged with condensation. Even sleep wouldn't free him from the game that controlled his life. "He'd call his assistant coaches at four in the morning and say, 'I know how we can run against the Oregon State defense. I just figured it out. I'll meet you right away at the athletic department,' " said Albert. "The assistants—Marchie Schwartz, Phil Bengtson, Jim Lawson—were all young guys, and had probably gotten home late from some party. Shaughnessy was driving them up a wall. He was a teetotaler and all he thought about was football. But Clark was so enthusiastic. He'd come out to practice that day and you could see the excitement in his eyes. 'If they use that same defense, Hugh Gallarneau, you'll score two touchdowns.' Damn if we didn't play the game and he's right. This really impressed the guys."

Frankie Albert was an average single-wing tailback for Stanford the year before. "I never cut up anybody running the ball. I was basically a passer," he said. "Pete Kmetovic was a runner who could hardly throw at all. We alternated at tailback, but it didn't matter. The defenses knew what to expect when each of us was in the game." The left-handed Albert took to the T-formation like a man on the desert takes to water. Albert was a born ball-handler, complete with sleight-of-hand tricks. Cocky and imaginative, he was the first and maybe the best of the bootleg quarterbacks, although Eddie LeBaron would enjoy later success.

"I loved the T from the start," said Albert. "I love fooling people anyway. I'd rather fool someone than overpower him, because I'm a little person. This formation gave me the opportunity to hide the football." Shaughnessy brought Bernie Masterson of the Chicago Bears, the first successful pro T-formation quarterback, out to Stanford that same spring to speed Albert's development.

That 1940 Stanford backfield was not only the first, but one of the best modern T-formation foursomes of all time—and they only played together that one year. Besides the leader, Albert, there was Norm "The Chief" Standlee, a 225-pound fullback who was a punishing runner and blocker. He averaged four yards a carry on the losing 1939 team. Shaughnessy knew he had the perfect short-yardage runner and lead blocker for Hugh Gallarneau's slicing runs between the ends. Gallarneau weighed 200, but his high school in Chicago didn't have football and so he concentrated on boxing and gymnastics. He turned out for freshman football at Stanford, where his body control and balance made him a perfect halfback, hard to knock off his feet. Pete Kmetovic was 175 pounds, like Albert, and the team's breakaway runner. Albert would get the defenses used to a diet of Standlee and Gallarneau coming through the middle, then pitch wide to the fast, elusive Kmetovic, who was most effective running outside.

Shaughnessy inherited a backfield, but that was about all. He had to revamp the offensive line. The center, Vic Lindskog, was a transfer from Santa Ana Junior College. Guards Chuck Taylor and Dick Palmer and tackles Bruno Banducci and Ed Stamm were sophomores up from the freshman team. The ends were Fred Meyer and Stan Graff. "With a new line, you can turn a losing record into a winning one," said Albert. "We didn't know how far we'd go that first season. But athletes are eternal optimists. We needed something new, our morale was down, and Shaughnessy and his staff were so refreshing. They were having an effect on us. I guess you could say that the T suited our needs and our abilities one hundred per cent."

Stanford was a touchdown underdog to USF, and probably should have been more. The Indians scrimmaged their freshman team two days before the USF game, "and they kind of beat us," Albert recalled. The freshmen knew what the varsity was doing. USF didn't, and was left spinning physically and mentally, 27–0. Stanford then knocked off Oregon 13–0, Santa Clara 7–6 and Washington State 26–14. "We won our first four games and we were the underdogs each week," said Albert. "Shaughnessy loved every minute of it. It wasn't until there was about three games left in the season that people began to say, 'Hey, these guys can go to the Rose Bowl.' This was a perfect situation for Stanford, because our players weren't reading all the time how good we were. I believe this helped our little team."

The Indians' fifth game was against USC, then as now the perennial powerhouse on the Pacific Coast. The Trojans had tremendous athletes in Jack Banta and Bob Peoples.

Before the game, Shaughnessy told Albert to put Kmetovic in motion, and have him come back as if he were going to block a Trojan defensive end. Albert then was to fake the ball to Standlee on an end run, and when Banta moved up from his halfback position thinking it would be a run, Albert was to throw the ball to Kmetovic, who had faked behind Banta. "It will be a sure touchdown," Shaughnessy predicted. It was, before the game was seven minutes old. But with four minutes left in the contest the score was 7–7. Meyer then made a fantastic catch of an Albert pass behind Peoples at the USC 5. Standlee slammed into the end zone, and Stanford intercepted an ensuing USC pass to make it 21–7, at the final gun.

"This is how we played all season," said Albert. "We just didn't get a new coach and new offense and run through everyone. We had a lot of tight games in 1940. In every game, we were fighting for our lives. But every game was a surprise." Stanford was pushed to beat UCLA 20–14, and then labored against Washington.

The Huskies had a 10–0 lead late in the third quarter and were driving again with a first down at the Stanford 9. The next play gained 7. Washington then ran three straight plays at Taylor, but the blond guard wouldn't give ground and Stanford took over inside its 1. Albert punted out of danger, Kmetovic intercepted a pass and scored, and Stanford caught fire in the last quarter to win 20–10. "You have to remember that there weren't many high-scoring games in those days—10–0 was a big lead," stressed Albert. "Yet people were calling us a wide-open team, even though we weren't. Heck, we only threw maybe nine passes a game. But this was the same year that the Bears

Stanford halfback Pete Kmetovic,
Player of the Game in the Indiana
21-13 win over Nebraska.

beat the Redskins 73–0 for the NFL title. Halas was sending us his game films every week, so we were one jump behind the Bears all season. You could say that we were a step toward wide-open college football, though. Shaughnessy opened the game up.''

Shaughnessy might have been the first college coach to call the plays for his quarterback. Only he didn't use the customary play messenger. Well, not quite anyway. "Clark always was thinking," said Albert. "He'd draw up plays right there on the sidelines while the game was going on. He'd use 5″ × 7″ cards. He didn't even have time to name the plays, but would give them to a guard who'd run on the field, hand me the card and say, 'Run this.' I'd show the card to the guys and say something like, 'This is what you do. On two!' Then I'd fold the card and stuff it inside the front of my pants and we'd go for 30 yards."

Stanford turned back Oregon State 28–14 and California 13–7, to finish the regular season 9–0. The year before the Indians hadn't won a game and now they hadn't lost a game. Shaughnessy was called a miracle worker, and the Indians received national attention. Shaughnessy was selected as College Coach of the Year. Albert was named All-America and after the season would star in *The Spirit of Stanford,* which was about his life and that incredible 1940 turnaround.

But if Hollywood had discovered Stanford, so had the Rose Bowl Committee.

SHAUGHNESSY'S "T"

Actually, Stanford was a shoo-in from the Pacific Coast Conference. Finding an opponent was more difficult. The Big Nine didn't allow post-season competition at that time, so neither Minnesota nor Michigan, whose Heisman Trophy hero Tom Harmon would also star in a movie *(Harmon of Michigan),* were available. Nebraska won the Big Six championship with an 8–1 record, its only defeat coming in the season opener to powerful Minnesota, 13–7. The Cornhuskers destroyed everything in their path after that, including Kansas 53–2. Nebraska had a colorful coach in Major Biff Jones and an All-America fullback in Vike Francis. And so it was decided, Stanford vs. Nebraska, in their first—and only—meeting ever.

By the time Stanford arrived in Pasadena, it had received the appellation "Wow Boys," a derivation of Stanford's "Vow Boys" of the mid-Thirties. "When you win, people spend a lot of time naming you," said Albert. "They didn't name us the year before."

Nebraska wasn't impressed and took the opening kickoff and scored quickly, Francis battering in from the 2 and kicking the extra point to make it 7–0. Albert could hear loud cheering from the 90,000 crammed into the Rose Bowl. "I kept thinking, 'Damn, this is a pro-Nebraska crowd,'" he recalled. "What happened was that a lot of the Stanford fans, with all the partying on New Year's Eve, came to the game late. We wore red jerseys most of the season, but were wearing white for this game. Nebraska's colors also were red and white, and they were wearing the red jerseys. Well, Nebraska scores —boom, boom—and the Stanford fans see the red jerseys, so they start screaming like crazy. Heck, our fans didn't know the T-formation from the single wing."

The remainder of the game proved that Nebraska was having the same problem. Stanford came back nine minutes later to tie the score, as Gallarneau ran over untouched from the 5 and Albert converted. Early in the second quarter, a punt by Nebraska's Herman Rohrig bounced off Kmetovic's chest and 'Husker back Allen Zikmund recovered at the Stanford 32. Rohrig, catching the Indians off-guard, threw a touchdown pass to Zikmund on the first play, but Taylor blocked the point-after and it was 13–7. Stanford fought back again to take the lead as Gallarneau took an Albert pass and turned it into a 40-yard touchdown play. Albert's kick gave Stanford a slim 14–13 halftime advantage. The Indians played the rest of the game without Standlee. The big fullback started the game with a severe ankle sprain, and six minutes before the half was gashed over one eye. It wouldn't be easy for the Indians, but then it hadn't been all season.

There was only one more touchdown, a sensational 38-yard punt return by Kmetovic in the third quarter, which is remembered as perhaps the most perfect example of team blocking in Rose Bowl history. Harry Hopp, from his end zone, punted high but short to Kmetovic, who started to his left but was trapped. Kmetovic swung back across the field to midfield as he looked for blockers. He soon found them, in numbers. Every Stanford player knocked down a Cornhusker—sometimes twice—as Kmetovic reversed his field once more. Palmer hit the unsuspecting Francis with a picture block, knocking him into the air and flat on his back. Kmetovic picked his way through the fallen bodies as if it were Verdun, not Pasadena, and slipped into the corner of the end zone to climax the ad-libbed, but amazingly executed play.

Albert built the score to 21–13. "I'm not a great blocker," he said, "but every time Pete changed directions, a Nebraska man turned around and ran into me. We'd both go down. It looked like I made fantastic blocks, when I was only trying to protect myself. But it was a super run."

Stanford failed to score again after Lindskog blocked a Nebraska punt at the Huskers' 16. It didn't matter. Stanford dominated the game after Nebraska's hurricane start, totaling 345 yards to 153 for the 'Huskers. The Indians, even without Standlee, dominated in rushing, 277–68, as Francis was stopped cold. Shaughnessy shifted the ball-carrying responsibilities to Gallarneau, who rushed seventeen times for 91 yards. Kmetovic was like a blur to Nebraska, cutting and darting for 130 yards in addition to his game-breaking, self-redeeming punt return. He was named Player of the Game.

Virtually everyone expected that Stanford would return to the Rose Bowl the next year, since only Gallarneau, Standlee and Graff were graduating. Albert and Kmetovic were juniors. But the Indians finished 6–3, losing to Washington State 14–13, California 16–0 and Oregon State 10–0, and Oregon State earned the invitation. "Injuries hurt us my last year," said Albert. "So did losing seven kids who were ruled ineligible for taking money, or some kind of favors, from alumni. The day that it all broke loose, Clark sat us in the bleachers. The old Swede faced the squad and said, 'Boys, I don't like penalties where the wrong people pay for them. The alumni should be punished, not you boys.' Shaughnessy had tears in his eyes, but they weren't selfish tears. Those seven kids were like his own. He fought for you. He was a fine man, so great."

But not without weaknesses. Shaughnessy knew so much football, a walking one-man clinic, that it was almost impossible for his assistants and players to keep up with, or even comprehend, his computer mind. He expected them to, and in time this failing would endanger, and eventually terminate, his coaching career.

"Clark over-coached," Albert admitted. "It wasn't so bad the first year when he put in the T-formation sparingly. By the second year he had given us so many tools—heck, we had seven different ways to hit a hole on the same play—that it became too complex. He was thinking football by pro standards, where guys have nothing else to do but concentrate on the game since it's their living. But our kids were also thinking about girls, studies, and good times."

Shaughnessy stayed only two years at Stanford. He had learned the school would be giving up football during World War II. Pearl Harbor took place less than a month after Albert played his final college game. Shaughnessy turned into a football maverick, becoming head coach at Maryland, Pittsburgh, then Maryland again, when he was also an advisory coach for the Washington Redskins.

All this time, his family remained home in Santa Monica, as Shaughnessy became a traveling salesman for the T-formation, attending clinics and banquets and counseling

Stanford coach Clark Shaughnessy, the man who brought the T-formation back to modern football.

other coaching staffs. He was now more engrossed with football than ever and more withdrawn. The Los Angeles Rams permanently lifted him from the college ranks by naming him advisory coach in 1948. By the start of the season he was the head coach. He came out to Ram practices followed by an assistant who carried an arm-load of two-foot by two-foot cards. The players rebelled. "If he can sit down and write out fifty percent of the plays he has given us this season, I'll learn the new stuff," grumbled quarterback Bob Waterfield. "Otherwise, nuts!"

Shaughnessy was fired after the Rams lost the 1949 NFL championship game to Philadelphia, 14–0. He was immediately hired as technical advisor to Halas in Chicago, with control of the Bears' defense. This lasted until the 1956 championship game with the New York Giants. Shaughnessy changed the Bears' entire defensive game plan on the day of the game, and Chicago was blitzed, 47–7. Halas rebuked him for this, and he became more withdrawn, icy, revolutionary; only now he was plotting defenses and plotting against Halas. Shaughnessy made the Bear defense a separate entity from the rest of the team. They met secretly, developing their own defensive codes by using men's and women's names, a technique which Shaughnessy advanced and which is in popular vogue today. On the Chicago staff at that time was George Allen, who hung around

Shaughnessy constantly, acquiring whatever knowledge he could from the older man, who lived as a recluse, in a flophouse in the Loop. Allen's workaholic habits, it is believed, were acquired by his watching Shaughnessy during their days together on the Bears' defense.

Shaughnessy began to alienate Halas by the secretive manner by which the defense was being run. Clark kept his plays in an army foot locker, which he carried around with him. One day, Stan Jones, an offensive tackle, was shifted to defense because of injuries in the defensive line. He found where the defense was meeting, but when they saw him walk through the door, they immediately closed up their playbooks and walked by the startled player and out the door. Jones was like an invader from another planet. He played defense that Sunday, with middle linebacker Bill George telling him what to do on each play.

Halas put up with Shaughnessy's eccentricities, even though "Papa" Bear didn't know from Sunday to Sunday what defenses his team would be using. Finally, the division grew so wide that Halas and Shaughnessy had a falling out, and Shaughnessy returned to Santa Monica in 1962—exactly one year after he successfully shut down the San Francisco 49ers' Shotgun offense, his final personal victory, and a year before the Bears won their last NFL championship, with Allen now in charge of the defense. Allen was awarded the game ball in a memorable post-game ceremony, as Shaughnessy watched on television, crest-fallen.

Shaughnessy did some scouting and tried to merchandise his knowledge of the game in several ways, all of which failed. Halas sent him checks regularly, which was believed to be his main means of support until he died in 1970, at the age of 78. His collection of diagrams, playbooks and films, was purchased by a Santa Paula, California, business-man with the idea of starting a sports academy. Nothing ever came of the idea, and Shaughnessy's true epitaph lies in an office building in Santa Paula.

Eight players from Shaughnessy's Rose Bowl team at Stanford went into professional football: Albert, Standlee, Gallarneau, Kmetovic, Lindskog, Taylor, Banducci, and Meyer. Taylor later became head coach and athletic director at Stanford, and took the Indians to the Rose Bowl, in 1952. Albert starred for the 49ers and then became their head coach from 1956–58, even though "I hadn't served my apprenticeship. I wasn't ready to be a head coach. I wasn't that dedicated a coach anyway, and didn't want to make it my career." Now 57, Albert has sold his limited partnership in the 49ers.

"Thirty-six years have gone by since we played in the Rose Bowl," he reflected. "Football really hasn't advanced that much offensively in the interim, nowhere near the changes on defense. I often wonder if Shaughnessy were a young man today, seeing all those innovative defenses, what he would do. I know this, he wouldn't just sit there and take a beating. He'd have two quarterbacks behind the center, one spinning one way and another the other way. Both at the same time. I mean it."

Albert smiled and then stared off into space, as if in the back of his mind he could still see Shaughnessy furiously drawing diagrams. Somewhere.

WAR TRANSPLANTS
THE ROSES

It rained in torrents in Pasadena on January 1, 1942, making conditions miserable for football. But the downpour didn't affect the Rose Bowl game between Duke and Oregon State, which was played that day in Durham, North Carolina, where the weather was misty, yet tolerable. It was the only time a Rose Bowl game was not played in Pasadena, and the only time a Rose Bowl game was played after having been cancelled. These complications can be explained easily enough: War.

Twenty-five days earlier, Japanese air and naval forces attacked Pearl Harbor.

A week after the attack, Lieutenant General John Lesesne DeWitt, commander of the Fourth Army and in full command of all military forces in the eight western states and Alaska, notified Governor Culbert Olsen of California to close down the Santa Anita race track and cancel the East-West and Rose Bowl football games.

There were reports of Japanese submarines shelling the coasts of California and Oregon. Steel nets were stretched across the Golden Gate to guard against a sub attack on San Francisco. Up and down the coast there were blackouts, for fear that Japanese planes would attack at night.

"I join General DeWitt in this request," Olsen said in a telegram to A. I. Stewart, chairman of the City Board of Directors of Pasadena, "which is supported from groups of the civilian population of the Pasadena and Southern California area. The congestion of the state highways over a large area incident to this (Rose Bowl) tournament and football game, the concentration of a large police force now needed for defense services, the unusually large gathering of people known to the enemy, requires that plans for the holding of this tournament and football game be abandoned."

General DeWitt, history will show, did not mince, or carefully choose, his words.

He warned the citizens of California that they must take proper air raid precautions or possibly die. "If I can't knock it into you with words," he declared, "we'll have to turn it over to the police to knock it in with clubs." General DeWitt would later assist in the evacuation of thousands of Japanese-Americans from the West Coast and place them in "internment" camps, taking away their American citizenship in some cases. "A Jap is a Jap," he was quoted by the U.S. Circuit Court of Appeals in San Francisco, which accused him after the war of holding to a "Nazi-like doctrine" in his treatment of Japanese-Americans, a number of whom had their American citizenship restored by the court.

Nevertheless, when General DeWitt spoke during World War II, everyone on the West Coast snapped to attention, regardless of whether or not they were wearing G.I. clothing. Everyone, that is, but the folks up in the farming community of Corvallis, Oregon.

Corvallis is the home of Oregon State College, as it was called back then didn't become a "university" until the Sixties. Oregon State had just been invited to play in its first Rose Bowl, and didn't like the idea of someone telling it that the game was off, even if it was the United States government.

"I wonder if General DeWitt intends to lock up all the department stores where people might gather, or restaurants, churches, and all the public meetings," challenged Bud Forrester, the Oregon State College publicity director, acting with more smite than might. "We feel the game will go a long way towards building civilian morale in a distressing time, and we believe that Army authorities during the last world war felt much the same way. We will do everything in our power to have the ban against the Rose Bowl game lifted."

A man with the wonderfully lyrical name of Percy Locey was then athletic director at Oregon State. Locey, who in 1977 was 83 and selling real estate in Corvallis, had the guile of all successful promoters.

"I had a meeting with the Rose Bowl people in Pasadena who said the game was definitely off," he recalled. "I drove all night to see General DeWitt and was allowed inside his office, but at bayonet point. He said, 'Gentlemen, there will be no Rose Bowl game in Pasadena even if I have to call out the troops to stop it.' The general moved a company of Army engineers into the Rose Bowl stadium, to prove he meant what he said. I called Governor Olsen four times, but it was no use."

Locey wasn't finished, though. He had an idea. If Duke couldn't be brought west to play Oregon State, why not take Oregon State back east to play Duke? "Where else could we go?" reflected Locey.

"I called Wallace Wade, the Duke coach, and asked him what he thought, and he said it was a marvelous idea. "The game's all yours," Wade told Locey. "Manage it in Durham, as you see fit. You handle the gate receipts and everything else." And so, in another Rose Bowl first, a contract was signed between two schools to stage the game free of any involvement of Tournament of Roses officials. It would be the Rose Bowl

Oregon State Athletic Director Percy P. Locey. When the government cancelled the Pasadena game Locey engineered its move to Durham, North Carolina.

The Rose Bowl was played in the stadium pictured here, but the stadium isn't the Rose Bowl because the game was shifted east under the fear of enemy attack on the West Coast. This is Duke Stadium in Durham, N.C. Pearl Harbor had been attacked just three weeks earlier.

in name only. Locey also assumed responsibility for returning the 65,000 tickets already sold for the game in Pasadena before General DeWitt stepped in. (The East-West Shrine game was played that year in New Orleans, the only time it hasn't been played in California.)

The official cancellation period of the Rose Bowl game lasted approximately twenty-four hours. The main reason Wade was so anxious to play in his own front yard—Duke is located in Durham—was that it would save him additional embarrassment. Exactly three years before, Wade brought an unbeaten, unscored-upon Duke team to play USC in the Rose Bowl, only to lose in the last minute, 7–3, on Doyle Nave's pass to Al Krueger. Wade was criticized then by the Southern California press for not shaking Nave's hand after the game. Wade, in addition, had told a Los Angeles newspaperman that he didn't particularly like Southern California or the manner in which the Rose Bowl was run. The press was sanctimoniously enraged, and attacked Wade through galleys of hot type. When the same group of sportswriters learned that Wade was coming back to Pasadena, old fires began to blaze. Locey spared Wade any further humiliation.

Oregon State, as the Pacific Coast Conference champion, had the right in those days to pick its opponent. There were several worthy candidates besides Duke, such as Fordham, Missouri, Duquesne and Texas. Minnesota was ranked number one in the nation, but Big Nine schools didn't play in post-season competition at the time. Duke was ranked number two. The Blue Devils were undefeated and had the country's highest-scoring offense. "Our boys wanted to play an unbeaten and untied team," said Oregon State coach Lon Stiner. "Minnesota was their first choice and Duke their second." And so it was Duke. The choice not only was unpopular on the West Coast, but in Texas. The Longhorns were angered at being passed over and destroyed their final opponent, which happened to be the University of Oregon, 71–7. Because of what the Texans still consider a slight, Southwest Conference champions have played in the Cotton Bowl ever since.

Oregon State and Duke represented a David and Goliath situation. The Beavers were picked to finish last in their conference, even by their coach. "Our situation is terrible," Stiner lamented before the opening game with USC. "We've lost eleven lettermen. We have the smallest squad in the league. We're so weak in several positions, we'll be murdered."

Quentin Greenough, a standout center-linebacker on that Oregon State team, remembers coach Stiner as "a real psychologist." But if Stiner was trying to soft-sell his Beavers or to "set up" the rest of the conference, he failed, because USC defeated Oregon State, 13–0. The Beavers edged Washington, 9–6, then pulled off a major upset by clubbing Stanford, 10–0, for the Indians' first defeat in two years under Clark Shaughnessy's T-formation offense. The undulating Beavers were knocked off the next week by Washington State, 7–0, and with two defeats appeared out of the conference race.

But they allowed only two touchdowns over their next five games in beating Idaho, 33–7; UCLA, 19–0; California, 6–0; Montana, 27–0, and Oregon, 12–7, and finished the season with a 7–2 record.

"We beat Oregon at their place," said guard Martin Chaves. "They stuck the thirty-three of us in a twenty-foot by fifteen-foot dressing room. Stiner was furious. Before the game he got down low and ran right through the closed dressing room door, knocking it off its hinges. He got back up and looked at the rest of us inside, and said, 'That's how I feel about this game!' You should have seen thirty-three guys try to get through the door at the same time."

Stiner was 38 at the time, but a powerful man at 230 pounds. He had been an all-America tackle at Nebraska before becoming the Oregon State coach in 1933. During his first year the Beavers held USC, which had defeated twenty-six straight teams, to a scoreless tie, even though Oregon State played only eleven men that day. The Beavers traveled to New York that same season and stunned powerful Fordham, 9–6. Stiner was an imaginative coach and during that game had both Beaver tackles hoist 6' 6" center Clyde Devine at the line of scrimmage when Fordham kicked its point after touchdown. Devine blocked the kick. Stiner had a respectable record at Oregon State, 74–48–16, before resigning in 1949. His only championship came in 1941.

That same Beaver team had a third-string end, Jack Yoshihara, who was a Japanese-American. "A few days after Pearl Harbor, Jack disappeared," said Chaves. "He was found and placed in one of those prison camps."

Oregon State's all-America center Quentine Greenough.

Greenough was the most-honored Oregon State player that year, a second-team all-America. "I didn't have that much ability," said center-linebacker Greenough modestly. "I wouldn't take no for an answer on the football field and I had a big heart. Heart makes up for a lot of things. If there was a star on our team, it was Durdan."

Don Durdan was the wingback in the Beavers' single wing, a runner, passer, and punter of the old triple threat style. Durdan would be voted Player of the Game, in the 1942 Rose Bowl game. The tailback was Bob Dethman, who would make the deciding play at Durham. "They were called the 'Three Ds' in the Northwest—Durdan, Dethman and Day," said Greenough. "Joe Day was our fullback and a good runner too. The 'Three Ds' were big in our neck of the woods, but the name never caught on nationally." It's a shame that Grantland Rice, that most gifted of namemakers, couldn't have covered that Rose Bowl game. If he could immortalize the names of Stuhldreher, Layden, Crowley and Miller, think what he could have done with Durdan and Dethman. Rice could have rhapsodized or eulogized at his best. Durdan and Dethman. They sounded literally like the horsemen from the apocalypse. Durdan and Dethman. What a shame they hadn't played for Notre Dame or Army. Duke wouldn't know the difference on New Year's Day.

Duke's 1941 season was awesome. Wade's 9–0 team had been acclaimed the greatest in the school's history, even greater than the 1939 Rose Bowl squad. The reason was that the Blue Devils had scored a whopping 311 points, and on defense, allowed only

Oregon State backs Bob Dethman (No. 26) and Don Durdan (No. 39).

a measly 41 points. They flattened Wake Forest, 43–14; Maryland, 50–0; Davidson, 56–0, and North Carolina State, 55–6, in an era when a three-touchdown victory was a rout.

Duke's quarterback, or blocking back in the single wing, was Tommy Prothro, who would later coach Oregon State in its two other Rose Bowl appearances.

"Duke was about as good as any team in the country that year," says Prothro. "I weighed 212 then and our tackles, Bob McDonough and Mike Karmazin, weighed 214 and 208. We were the only players on the squad over 200, but I don't remember playing anyone who was bigger than our team." Or better. The Blue Devils had several well-known players like center and captain Bob Barnett, end Al Paisecky, and Karma-

Tommy Prothro, quarterback-blocking back for Duke. He later coached Oregon State in the 1957 and '65 Rose Bowls, and UCLA in the 1966 Rose Bowl.

zin, but their best player was second-team all-America tailback Steve Lach, who averaged 8 yards per carry, 45 yards a punt, and caught twenty-two passes. Lach was even more outstanding on defense.

"In those days you didn't substitute much," said Prothro. "I would guess that eight or nine of our players went sixty minutes in most of the close games. I received a cracked collarbone in the Rose Bowl, and was out one play." Duke's "closest" win that year was a 14–0 victory over Georgia Tech.

The Blue Devils didn't envision Oregon State as anything resembling a threat. The Beavers had scored only 123 points, a little better than one-third of Duke's total, although the Beavers fared better on defense, yielding just 33 points. However, Duke felt Oregon State hadn't played an offense as destructive as its own. Yet the Duke players only agreed, in a 27–0 vote, to play the Beavers because it meant a trip to California. Opinions changed when the game was shifted to North Carolina. The players voted 25–2 against playing in the game.

"After Pearl Harbor, we didn't care about playing another game in Durham," explained Prothro. Wade stood in front of the team and expounded on the importance of having the Rose Bowl come to Durham, then left the room. The players voted again, but it was still 17–10 against. Desperate, Wade went against all coaching principles and agreed to let the team off for a ten-day period over the Christmas holiday. On that condition, the Duke players accepted, but only by 15–12. So the Duke players went home for Christmas.

"We knew they weren't too hot to play the game," said Greenough. Oregon State had gained an important psychological edge.

It took six days for the Beavers to travel by train from the Northwest to Durham, with some sightseeing in Chicago and Washington, D.C., included. A brass band and welcoming ceremony awaited them at the Durham station. Chaves, who would be the Beavers' game captain against Duke, was named honorary mayor of Durham for one day. "Honestly," Stiner told the crowd at the railroad station, "everybody's being so nice to us that I don't see how we can politely win the Rose Bowl game. I've never seen such people." The Beavers were being killed with Southern kindness.

The Oregon State team stayed and trained at the University of North Carolina campus in Chapel Hill, ten miles from Durham. After dinner one night in a Chapel Hill hotel, Stiner was approached by a young man. "Mr. Stiner," he said, "I work at the bank here in town. If you want to cash any checks, I'm the man to see." Stiner thanked him and said, "The way the boys have been borrowing money from me on the trip, I'll be seeing a lot of you." Someone else offered his car to Stiner, who had already been given a brand new one to use. A well-fed, obviously well-off tobacco man asked Stiner how he liked the South. "Wonderful," the coach replied loudly. "And the Southern hospitality, that's wonderful, too."

While the Duke players had Christmas off and wouldn't begin practicing until four days before the Rose Bowl, Stiner was working the Beavers hard at Chapel Hill. "Lon was a hard-nosed coach," said Greenough. "He was a real character, but he didn't fool around when it came time to practicing football. He was a tremendous coach."

Duke was made a three-to-one favorite. "This game is going to be a lot closer than the people around here think," Stiner told the press. "I don't know much about Duke's team, but I do know something about my boys. Nobody's managed to score more than two touchdowns against us all year, and we don't intend to start the new year off on the wrong foot."

Chaves said, "Ever since we hit North Carolina, people have been telling us how tough Duke is supposed to be. All right, so they talk. But what are we supposed to be, pushovers? We've met tough teams before, and we were tougher than most of them."

Wade, at least for the record, called the game "a mystery. Whatever we know about Oregon State and whatever they know about us is all second-hand information. We're both playing a guessing game."

The stadium at Duke was increased from 35,000 to 56,000 seats, as Locey installed temporary bleachers.

The Duke team, regardless of how little practice it had, was confident. This would be Wade's sixth Rose Bowl appearance. His first was as a Brown University guard in the 1916 game, won by Washington State, 14–0. Wade then coached Alabama to Rose Bowl victories over Washington, 20–19, in 1926, and over Washington State, 24–0, in 1931, and to a 7–7 tie with Stanford, in 1927. Wade was looking for revenge from his defeat by USC in the 1939 game. He was confident.

So was Governor J. Melville Broughton of North Carolina, who gave up his covered press box seat to accommodate an overflow of newspapermen, thinking that Southern hospitality naturally would include the weather. It rained that morning and lightly at times during the game, taking away from the governor's optimism and increasing Oregon State's. "It was, as I remember, a typical Oregon day," said Greenough. What better omen?

Stiner, a showman all the way, saved his last act, strictly impromptu, for the bus ride to the stadium on the morning of the game. He convinced the highway patrolman who was at the head of the motorcade to stage a mock argument with him for the Beaver players to observe. The patrolman and Stiner went at it jaw-to-jaw. "I called him everything in the book," said Stiner. By the time he climbed back on the bus, the players were ready to walk on hot coals and eat broken glass. "It worked," Stiner said to himself as he leaned back in his seat.

Duke's tailback was Tom Davis, a sophomore pressed into starting because of an injury to Moffet Storer. Davis received the opening kickoff and started upfield to his 30, where Oregon State tackle Lloyd Wickert slammed into him. The ball popped loose, and George Peters recovered for the Beavers, at the 29. Duke held, but couldn't move the ball, and Lach punted out of trouble. Then Durdan punted 70 yards out of bounds at the Duke 1. Lach punted to his 45, and the Beavers began their first scoring drive.

Oregon State created problems for opponents with the left-handed Durdan and the right-handed Dethman passing or running, which was precisely what happened to Duke. From the Blue Devils' 15, Dethman spun around and gave the ball to Durdan, who looked to pass, but saw an opening in the line and darted through it, and into the end zone, practically untouched. Warren Simas' conversion kick made it 7–0.

Wade's favorite play was the "Duke reverse," and the Blue Devils executed it in a variety of ways. Davis ran for 29 yards, Lach for 22 and then Lach the final 4 yards —all on reverses—for Duke's first touchdown. Gantt's kick tied the score at 7–7, and that's how the game stayed until halftime.

While Stiner was talking to his team in the locker room, there was a commotion at the door. An intoxicated soul, feeling his own Southern comfort, staggered in looking for a rest room. "Over there," said an unperturbed Stiner, pointing the way. The Beaver players laughed. They would have the day's last laugh, too.

The orange-jerseyed Beavers scored quickly in a wild third quarter as Gene Gray circled end for 23 yards against Duke's 6–2–2–1 defense, and Durdan threw a 32 yard touchdown pass to end George Zelleck. Then Duke's Lach bolted 38 yards on another reverse to the Oregon State 25. An unnecessary roughness penalty against the Beavers gave Duke a first down at the 1. Fullback Winston Siegfried plunged into the end zone and the score was deadlocked once more, 14–14.

Two minutes later Oregon State went ahead permanently, on a spectacular play. Dethman threw a long pass to Gray, who side-stepped a tackler at the Duke 28 and scored. Jack Guenther, covering the game for United Press, said the play covered 62 yards. Rube Samuelsen reported it was 68 yards. Rose Bowl records place the distance at 70 yards, officially (they say) the longest pass in Rose Bowl history.

Oregon State led 20–14, as Simas' kick was blocked. The Blue Devils were perplexed. In ten years at Duke, no Wade team had given up more than two touchdowns in one game. However, the Blue Devils weren't through.

"We drove to their 9 where we had second and a yard to go for a first down," said Prothro. "I called the offensive signals for the team and had decided on a running play in the huddle. Then I noticed that their linebackers were up close and the safeties deep, and I thought we could throw between them. I checked off at the line of scrimmage and called a pass play. The pass was slightly high. It bounced off our receiver's hands, and their safety intercepted." It was Oregon State's fourth interception, on top of three recovered Duke fumbles.

Karmazin tackled Durdan in the end zone for a fourth-quarter safety, but it wasn't the Beaver star's fault. "I was responsible for the safety because I made a bad pass from center," said Greenough. "That play may have been a blessing in disguise. Instead of having to make a pressured punt out of our end zone, we had a free kick from our 20. Durdan got away a booming kick and we pinned them back against their goal. Durdan was the difference that day."

Oregon State's 20–16 victory shocked Duke and Wade, who watched another perfect season shattered in the Rose Bowl. However, remembering the problems following the

Two Rose Bowl coaches flank famed sports writer Grantland Rice in 1942. At left is Wallace Wade whose Alabama teams appeared in 1926 and '27, and whose Duke teams played in 1939 and '42. At right is Robert Neyland, whose Tennessee team played in 1940.

1939 game, Wade visited the Oregon State dressing room and offered congratulations. "You played a nice game, boys, a mighty nice game," he said.

Wade took the blame for the defeat, declaring he had erred in letting his team have so much time off before a big game, even though his hands were tied. "It looks like my Rose Bowl luck has run out," he commented wryly.

Stiner told writers after the game, "We played pretty good ball, but not our best."

Chaves was quoted as saying, "If I get killed, I can die happy now. That's what winning a Rose Bowl game can do to a fellow." Now a retired lumberman in Corvallis, Chaves was asked about the accuracy of that quote. "It's true, I said it," he verified. "We were gung-ho back then."

It was necessary. The world was at war.

THE BEAUTY
AND THE BULLDOG

Football was an afterthought in 1942. With the nation facing military juggernauts on its oceanic flanks, touchdowns weren't high priorities. Yet, there were games; there would always be games, which would provide momentary distractions from the grim news overseas. Even for the players, the games served only as flitting diversions from expected calls to military service. Conscientious objectors and draft evaders were relatively few then; it was the last American war in which, to most of us, the killing almost made sense; the times, and the national fabric, were different from what they've become. What seemed then like our "finest hour" has since evolved into the good old days.

Frank Sinkwich was the star of the 1942 Georgia team that went to the 1943 Rose Bowl. Charlie Trippi was the star of the Bowl itself, in which Georgia defeated UCLA in the most one-sided 9–0 game one could imagine.

The Georgia Bulldogs had been to a Bowl game a year earlier, defeating Texas Christian at the Orange, 40–26, on the same day the Rose had been transplanted to a North Carolina garden. Sinkwich always believed the Bulldogs of the 1941 season were a better team than his Rose Bowl crew of the next year. "We had more ability in 1941," he said. "More depth. Our 1942 team that went to the Rose Bowl had a lot of individual ball players who possibly were better than some of the 1941 guys, but the 1941 bunch was just better as a team. I remember that right after our Orange Bowl game, a lot of boys on our team went into military service. And by the time we finished the next season and were heading for the Rose Bowl, there were just so many other things to think about besides football. I mean, so many of our guys would be going to the service, either a few weeks after the game or when they graduated."

Sinkwich (in the old country it had been Sinkobic) had come to Youngstown, Ohio, from Yugoslavia, at the age of three. The eventual Heisman Trophy winner spent many after-school hours and summers working in the family restaurant.

One year ahead of Frank in high school was a football player named George Poschner. The two eventually began their college careers together, down in Athens. Georgia coach Wallace Butts was advised of the Youngstowners' abilities by a coach from Ironton, Ohio. Good advice. Both Poschner and Sinkwich would become all-Americas.

Butts recruited well in northeastern Pennsylvania, too. Trippi remembers that "a man who ran the Coca Cola plant near Pittston had played and coached a little at Georgia. His name was War Eagle Keplon, and he took an interest in me. I went down there to take a look. I knew they had a good football program and was impressed, so I decided to stake it out. And here I am nearly forty years later, living in Athens."

War Eagle apparently recommended some neighbors of Trippi's to Butts, for on the roster of the 1943 Bulldog Rose Bowl team appear the names of Joe Tereshinski and Andy Dudish.

In the 1942 season, Trippi was a sophomore playing his first varsity year, while Sinkwich and Poschner were seniors. "It was difficult breaking into that team," said Trippi. "Any time you got a guy like Sinkwich, it's difficult. I had to prove myself, and then Coach Butts moved Frank to fullback and made a tailback out of me." During that season, Sinkwich's Heisman year and the year in which the AP named Frank the "athlete of the year" in all sports, Georgia was 10–1, losing only to Auburn in the next to last game of the regular season. The Tigers were the only T-formation team Butts' single wing squad met that year. "Not enough preparation time, I guess," said Trippi. The next T team Georgia would face would be UCLA, in the Rose Bowl. "We had a month to get ready for them, so it worked out better."

Not for Sinkwich, however. "Just before we got ready to go out West, I hurt my left ankle in a practice," said Frank. "Then a day or two before the Rose Bowl game, we had just finished a workout and Coach Butts said, 'Let's run one more play.' So I made a long run and had to pull up just before I reached the end zone. I'd hurt the other ankle." But Frank was in uniform on the bench in Pasadena. "I was going to try and play," he said. "I did want to play."

"Nobody on our team was really surprised that Frank got in the game," said Trippi. "He was dressed out, and anybody who Coach Butts dressed out was going to play. Coach Butts was tough. Quite a disciplinarian. When you played for him, you knew you were prepared to do almost anything. The impact he had on me made my professional career so much easier. The only two people I ever feared in my whole life were my dad and Coach Butts."

The Bulldogs of 1942 were potent offensively (367 points in the eleven games) because Butts ordered more passing than most teams of that time. "We used both balanced and unbalanced single wings, and threw maybe forty or fifty percent of the

Georgia backfield stars Charlie Trippi (left) and Frank Sinkwich, whose club breezed past UCLA 9-0.

time," said Sinkwich. Trippi recalls Georgia averaging perhaps twenty-five passes a game. The Bulldogs could move the football.

The 1942 UCLA Bruins were something new on the West Coast. Until that season, the Bruins had never defeated Southern Cal on the football field. Then they knocked off the Trojans 14–7, for a Rose Bowl slot. Actually, the short trip to Pasadena— UCLA's first visit—was rather anti-climactic after the much-celebrated victory over USC. The Bruins, coached by Edwin C. "Babe" Horrell, had come out of nowhere that season—riding the arm and kicking toe of quarterback Bob Waterfield into brief Pacific Coast Conference glory. But for the next several decades, the Bruins were continually obscured by their Trojan neighbors. Year after year, USC prevented UCLA from reaching Pasadena, with victories over the latter in their late-season, emotional rivalry —a matchup that would take on all the fervor of the later Ohio State-Michigan tradition in the Big Ten. Through 1977, the Bruins managed just seven trips to the Rose Bowl, winning only two. That first visit, that meeting with Georgia, set the tone in Pasadena for the Bruins.

Until late 1942, no one was certain the Rose Bowl could return to Pasadena or, for that matter, if it could be played any place at all on January 1, 1943. The military had a hold on transportation.

The Bulldogs actually had their choice of Bowl invitations, but wouldn't pass up the Rose once the game was approved. "Anybody playing football wants to play in the Rose Bowl," said Trippi. "Let's face it. It's *the* game, regardless. I was very young then, and I knew how important it was to play in the Rose Bowl. It's a game that has a lifetime impact on you."

The lovely film actress Rita Hayworth had a momentary impact on the Bulldog team. Samuelsen says that the Georgia team train was "detoured to a siding barely three hours out of Pasadena"—most likely to allow a troop train the right-of-way. "Some of the Bulldogs got out to stretch their legs. The Santa Fe's El Capitan was ahead on the same siding ('facing the other way,' remembers Sinkwich) and the rumor spread that the glamorous Rita Hayworth was aboard."

Sinkwich chuckles over the recollection. "George Poschner heard that Rita was over there, so he went on her train yelling, 'Telegram! Telegram for Miss Hayworth!' She opened her compartment door, and George stuck his foot inside."

Samuelsen reports Miss Hayworth was "clad only in undies and negligee" and "let out a scream."

"Somehow the publicity got out," said Sinkwich, "that she wasn't very favorable to what George had done. But she was a very lovely girl. She came over to see some of the team at the Huntington Hotel and apologized if she'd done anything wrong. And she hadn't."

Georgia wasted little time threatening UCLA. Only a fine tackle by safety Waterfield on the opening kickoff prevented Bulldog Lamar Davis from returning the boot for a touchdown. Poschner brush-blocked Waterfield, but Bob sidestepped to make the tackle on the Bruin 45.

Neither Trippi nor Sinkwich remembers hearing much before the game about Waterfield. But they'd hear plenty about him later, when Bob became one of professional football's fine T quarterbacks, with the Rams in Cleveland and Los Angeles. He would marry another Los Angeles star, chesty actress Jane Russell. Ah, but back to football.

Twice in the first half, Georgia knocked on the Bruin door. On the first occasion, Butts sent in Sinkwich, but UCLA held at their 2. Then just before the end of the half, a Georgia drive, with Sinkwich again testing his wounded ankles, stalled at the UCLA 8. The game was scoreless at halftime.

"I wasn't really capable of playing at full speed," said Frank. "I could get maybe a yard or two on a carry, but that was all."

Georgia had so dominated the first half the club was more confident than frustrated, despite the score. "We knew we were capable of scoring," said Trippi. "We knew it was just a matter of time until we got into their end zone because we'd been going up and down the field all day. We probably should have scored at least two more touchdowns."

#301 01-12-2011 12:16PM
Item(s) checked out to GROCKI, JON S.

TITLE: Rose Bowl football since 1902
BARCODE: 51000001661782
DUE DATE: 02-02-11

TITLE: W. [videorecording]
BARCODE: 51000003647951
DUE DATE: 01-19-11

UCLA quarterback Bob Waterfield married pinup girl Jane Russell a few months after his Rose Bowl appearance in 1943.

Still, the game remained scoreless after three periods. Sinkwich had tried again in the third quarter. The Bulldogs had marched from their own 38 to inside the Bruin 5. Trippi had thrown or run on nearly every play in the drive. "If you played for Coach Butts, you never got tired," said Charlie.

From a few feet out, Sinkwich carried—and fumbled, with Bruin Al Izmarian recovering on the UCLA 3. "The center hit me in the knee with the football," said Frank. "I just messed it up."

Finally, Poschner and Red Boyd put a big rush on Waterfield in a UCLA end zone punting situation, moments after the Sinkwich fumble. "And Red blocked it," said Sinkwich, who then recalled that Boyd had died sometime in the late 1960s.

After the block, the football bounced out of the end zone for an automatic safety. Georgia at last had a couple of points for all its effort.

On the next UCLA series, the Bulldogs reinforced their dominance, as Clyde Ehrhardt intercepted a Waterfield pass and returned to the Bruin 25. Butts once again sent the hobbled Sinkwich into the game—but this time kept Trippi in the backfield, too.

Charlie ran for 11 yards. Frank lost one. ("Barely able to get back on his feet, and then only to limp badly, his teammates urged Frankie to take himself out, but he refused," wrote Samuelsen.) Charlie carried to the Bruin 8, and Van Davis then picked up a first down on an end-around. Another Davis run moved the ball to the 2—and Sinkwich then lugged it in for the touchdown.

All the Bruins raved about Trippi, after the 9–0 result. As did Sinkwich. But Frank still savors his memory of the train trip. "I'll never forget," he says, "that time George got a look at Rita Hayworth."

EAST-WEST
MARRIAGE

Iowa defeated Oregon State, 35–19, in the 1957 Rose Bowl to give the Big Ten a record of ten victories in its first eleven "contracted" games with Pacific Coast teams. This prompted *Los Angeles Mirror*'s Sid Ziff to write, "The Humane Society will have to step in if this keeps up."

This Bowl marriage was so inequitable in its formative years, it is amazing teams from the coast continued to honor the contract. Big Ten teams won the first six, lost in 1953 (USC 7, Wisconsin 0), then won the next six, to give them twelve out of the first thirteen.

"This is a case of men playing boys," wrote George Davis in the *Los Angeles Herald-Express.*

Columnist Ray Haywood of the *Oakland Tribune* fiddled with the safety pin he used to secure one of the stems of his spectacles, and typed, "With the Big Ten, football is a science. With us in the West, it's a game."

When the game count was only six-zero Big Ten, craggy L. H. Gregory of the *Portland Oregonian* sought a glint of optimism, as he wrote, "The only hope for the future that I can see is that, having fulfilled the Biblical prophecy of a long famine, the Pacific Coast should now have many good years to come."

Washington won back-to-back games in 1960–61 to turn the tide. By nightfall of January 1, 1977, the famine was on the other foot. With USC's 14–6 domination of Michigan that day, the score now stood eighteen-thirteen Big Ten, and coast teams had won nine of the last twelve, seven of the last eight.

Before 1969, observed Robert W. Creamer of *Sports Illustrated,* "The Big Ten had a sixteen-six edge and every school in the conference made at least one trip to the Rose

Bowl. Since 1969, when Michigan and Ohio State took over, only those two over-inflated powerhouses have gone to Pasadena. And they have lost seven of the nine games they've played there. The obvious conclusion seems to be that the Big Ten was far more effective when it was a competitive conference, when playing talent was more evenly distributed, when its eventual champion had to win more than a two-team race."

In the early years, the ground rules for selection of the Rose Bowl teams were simple.
• Until 1923, the Tournament of Roses Association invited both the Western and Eastern teams, usually the West entry first.
• Between 1923 and 1935, the Association continued to invite the coast club, which then selected its own foe.
• After 1935, the old Pacific Coast Conference selected its Pasadena representative, which then tabbed its Eastern playmate.
• The Pacific Coast-Big Ten agreement began with the game of 1947 and, except for minor variations in the team selection process and actual names of the conferences, continues unabated.

Before 1947, only two Big Ten teams had ever played in the Rose Bowl: Michigan in the 1902 opener and Ohio State in 1921, a 28–0 loser to California.

Prior to the East-West twain meeting, the West had for fifteen years "wooed the Big Nine only to meet with constant frigidity," notes Rube Samuelsen. (To digress momentarily, at the time of the Bowl agreement in late 1946, the Big Ten was indeed known as the Big Nine. The University of Chicago had abandoned conference football, and Michigan State (then MSC and not yet MSU) had not as yet been admitted to membership.) The Western group of schools at contract time was called the Pacific Coast Conference (PCC).

But the emergence of competition from some of the newer bowls for the Southern teams which had befriended Pasadena and the need for upgraded collegiate football financing finally drew the Big Nine and PCC together.

Just as California fans were clamoring for a New Year's Day look at the great Blanchard-Davis Army team, the Big Nine voted on November 15, 1946, to move toward a bond with the West. (Trivia fans will be pleased to know the vote was seven-two, with Minnesota and Illinois in the minority.)

The Big Nine even called its own terms: it would not necessarily have to send its champion to Pasadena. And the PCC, which then had ten teams (Idaho and Montana would be the eventual dropouts), bought the deal on November 21. (The vote was six-two-two, with USC and UCLA opposed, and Oregon and Oregon State abstaining.)

There was instant enmity to the deal. Johnny Mack Brown, the star of Pasadena (1926) and cowboy filmdom, called the contract "all wrong. The honor should be spread around," he said. "Every football player all over America dreams of playing in the Rose Bowl. The Rose Bowl has cut out its heart. It's a crying shame."

Veteran Rose Bowl reporter Maxwell Stiles of the *Long Beach Press-Telegram* barked, "We don't like being told by a bunch of professors in Missoula, Montana, and Moscow, Idaho, and Ann Arbor, Michigan, that we *must* play a Big Nine team *every* year. The closed shop has no place in intercollegiate football."

That very week, UCLA knocked off USC and Illinois blanked Northwestern to become the first honeymoon couple in this new marital agreement.

From 1947 through 1959, the PCC and Big Ten selected their own representatives with only minor shadings in the selection process.

However, the early years of the arrangement were not without discord. After the 1949 game, for example, University of Minnesota President Dr. J. Louis Morrill said he wanted the deal discontinued because of the pressures on individual coach and school. Yet, in 1953, the deciding vote to renew the pact was cast by the University of Minnesota.

Before the 1957 game, the PCC barred four of its members (Washington, USC, UCLA, California) from bowl participation for rules infractions, and so Oregon State got the opportunity to lose at Pasadena.

Two years later, the PCC became the five-member Athletic Association of Western Universities (AAWU) with the Oregon schools and Washington State briefly dislodged from the ranks. At the same time, the Big Ten split five-five on renewing the contract but permitted its schools to negotiate individually. That result bore bitter fruit after the 1961 season. Ohio State won the Big Ten title, but its faculty rejected the Bowl opportunity. Naturally, there was a riot on the Buckeye campus and in downtown Columbus.

Thus, there was a new shuffling of the cards in 1962, which resulted in a new contract, for an indefinite period, between the two conferences.

Ultimately, the AAWU once again became an eight-member operation, called the PAC-8, until it swelled with the addition of Arizona and Arizona State, in early 1977, to the PAC-10.

From a monetary point of view, the arrangement turned out splendidly. As Joe Hendrickson of the *Pasadena Star News* pointed out in the 1977 game program, "Public interest from coast to coast in this present duel between football powers has made possible an annual five million dollar attraction in receipts at the gate and from television. The entire Tournament of Roses project is financed by Pasadena's fifteen percent cut, and the two conferences divide some four million dollars among their member schools."

It has been, wrote Hendrickson, "a multi-million dollar marriage."

THE TINY GIANT

The name Buddy Young doesn't mean anything more to the present generation than Fred Allen, penny candy, Dagmar, and the one-button roll. Claude "Buddy" Young was the scatback of his time, although scatback is as outdated now as the leather helmet. You can't even find a halfback or a fullback any more. They're all running backs, a designation so cold and impersonal and computerized, the implication is that you can't tell one from another. More often than not, you can't. A running back is programmed at between 6' and 6'3" and 200 to 230 pounds. Anything smaller will be returning punts and kickoffs, or coaching high school back home. Anything as small as a Buddy Young, and he's not even scouted.

No scatback or halfback or fullback or running back ever ran more successfully against the odds than Young. He stood 5–4, the smallest man ever to play professional football. He ranged from 155 pounds, his weight at the University of Illinois three decades ago, to 168 in the NFL.

Looking at him, reminds you of standing in the house of mirrors at a carnival, at the mirror that makes you look twice as small as you are. But Buddy Young could run the 100-yard dash in 9.5, when the world record was 9.4. And he was so tough, so durable, that he actually played fullback, a tiny sports car at a position meant for tanks.

"When I think of Buddy Young, I think of a rubber ball exploding," said Frankie Albert, a quarterback for the San Francisco 49ers when Young played for the New York Yankees of the All-America Football Conference, in the late Forties. "Buddy used to wear these dime-store shoulder pads and no hip or thigh pads. He was 9.5 when he hit the line. Defensive linemen lived in fear of making an error, because once he got

Illinois halfback Claude "Buddy" Young was instrumental in the Illini's win over UCLA, in the first Rose Bowl game played under the Big Ten-Pacific Conference pact.

behind you he was a blur. He was so low to the ground that linebackers could hardly see him. He didn't try to run over you, but he was gutty and never ran for the sidelines."

Not only could Young run the draw, but he was a draw at a time when pro football was struggling to gain acceptance. "Buddy was a ticket seller, even though he didn't play on many winning teams," said Albert. "You'd have to say that he was the O.J. Simpson of his time. I mean if you asked who was the NFL's premier scatback of the early Fifties, you'd hear the name Buddy Young."

THE TINY GIANT

Jack White, retired as the player personnel director of the 49ers, coached Young both in the military and with the Yankees, and practically has total recall in describing his extraordinary talents. "Buddy played for the Fleet City team during the war. We played the El Toro Marines in a big game and they were leading 14–0 in the first half. Buddy caught a punt and went for a touchdown. El Toro came back and scored, kicked off, and Buddy took the kickoff for a touchdown. We held them, pitched out to Buddy, and he went for still another touchdown. We tied them 21–21 at halftime, and eventually won the game. But Buddy had his hands on the ball three times in the first half, and scored each time. He was a great clutch performer."

White said that Terry Metcalf of the St. Louis Cardinals, among the players of the Seventies, reminds him most of Young. "Metcalf probably had a little better hands, but Young was more compact and powerful and just as dangerous in the open field. You didn't catch Buddy Young in the open very often. He truly was one of the greatest speed backs who ever played—he had violent speed. He also had great strength in his legs and could run just as well inside as outside. It was surprising how much short yardage he could get you. He'd hit into the hole so quickly, guys didn't have time to react. And he was one of the best open field blockers I ever saw, a man of great courage. I can still see him against the Cleveland Browns. Spec Sanders, our great single-wing tail-back, broke for a long run. One of their big tackles has a shot at him. Buddy rolled up in a ball, and cut that tackle like a knife."

Young was one of the early blacks in pro football, but it wasn't a problem even on a team like the Yankees, which was dominated by Southerners. "Buddy was extremely well-liked by his teammates," said White. "We had this end from Texas, Bruce Alford, who requested that Buddy be his roommate. Buddy was a leader, highly intelligent, and a great person. I guess the only bad thing I could say about him was that he was short. If he had been 6' he would have weighed 215. Football was a big man's game even then, although not like it is today. Buddy's size never really hurt him, though. He was a champion."

Always a champion, although it was hard to detect this when he was the smallest kid in class, Buddy grew up with four sisters and four brothers in Chicago. Young's mother played basketball and volleyball in her youth. She understood sports and told Claude that he might have to look up to others in height, but that he could always look at them eye-to-eye in ability. A sister, Claudine, later would become a sprinter with a Chicago track club. Claude and Claudine were two teen-agers on the move. Buddy pulled off a tremendous coup with teammate Ranis Thomas as they led Wendell Phillips High School to the 1943 Illinois state track and field championship. Young won the 100-yard dash and the 220-yard low hurdles. Thomas captured the 220-yard dash and placed second behind Young in the 100. Their two-man total of 19 points was enough to defeat 32 other schools.

A number of colleges studied Young's accomplishments, regardless of his size. He was running 9.7 as a high school senior. Young selected Illinois, although there was little choice. "My grandfather wouldn't have had it any other way," he said. Buddy enrolled at Champaign in the spring of 1944, running the dashes in 9.5 and 20.9 and broadjumping (this was before the term became long jumping) 24–0½, tremendous versatility for a college freshman. He never realized his full potential in track and field because that was his last season competing in the sport. Young set a world indoor record of 4.5 in the 45-yard dash, before he was through. He won both the NCAA indoor and outdoor championships in the 100 and 220 sprints, a superb achievement, as Illinois won the outdoor title. "I believe I may have been the first trackman ever to make it big in football," he said. "I was an all-America in both sports."

There have been many world class sprinters who tried to make it in football and failed, names like Ray Norton, Frank Budd, Jimmy Hines, and John Carlos. They didn't like the fierce pounding or didn't have the hands to hold on to anything but a baton. Young was just as spectacular in football as he had been in track. As an Illinois freshman, he scored 13 touchdowns to tie the legendary Red Grange's school record. Young blazed 98 yards against Pittsburgh, 93 yards against a Great Lakes Naval Air Station team coached by Paul Brown, and 76 yards against Notre Dame, all for touchdowns. Combining his track and football accomplishments, no college freshman ever had a year like Buddy Young.

However, any signs of immortality would have to wait. The country was at war, and Young was eligible for the draft. As soon as football season was over, Young found himself in the Navy. He was assigned to Great Lakes in Illinois, but never played for Brown because he was transferred to Camp Shoemaker in Pleasanton, California, thirty miles from Oakland. Commander O. M. Forster, the camp's commanding officer, believed winning football was good for morale and, perhaps, rank. He formed the Fleet City Bluejackets, coached by Bill Reinhart, which included names like Bruiser Kinard and Bill Daddio. Fleet City was one of the best service football teams of World War II, and appropriately named. Young was running between 70 and 90 yards for touchdowns, almost at will. Playing against the Hawaii Naval All-Stars, at Kezar Stadium, in San Francisco, he ran approximately 130 yards for a touchdown, counting his cuts back and forth across the field.

"Nobody caught Buddy Young, nobody!" said Frankie Albert. "I was playing for St. Mary's Pre-Flight at the same time, and one day I caught Buddy in the open. Suddenly I had the reputation as a great defensive player. Heck, I couldn't play defense. What happened was that Buddy was going down the sidelines for the winning touchdown. He slowed up when he saw me coming, figuring he could fake me. Only I don't slow up. I know I had the sideline to my advantage, and I knocked him out of bounds. I told Buddy years later, he should have kept on running, because I couldn't have got him. What chance did any defensive back have against him in a situation like that? This was how good he was."

Buddy Young was being compared to Glenn Davis of West Point and even Grange. Young was live newspaper copy in the Forties, and there was rampant speculation about where he'd resume his education. There were rumors he would select UCLA over Illinois. UCLA had had a number of star black athletes, such as Kenny Washington and Jackie Robinson; it was the first school to actively recruit blacks. Young visited the UCLA campus with Kenny Washington. UCLA wanted Young as badly as Illinois. Coach Bert LaBrucherie knew he had a strong Bruin team coming up in 1946, and that Young could make it fearsome. "People of my race contacted me about attending UCLA," said Young. "I went home on leave and talked with Illinois track coach Leo Johnson, football coach Ray Eliot, and athletic director Doug Mills. We talked at length about my return, but I told them I wouldn't make up my mind until I got out of the Navy."

Young stretched out the speculation until he was discharged in July, 1946. Then he said it would be Illinois. "Once again, my grandfather would have been furious if I had gone any place else," he said, committed in the end by a strong family bond. UCLA would become familiar to him a second time in the not-so-distant future.

Illinois was favored to be a national contender in 1946 because of a great number of players coming back from the service—athletes such as Alex Agase and Julie Rykovich. Perry Moss, who had quarterbacked at Tulsa, transferred to Illinois to become part of the fun. Only it wasn't good times in the beginning. "It was almost chaos," declared Young. "The older players couldn't adjust to the college environment. Some had been fighting overseas, and coming back to college football was not the easiest thing in the world. Some were angry and frustrated because they once had all-America potential, but felt the war had robbed them of their speed and ability. So dissension began to raise its ugly head." Illinois rolled over Pitt in the opener, 33–7, then was crushed by Notre Dame, 26–6. Young felt more than the effects of a defeat. "I played the whole season with two sprained ankles I received on one play in that Notre Dame game, when Johnny Lujack hit me with a shoetop tackle," said Young. The Illini rebounded to trounce Purdue, 43–7, only to lose again, 14–7, to Indiana. "After those two defeats, the student body petitioned that Ray Eliot be fired as football coach," said Young. "Things were at their worst. Eliot was one of the greatest coaches I've ever been in contact with. We had the depth and talent, but we were defeating ourselves. We finally turned it around. We had so much talent that we *had* to win."

The Illini won their last five games—over Wisconsin, 27–21; Michigan, 13–9; Iowa, 7–0; Ohio State, 16–7; and Northwestern, 20–0. Illinois had won the Big Nine championship and something historic was about to happen—the first of the annual Rose Bowl games between what was then the Pacific Coast Conference and the Big Nine (Michigan State would later join the conference), as part of a contract which exists to this day.

Not in 26 years, or when California flattened Ohio State, 28–0, in the 1921 game, had the two conferences met in the Rose Bowl.

Illinois' opponent would be UCLA, which although failing to land Young, had completed a 10–0 season. The Bruins had a fine quarterback in Ernie Case, and great ends in all-America Burr Baldwin and Tom Fears, later a great pro with the Los

Angeles Rams. UCLA had a victory margin of 31–7 over its ten opponents, fattened by a 61–7 assault of Montana. Illinois' margin was 19–10. At least on paper, the Bruins looked stronger, and the West Coast press made them seem twice as strong. LaBrucherie had been named Coach of the Year.

"The papers out there weren't too happy because we had lost two games. They said that we were demeaning to the Rose Bowl," recalled Young. "I'm sure they wanted Army, with Glenn Davis and Doc Blanchard, which had just played the famous scoreless tie with Notre Dame. But they were stuck with us because of the new contract. We had no doubts in our minds that we were a good football team and, in the tradition of our conference, the roughest and the toughest. We knew we would do all right."

The Illini boarded the Illinois Central in Chicago, changed trains in New Orleans, and continued their fifty-hour journey to the West Coast. The team registered at the Huntington Hotel in Pasadena, where disciplinary problems surfaced again. Two second-string players didn't make it back from Los Angeles to Pasadena before curfew and Eliot sent them home to Champaign. The Illini somehow made it to the Rose Bowl on New Year's Day with the rest of the team intact. "Ray Eliot made one of the most outstanding pre-game talks I ever heard, before we played UCLA," said Young. "It was a fiery thing, eloquently done, pitched very well. Oh yes, he reminded us about what the papers had said about us. After that speech, we knew nothing could stop us."

Nothing did. UCLA looked like Don Quixote trying to joust with a windmill. Illinois had a potent split-T backfield of Moss, Young, 200-pound Rykovich, and fullback Russ Steger, a lead blocker and third-and-two-type runner. There was tremendous blocking up front in Sam Zatkoff at end, brothers Lou and Alex Agase at left tackle and right guard, and captain Max Wenskunas at center. There was defensive pressure in the line from 300-pound Les Bingaman and Ike Owens. Bingaman would later star for the Detroit Lions, Alex Agase for the Cleveland Browns, and Rykovich for the Chicago Bears.

Illinois took the opening kickoff, and caught fire at once. On the first offensive play, Moss and Rykovich teamed on a 44 yard pass play to the UCLA 16. Rykovich scored six plays later, but Don Maechtle missed the conversion kick. Case retaliated with a UCLA touchdown seven minutes later and then kicked the PAT to put the Bruins on top, 7–6. While the Bruins thought things had turned around, Illinois had a surprise waiting for them. A big surprise.

"We had a flea flicker play worked up for the Rose Bowl," said Young. "We were on about the UCLA 38, third and 11, lined up on the left hashmark. I was set out on the right hashmark, then started in motion towards the quarterback. Moss faded to pass just as I had reached the line of scrimmage. I turned back towards the direction from where I had come, and Moss shoveled me the ball. We had a wedge set up outside the end, and the play went for 16 yards, setting up a touchdown. What I remember most about this play is that Lou Agase caught Burr Baldwin with a blind-side block and knocked him out of the game for good. The whole thing might have had a lot to do with demoralizing UCLA."

Young punched the ball across at the end of the drive, and Maechtle made it 13–7. Illinois scored twice more on a 4-yard counter by Paul Patterson, a reserve back who was black and had played with Young at Fleet City, and a 1-yard sneak by Moss. Maechtle missed one conversion and had another blocked, but it was 25–7 and UCLA was all but finished in the second quarter. "We did everything we wanted to do against their team," said Young. "We had no trouble moving the ball at all. We had confidence, a great game plan, and a damn good defensive team."

UCLA narrowed the score to 25–14 at halftime, with one of the more memorable plays in Rose Bowl history. A substitute halfback, Al Hoisch, took an Illinois kickoff 3 yards deep in his end zone. He started out for the right sidelines, faked two tacklers, and received several blocks that left him with just one man to beat at his 35. Hoisch cut sharply by the defender towards midfield and outran three Illini to the end zone. Hoisch's 103-yard kickoff return is the longest ever in the Rose Bowl, and remains clear in the mind of Young, who watched from the sidelines. "Hoisch juked a few people —although in those days they didn't call it juked—got to the outside and ran like a guy going to his breakfast," said Young. "It was a heckuva run, but it didn't do them any good because we were ahead by three touchdowns at the time."

Illinois marched 66 yards in fifteen plays to score on the first series of the second half, Young punching across from a few inches out. Maechtle made it 32–14. The Illini kicked off and held their breath as Hoisch exploded a second time, twisting 51 yards before Illinois managed to run him out of bounds, at its 38. Two plays later, Case's pass

USLA halfback Al Hoisch. He returned a kickoff for 103 yards and a touchdown in a losing cause. His run is still the longest in Rose Bowl history.

Illinois coach, Ray Eliot, showing sideline enthusiasm, as his club smashed UCLA 45-14 in the 1947 Rose Bowl.

was intercepted by Steger, playing linebacker, and he lumbered 70 yards for a touchdown. Case later tried a flat pass near his goal line, and Illinois tackle Stan Green intercepted at the 12 and practically walked in with the final touchdown.

Illinois' 45–14 victory, at the time, was the second biggest defeat of a West Coast team in the Rose Bowl. The worst drubbing was Michigan's 49–0 defeat of Stanford, in the 1902 inaugural. Young and Rykovich, who shared Player of the Game honors, each rushed for 103 yards, as Illinois amassed 326 on the ground to UCLA's 58. The Illini dominated the Bruins all around, with a 403–261 margin in yardage gained, and a 23–12 advantage in first downs. It was strictly no contest.

The Illini gloated after their easy win, calling UCLA "weaker than the weakest Big Nine team" after their snow-decked train pulled into Chicago. Rykovich descended from the train chomping on a cigar. Young told the press that UCLA's "inferior tackles" made it possible for Illinois to gain so much running yardage. But the Bruins weren't really all that bad; the Illini were just fantastic.

And built too low to the ground.

HOPALONG HALFBACK AND WOODY

The bitter chill of winter only three weeks before had closed down Ohio State University and a number of businesses in Columbus, Ohio. In addition, one of the worst snowfalls of the century in the Midwest made driving treacherous for those brave residents who crawled out of their enforced hibernation. Regardless of the elements, Wayne Woodrow Hayes wasn't one to malinger. The arrival of letters of intent—those signed certificates of indentured servitude, which turn over eighteen-year-old fullbacks and linebackers to football coaches for four years—was rapidly approaching. Michigan might be gaining an edge with a recruit, which is more than Woody can bear, and so Hayes, who had just turned 64 on Valentine's Day of 1977, threw on an overcoat (he no longer attacks the cold in just shirtsleeves) and went out to fool Bo Schembechler and Mother Nature.

"I do more recruiting every year. I go hard at it," Hayes was saying from his snowbank-surrounded office, two weeks after his birthday. "Sometimes it involves eighteen hours a day, although a lot of it is traveling. A few nights I don't get much sleep, and some nights I don't get any. But when you get older you don't need much sleep."

Woody Hayes sets his own rules, whether it involves personal health, or his ultra-successful football program. Apparently, it matters not to him that he had a heart attack in 1974. He weighs more than a heart victim his age should, but that doesn't slow him down either.

"I'm about ten to twenty pounds above where I should be," he said. "But with all this snow around here, I don't get the exercise I should. Sometimes when I get to an airport, I'll take a walk for a mile or two before I catch my plane. But I'll get my weight down in the summer, when I can do some hiking."

154

He doesn't think about retirement, although Ohio State has a mandatory retirement age of sixty-five that caught up with Woody's athletic director, Ed Weaver, in June of 1977. "I'll do something else when I find a job I like better," said Hayes, intimating he may never be ready to retire. "My eyesight is still good. In our last home game of the 1976 season, there was a play on the 7 yard line that I caught and the officials didn't. The films proved I was right. The only trouble I have with my eyes is that my glasses won't stay in place, because I've got this peanut nose."

Hayes has a soft voice, almost grandfatherly in tone, that seems out of proportion to his large frame and often irascible behavior.

The letters of intent had just arrived in his office, and although he was highly pleased there was no animation in his voice. "We've gotten some of the best athletes we've ever gotten. Academically, too," he said. "We're a little short of interior linemen, but I believe this group will do very well."

It's reasonable to believe that if Woody Hayes can't find an interior lineman, he'll make one.

Woody Hayes has been Ohio State's head coach since 1951. Only Paul "Bear" Bryant has more college coaching victories. Both are legends in their time. "A good general makes you search for his weaknesses," said Hayes of his approach to coaching, which has been influenced more by Patton than by Rockne. Woody is well-read on the intracacies of modern warfare. He doesn't send a player out to beat Michigan; he deploys him. Hayes invades Ann Arbor in November while remembering the lessons learned from Napoleon's attempt to take Russia in February. Hayes is half-coach, half-general.

"Woody lived without friends," wrote Dan Jenkins in *Saturday's America*. "His closest associate was a blackboard with circles and X's on it, or a film projector. He breathed football the way he breathed fire on the practice field, which was excessively. In practices, Woody was seen to bite his wrist when a Buckeye blew an assignment. He would throw his baseball cap down and stomp on it. He would hit himself in the jaw with his fist. He would growl, grumble and groan. He would slam a lineman on the shoulder pad and read him out for all the world to hear. 'We have to avoid being nice, that's all,' Woody said. 'That's what I tell the boys all the time. It's this niceness from people complimenting you that can be killing. I can be deceiving. Yes, sir, Emerson was hitting the ball square when he said, 'As soon as honeyed words of praise are spoken for me, I feel as one who lies unprotected before his enemies!' "

Woody hasn't left himself unprotected. He has had just two losing seasons out of twenty-six at Ohio State through the 1976 season, which is testimony to his indomitable energy, great love of work and also his scheduling. Ohio State, since Hayes has become head coach, has not played Notre Dame, Oklahoma, Alabama, Texas, Nebraska or Arkansas. Edward "Moose" Krause, Notre Dame's long-time athletic director, said Hayes overruled the Ohio State Athletic Board and canceled a series between the two schools that was to begin in 1977. "In his early days at Ohio State, Hayes came to our place to scout USC before the Rose Bowl," recalled Krause. "I said, 'How about getting together for a series of games?' He told me that he would never play us as long as he was at Ohio State. But if he doesn't want to play us, why doesn't he say it publicly?" Because, this way people only remember Hayes' 10–1 records, which he builds, calculatingly, with a steady diet of Texas Christians, North Carolinas, and Oregons.

Hayes' image to those who only know him through television is one of a storming, raging tyrant. He has stomped on sideline markers, shoved a Michigan State student, and allegedly shoved a camera in the face of a *Los Angeles Times* photographer who ventured too close on the sidelines at the Rose Bowl. The photographer, Art Rogers, sued, then later dropped the suit. "I have never thought of divorcing Woody," his wife once said. "Shoot him, yes." Yet Hayes isn't without redeeming qualities. He is both impatient and generous to a fault. He charges you one moment, consoles you the next. He is unpredictable, unselfish, unreasonable. He is deeply patriotic. He is controversial, to say the least, and he seems to enjoy it.

"Woody is a great coach and a great person," said Howard "Hopalong" Cassady. "He has always gone to bat for his players, even after they have left school. His principles haven't changed over the years, but he has mellowed some. I wouldn't say he was my toughest coach. My high school coach was tough. Buddy Parker and George Wilson were tough. They just demand in different ways."

Hopalong Cassady was Woody Hayes' first football hero, actually a catalyst to Hayes' ensuing success. Woody's first Buckeye team finished 4–3–2, and both students

Ohio State coach Woody Hayes and his star halfback Howard "Hopalong" Cassady.

and alumni screamed for his scalp; Coach Paul O. Bixler lasted one year in Columbus with an identical record in 1946. Hayes managed to survive that turbulent beginning, and have identical 6–3 records during Cassady's freshman and sophomore years. The breakthrough came the next year. Ohio State finished 10–0, one of only two times a Woody Hayes' team from Columbus has been both unbeaten and untied. The Buckeyes of that year won the national championship and defeated USC, 20–7, in the Rose Bowl. Woody Hayes was here to stay.

Cassady was a two-time all-America in 1954–55, a Rose Bowl star, and both Heisman Trophy winner and Associated Press Male Athlete of the Year in 1955. The nickname "Hopalong" of course was derived from the movie-television cowboy, Hopalong Cassidy. "I was a single wing tailback in high school in Columbus," said Hopalong Halfback. "My friends called me Red. In fact, if someone calls me Red today, I know that I went to high school with him. But I was always jumping over the line when I ran. So a number of writers stuck the name Hopalong on me. There are people now who call me Howard. A lot of others call me Hop. My wife calls me Hop and Howard, among other things." The voice from the other side of the continent chuckled over the phone.

The heroes Hopalong met often. "As he was raised in Hendrysburg, Ohio, which is only thirty miles from Columbus, he used to appear in parades and state fairs back home," said the halfback of the cowboy, whose real name was William Boyd. "I made some appearances with him, and when we went out to the Rose Bowl, he came to several of our practices. I had some pictures taken with him, one in which I'm wearing his guns and he is carrying the football. He sent me a picture of him, which he signed, 'From one Hopalong to another.' I guess you could say I inherited his nickname, but not his money. I was proud, though, to be named after him. He was a great person, a wonderful man."

Although Hopalong Halfback hitched his wagon to Hopalong Cowboy's immense popularity in the Fifties, the football player didn't need a gimmick. He would have won the Heisman in 1955, had his name been Howard Schwartz. "I'm sure the name Hopalong didn't hurt, but Cassady won all those awards on his own ability," said Hayes. "He was a very inspirational player because he was able to turn around a game at any time. Time and time again, he'd make the big play. He was a gamebreaker, a climax player."

Both Hayes and Cassady remember the 1954 game against Wisconsin, the nation's number one-ranked team at the time, and led by fullback Alan "The Horse" Ameche, the Heisman winner that season. "I had a big interception and went 88 yards for a touchdown to break the Wisconsin game wide open," said Cassady. The Buckeyes broke Wisconsin's spirit as well, 31–14. The week before, Cassady was the difference in a 20–14 win over a good Iowa team. "Hop had been beaten on a pass early in the game, and was mad as heck," Hayes remembered. "The first time we had the ball, near midfield, he went all the way on the first play. Hop just made things happen. He caught a fumble in mid-air and ran for a touchdown against Indiana. Hop was also a darn good blocker."

Howard "Hopalong" Cassady only wanted to play for Ohio State, although he had contemplated Notre Dame. "I was just hoping Woody would give me a chance," he said. That never was a problem, although Hayes was reluctant to play the freshman halfback. "This was during the Korean exigency, and freshmen were eligible for varsity play," said Hayes. "Hop was a mid-year high school graduate and turned out for spring practice. In every scrimmage, he'd break away for a touchdown. Otherwise, he wasn't doing much. But he kept breaking off these long runs. All we had to do was add things up, and we decided he should be playing." Cassady made some big defensive plays at Ohio State, including two in the Rose Bowl triumph over USC. "No, I wouldn't say that he was a good defensive player," said Hayes. "We played him on defense because the rules said we had to play a man both ways. But he could make the big play. I'm sure on that interception against Wisconsin, he had overplayed his man. Sometimes he'd come out all right."

There never was any question about Cassady's offense. He set Ohio State records for rushing, total offense, scoring and kickoff and punt returns. He was a "do it all" kind of player. Cassady never was better than his senior Heisman-receiving season. The Buckeyes had no passing attack, and opponents knew that Cassady was the man to stop. In nine games he rushed for 958 yards in 161 carries (5.9 average) and fourteen touchdowns, and also scored on a 37-yard punt return. The Buckeyes repeated as Big Ten champions but were prevented from a second trip to Pasadena because of the conference's illogical no-repeat rule, since voided. "Probably no one in the history of our university has had so much favorable publicity," said a high Ohio State official of Cassady's four years at the school.

There was also honesty and virtue about Cassady, similar to that which was projected on the silver screen by the silver-haired other Hopalong. The football player won by a comfortable margin in the Male Athlete of the Year balloting over boxer Rocky Marciano and baseball pitcher Johnny Podres. College basketball star Bill Russell finished fifth, and baseball great Ted Williams was tenth. "Why not someone like Rocky Marciano or Johnny Podres?" asked Cassady in accepting the award. "Their accomplishments were made by themselves. I had a whole team to help me. Football is the most integrated sports there is. I don't know how many times I might have been stopped if a teammate hadn't thrown a key block and then went downfield to throw another. I hope I can uphold the reputation of this honor."

Hop didn't do it alone, as he said. "Jim Parker was our left guard, and Cassady made a lot of yardage running quick-hitters or traps through Parker's hole," Hayes pointed out. "We played Hop at left halfback, so he had the advantage of having Parker, who even blocked for him on sweeps. Jim had a super year in 1955, and Hop averaged just about six yards a carry." Parker eventually would block his way into the college and pro football halls of fame. "Jim didn't start at the beginning of his sophomore season in 1954, but he worked his way into it," said Cassady. "Woody depends a lot on his linemen. Linemen become great blockers at Ohio State, or they don't play. You see a lot of Woody's linemen in the pros. They say Woody is a fullback-type coach because he had Bob White, Bob Ferguson, Jim Otis, and John Brockington. But I was a halfback and so was Archie Griffin. The whole thing has to do with the caliber of Woody's line."

"That 1954 team has a fond place in my mind," recalls Hayes. "It played great football—great team football. And it destroyed Michigan!" Which is always the final determinant for Hayes, because he plays Michigan twelve months of the year in his mind, not just on a November afternoon. "We had a lot of tough games that year. We just didn't walk through the schedule," says Cassady. "Michigan was leading us 7–0. We stopped them on our 1-foot line after they had six plays inside our five. Instead of 14–0, we went right down the field and scored on them and eventually won (21–7). We had a number of games we broke open in the fourth quarter."

Ohio State had a tremendous backfield—one of the best in the school's football-rich history—that 1954 season. Dave Leggett was the quarterback and good enough to bench John Borton, co-captain and the school's all-time single-season passing leader. Cassady and Bobby Watkins, the first Ohio State player ever to score four touchdowns in one game, were the halfbacks. The Buckeyes had an unusual fullback with the unusual name of Hubert Bobo. Bobo played to a different drummer, one who didn't always march to the Hayes' beat. "Bobo got on the bad side of Woody," said Cassady, "and then hurt his knee real bad the next year." Bobo, who also punted, only played his sophomore year, but was splendid. The Buckeyes had outstanding ends in co-captain Dick Brubaker and Dean Dugger.

The Buckeyes struggled to get by California, 21–13, and Northwestern, 14–7, while having an easier time against Indiana, 28–0; Illinois, 40–7; Pittsburgh, 26–0, and Purdue, 28–6. In those days, the Big Ten representative was almost a guaranteed winner at Pasadena. "The Big Ten was tough then, while the other leagues weren't that tough," said Cassady. "The Big Ten is still as tough, it's just that the other leagues have gotten so doggone strong."

Ohio State and USC met for the first time in the Rose Bowl, but it certainly will not be their last meeting. USC wasn't in Ohio State's "league" that season. Coach Jess Hill's Trojans were 8–4, but finished the season in a tailspin, losing their last three games, including the Rose Bowl. USC battered Washington State, 39–0; Pittsburgh, 27–7; Oregon State, 34–0, and Washington, 41–0, then fell flat on its face against UCLA, 34–0. But since the Pacific Coast Conference also prevented its champion from going to the Rose Bowl two years running, the Trojans appeared in Pasadena, on New Year's Day, instead of the stronger Bruins. Hayes watched as Notre Dame defeated USC, 23–17.

"I said before that Rose Bowl game that the team which played the most foolproof football would win," repeated Hayes. "We had the ball eighty-two times and didn't fumble once, and they had the football thirty-two plays and fumbled seven times. Our not fumbling was remarkable considering the conditions." Rose Bowl records show the Buckeyes with one lost fumble that game, and USC with three. Nevertheless, the Buckeyes proved superior at mudding and mudslinging.

It was the last time the Rose Bowl was played in a downpour. The rain and mud were ankle deep. "On the opening kickoff, I couldn't even see the ball," said Cassady. "I heard something splashing in the mud, saw the football and picked it up." The Buckeye backfield sloshed through USC for 295 yards rushing. Cassady led the way with 94 yards in twenty-one carries (4.4). Watkins and Leggett each rushed for 67 (4.2), Jerry Harkrader for 49 (7.0) and Bobo for 19 (3.1). Hubert also punted for a 38-yard average.

"The bands marched at halftime and didn't help the field," Hayes recalls. "USC's band did a ring-around-the-rosy and destroyed the middle of the field. Their little linebacker, Marv Goux, who's still one of their coaches, made fifty percent of the tackles. If he was making that many, then someone else wasn't. I said after the game that I didn't think they were a great team because of that, and it created a little turmoil." Just a little. Hayes is regarded with about as much warmth in Southern California, and at USC, as a plague.

"The worst thing about the game," recalls Cassady, "was that the rain softened the field and exposed the sand that was beneath the turf. We all had sand burns, and some of us had the skin torn right off. You know the 'strawberries' you get in baseball from sliding? We got those." Meanwhile, the Trojans were getting the raspberries from the Ohio State rooting section, which gleefully watched the Buckeyes march up and down the muddy Rose Bowl terrain like Patton's tanks in Germany.

USC had talented players in end Leon Clarke, quarterback Jim Contratto, Goux and junior halfback Jon Arnett, later an all-pro with the Los Angeles Rams. Contratto had the greatest difficulty holding onto the football. He committed the first Trojan fumble, ending a drive at the Buckeyes' 31. Cassady, Leggett, and Harkrader methodically worked the ball to the Trojan 3, as Parker was knocking USC tacklers every which way. Leggett scored on the next play, and little Tad Weed's conversion made it 7–0. Ohio State scored again three minutes into the second quarter after Arnett lost control of Contratto's wobbly pitchout and the Buckeyes recovered. Watkins ran for 14 yards and then caught a 21-yard touchdown pass from Leggett.

USC's only moment of glory came in historic fashion. Aramis Dandoy, a reserve senior back, fielded a Bobo punt at his 14, broke to the sidelines and behind perfect blocking ran 86 yards for a touchdown—the longest punt return to date in a Rose Bowl game. "All I remember about that run," said Hayes, "was that despised USC bullhorn, which it seems like I've been hearing since 1920. Now it was 14–7 and we had to come back and take control of the game again—which we did."

USC was never in the game again. They lost the first-down battle, twenty-two to six, and were outgained, 360 yards to 206. The Trojans did have chances for big plays that

USC halfback Aramis
Dandoy, who set a Rose
Bowl record with an
86-yard punt return in the
20-7 loss to Ohio State.

would have changed the complexion of an otherwise lost afternoon, but Cassady rebuffed them each time. Jaguar Jon, as Arnett was known, broke loose on a 70-yard run before Hopalong caught up to him, at the Ohio State 26. "I took a deep angle and cut him off before he could get away," said Cassady, who later knocked down Contratto's fourth-down pass to Arnett from the 23. Later in the game, Arnett slipped away again, racing for 31 yards to his 43, where Cassady smacked into him, jarring the ball loose, which Ohio State's Bob Thornton recovered.

With those isolated incidents taken care of, Ohio State put the game out of reach. Leggett ran for 22 yards later in the game, then completed a 15-yard pass to Harkrader, at the Trojan 9. Harkrader scored standing up on the ensuing play. USC's only consolation at that point was Clarke's blocking Weed's PAT attempt, and Goux' stopping another Buckeye drive at the 4.

"We used our 'twenty-six pass' three times that day, including the pass to Harkrader that set up our last touchdown," said Hayes, the game still clear in his mind. "We hit Watkins with it another time, and overthrew Brubaker, who was clear in the end zone."

Leggett completed six of eleven passes for 65 yards, in addition to his 67 yards on the ground. He ran for one touchdown, threw for another, engineered the third touchdown drive, and was named Player of the Game.

But for all-around play, offensively and defensively, there wasn't a finer player on the field than Hopalong Cassady.

Cassady now living in Florida and employed by the New York Yankees as a scout and spring training physical fitness director, thought that Rose Bowl game was much closer than did Hayes. He especially remembers Arnett, who rushed nine times for 123 yards (13.7). "We knew that Arnett was a great back just by watching the films before the game," he said. "I'm glad it was raining. He would have been a bitch on a dry field."

Hoppy! For shame!

BUCKS AND DUCKS

Galen Bernard Cisco was a senior at St. Mary's, Ohio, High School when the Bucks were in the 1955 Bowl. The muscular fullback-linebacker had attended several 1954 games in Columbus "as a prospective player." Cisco was getting bids from Wisconsin, Michigan State and Purdue.

"But I was an Ohio boy," he recalls, "and Woody did the best selling job on me. He convinced me my home state university would produce more for me after I got out of school. And, of course, Columbus was closer to home. My choice amounted to his interest in me, really. I was awed by being able to go to a Big Ten school, even though a lot of people told me I was making a mistake, that I would get lost in the shuffle. And you know, I still hear that all the time from people who talk about boys going down to Columbus to play, or even just to attend, Ohio State. But I think it's best if you go to a big school like that, because if you can get through it and not get lost in the shuffle, I think you can cope with almost anything. And that's pretty much what life is, anyhow."

At the moment, Galen Cisco was coping with his suitcase in an Oakland, California, motel room. His latest team, the Kansas City Royals, had a baseball game across the freeway in a few hours with the Oakland Athletics. Later they'd move on to another town and another motel room, and so would Cisco.

He has now been a sports itinerant for eighteen years. He played in the 1958 Rose Bowl for Ohio State and Woody, and then went on to a baseball career as a pitcher in such towns as Raleigh, Corning, Allentown, Waterloo, Minneapolis, Seattle, Boston, New York (Mets), Jacksonville, Toronto, Pittsfield, Louisville, Omaha and, finally, to Kansas City as the team's pitching coach. He would be forty years old in 1977; a quiet, contained, quite strong figure—still 6', 197 pounds.

Apparently, no one had interviewed Cisco about football for years. Pitching coaches always are asked about the conditions of the arms of their young starters, not about Rose Bowls.

The 1957 Buckeyes were the best Galen played on during his three varsity years in Columbus. It was the best in the land that season, and featured a half dozen fellows who had come together as freshmen in 1955. Cisco and Leo Brown, co-captains, were two of them. Then there were Dick Schafrath, Joe Cannavino, Joe Trivisonno, and Dan James.

Among the younger players were Jim Houston, Dick LeBeau, Bill Jobko, Bob White, Don Clark, Frank Kremblas, Don Sutherin.

"I figured once," said Cisco, "that in the years I was at Ohio State our teams sent at least seventeen guys into the NFL."

None, however, was the star of the 1958 Rose Bowl game. That MVP honor befell Jack Crabtree, of Oregon. Before Pasadena, the Bucks did not know a great deal about Crabtree. "But he sure impressed me that day," said Cisco. "Heck, their whole team impressed me that day."

"The one thing I remember most when thinking back on Ohio State and football is that in those days, in the Fifties, there was more of a premium put on your studies than on the game," Cisco was saying, as he checked the motel room closet to make certain he would be leaving nothing behind. "But that thought really didn't sink in while I was there. Only when I look back do I remember the pressure put on the books, on getting an education. Over the years I think that Woody has had a great percentage of his athletes graduate. His program is total football, no question about that, but I think he'll do anything he can to get you to graduate."

Cisco was an Ohio State fullback in the days before the fullback represented THE offensive weapon for the Buckeyes. "His offense didn't start changing until Bob White came along—and he was starting to play just as I was leaving," said Galen. "Until then, the offense revolved more around the halfbacks (like Howard 'Hopalong' Cassady of the 1955 Bowl) than fullbacks. But even then, there was really not much passing at Ohio State. If we threw as many as seven or eight times a game, we thought something had gone wrong. No, the history then was great halfbacks and blocking-back fullbacks. After I left, the Whites and Fergusons, and Brockingtons came along.

"Our team had an outstanding class of boys. We were a bear-down bunch of boys who weren't afraid of anything. A little wild maybe—but in a positive direction. We had a lot of fun and everybody loved to play football."

Soon after mid-season in 1957, Cisco says the players knew they would probably win the conference and move on to Pasadena. "No question, we were looking forward to that," he says. "I was due to be married the following February, but then I decided to move the wedding with Martha, (a girl from Waverly, Ohio, whom he met in

Columbus), to December first, because the wives would be permitted to make the trip West with us. I thought that would be a honeymoon for us. But it didn't turn out that way. In fact, we've never had a real honeymoon."

Cisco remembers the Bucks had to work out in the campus fieldhouse in Columbus, because it was so cold and the ground was frozen, just before departing for Pasadena. Once in the West, Woody had the Bucks working twice a day, ninety minutes in the morning then another ninety after a "light lunch and nap. We started tapering off a couple of days before the game," recalls Galen, "By then everybody was back into respectable shape, and we were really ready to play." Football, that is.

Cisco remembers that Hayes "kept all of the players together, once we got to Pasadena. When we were at the hotel, our wives (about ten women made the trip) were out on sightseeing tours. When we were in our rooms, it seemed that they were always gone. And when they were in our rooms, it seemed that we were always at practice. I mean, some nights went by I didn't get to see my wife at all. By some coincidence," and here Galen chuckles, "Woody made sure we didn't get to meet often. Not that he had a tight curfew. It was just that whenever the players went out—and we never left the hotel all that much—we were all out together, and he was with us."

Hayes approached the 1958 Rose Bowl much as he would any other game, says Cisco. "Except I don't recall that we had too much information on Oregon. We didn't seem to know too much about their personnel. All we knew was what we read. I honestly don't remember if we saw any of Oregon's game films or not.

"Maybe we went into that game with an attitude of shrugging off Oregon. I remember feeling it was just a great thing to be picked for the Rose Bowl. Kind of a dream come true.

"Not like just another Michigan game. We always used to start thinking about Michigan at spring practice. A lot of days during the year you'd spend the last ten minutes of a practice just concentrating on the Michigan offense and defense. So by the time the Michigan game came around, we pretty much knew what we had to do and what they were going to try to do."

But the Ducks were, in Cisco's recollection, an unknown quantity. "We were going to go with five or six plays in our basic ground game," he says. "Woody's thinking was that if we could run those five or six we'd be all right, because we could run those plays better than anyone else. Our timing was perfect. Our blocking was perfect. At least we thought it was."

The Bucks, he says, were fretting a bit in advance about the passing ability of Oregon's Jack Crabtree. "We knew he was a great passer. We decided we would give him the short passes but not the long ones. We had run into a lot of good quarterbacks, but it was very seldom we'd give up a pass deep. I was the outside linebacker, in charge of covering the flat on my side or covering the deep outside, if the play went to the opposite side. I was never a flashy running back or anything like that. My specialty was on defense. I took more pride in that because I didn't have outstanding speed."

On this day, Cisco played almost full-time defensively, and slightly less than half-time on offense. Specialization, he believes has made "football a better game than it's ever been. When you are a two-way player, you learn more about the game."

Much of his day was spent trying to stop the Oregon attack. He had only one major offensive thrust personally: "I think I carried for maybe 29 yards, on a freak play. Fullbacks at Ohio State then ran—when they did run with the ball—usually just straight ahead. That was Woody's policy. But for some reason, this long-gainer of mine wasn't an average, ordinary fullback play. When I got through the line a yard or two, there was such good pursuit that I cut in behind the pursuit and was able to make an end run to the left. Of course, Woody doesn't like to run sideways. But because I was able to pick up some yardage, I didn't hear anything from him about it."

Oregon, however, amassed a great deal of yardage. So much, in fact, that the Ducks didn't have to punt during the entire game. Ohio State punted only twice in the game —both boots going out of bounds. So all day long, there wasn't a single runback of a punt or a fair catch.

Oregon coach Len Casanova later suggested that his lads had been "humiliated . . . derided by everybody" before the Rose Bowl meeting with Ohio State. He said his Ducks went "out there to show the Los Angeles sportswriters how wrong they were" in making the Buckeyes such heavy favorites.

The 19-point favoritism appeared justified as State grunted a 79 yard touchdown march, immediately after the opening kickoff. White and Clark reeled off steady gains on the ground, and the normally non-passing quarterback Frank Kremblas, tossed a 37-yard bomb to Jim Houston. Kremblas scored from the 2, and the Bucks had a quick 7-zip lead.

Easy. Or so it looked.

As usual, Hayes called all of the plays, says Cisco. "During the week Woody schooled Kremblas on the game plan. He did the same thing during timeouts in the game. Otherwise, he'd signal from the sidelines"—even though coaching from the sidelines was illegal in college ball until 1967.

But coaches "have always found ways to impose their wills on quarterbacks," a recent *Sports Illustrated* story reminds us. "Late in the 1956 Rose Bowl game, with the score tied 14–14, UCLA had the ball near its own goal line. The Bruin coaches wanted quarterback Ronnie Knox to pass, not run. Assistant Coach Jim Myers got Knox' attention and made a passing motion, but an official saw the gesture and penalized UCLA. Capitalizing on strong field position after the ensuing punt, Michigan State won the game on a 41-yard field goal by Dave Kaiser." So much for the 1956 game.

In the second quarter of the 1958 game, Oregon marched 80 yards to tie, on a drive which featured Crabtree pitchouts and keepers. The biggest gainer was a pitchout to Charley Tourville, and the TD came on a Crabtree pitch to Jim Shanley, on the 5.

"We had trouble on their keeper play," Cisco remembers. "And with their short passing game, too. We knew we couldn't let their deep men get behind us, and we had to keep their short passes down to minimum yardage. But their short ones were a little too long, and it seems to me that's how they put that touchdown drive together.

"I had very little area to cover defensively, because I was on the short side most of the time," says Cisco. "And they didn't do much cross-field passing, so I wasn't much affected by their offense. But they did run into the short side lots of times. We tried to mix our defenses to throw them off, but they adjusted to it. Their game plan was great."

The score was tied 7–7 at the half, but neither Hayes nor his players evinced much concern, says Cisco. "We thought that if we didn't have a lot of points to make up, we could get them in the second half. All season long we had outscored our opponents pretty badly in the fourth quarter. So we thought we could wear Oregon down. Didn't turn out that way, though.

"Woody didn't seem to be bothered in the locker room during halftime. No matter if you were ahead or behind or tied, his halftime talks were always pretty much the same. He talked about any necessary changes offensively and defensively. And you always walked out of that dressing room, for the second half, with the feeling you could beat anybody."

The second half was rather non-productive.

The Ducks' Jack Morris missed a 35-yard field goal attempt. In the first minute of the fourth quarter Don Sutherin was called on to boot a 34-yarder for Ohio State. "He'd had a bad back and a bad leg, and he hadn't kicked for a long time until a week before the game," said Hayes.

"I was sure I would make it good," says Sutherin. "I didn't look up. It felt good. I didn't know it was good, though, until my holder, Frank Kremblas, jumped up and said, 'Thank God!'"

And that was that; 10–7 Buckeyes. The Ducks did threaten after the go-ahead field goal. Crabtree hit end Ron Stover with a pass on the Ohio State 24. But Stover fumbled, and Cannavino recovered. Stover ended the game with ten pass receptions; but that one fumble outweighed the good he had done. The Bucks ate up the clock by controlling the ball.

Crabtree had had a fine passing and running day; Oregon finished with an advantage both in first downs (21–19) and total yardage (351–304). But Ohio State had intercepted two passes and recovered two fumbles. "Their attack was pretty good," said Hayes. "And their defense was good. Oregon was better than its three losses during the year suggested and better than its 19-point underdog role."

The tense fourth quarter—except for Sutherin's boot and Morris' miss—was something of a blur for Cisco, eighteen years later. "It's hard for a player to remember moments or turning points in a game," he says. "Unless you score a lot of touchdowns yourself, you forget things. Writers pick things out. Not players."

When it ended, as Galen recalls, "Hayes told us we'd played a pretty good game, and showed leadership. He said he was pleased we didn't lose our composure in such a close game. He said we'd been heavy favorites but hadn't bowed to the pressure of that favoritism, by falling apart when things weren't going our way."

A young member of the Oregon team remembered how the Bucks kept their composure in the final moments. John Robinson, who coached USC in its 1977 Bowl victory over Michigan, recalls, "I went in for the last fifteen seconds. Ohio State had the ball. Their quarterback took the snap, fell on the ball, and the game was over. Obviously, they were afraid of me."

"We showed 'em," said Oregon's Casanova. "In my mind, I have the best team in the country. It out-gutted everybody and came from nowhere." And the pundits agreed.

The *Milwaukee Journal*'s Oliver Kuechle suggested the Bucks were the Big Ten's weakest Pasadena representative to date. "Oregon deserved to win," he wrote. "And I'm sorry they lost."

Crusty Jim Schlemmer from the *Akron Beacon-Journal* observed, "Oregon won everything but the score."

"We hate to pull against our own territory," wrote Charles Johnson of the *Minneapolis Star-Tribune,* "but we wish Oregon had won today. Ohio State had to fight for its football life, and only one bad break kept Oregon from the upset of the season."

"The Ducks," wrote Pasadena columnist Joe Hendrickson, "won the heart of the spectators."

But Woody had won his second Rose Bowl game. He was now two for two, and would not return to Pasadena for another eleven years.

Cisco coached freshman football at Columbus briefly, after finishing his active gridiron career in Pasadena. Then came the baseball life. "I had a few opportunities in pro football, I guess," says Galen. "The San Francisco 49ers once were interested in me. And I might have caught on with one of the AFL teams that were just getting started then. But I stuck to baseball. Still, I've always wondered how I would have made out if I'd tried pro football. When you miss something like that, you always wonder."

Galen finds that when he is in St. Mary's or travelling around Ohio, sports fans still tend to identify him as a football player. Not specifically as a blocking fullback or tough linebacker or participant in the 1958 Rose Bowl. "The one thing people remember," he says, "is just that I played football at Ohio State."

ONE-EYED QUARTERBACK

Bob Schloredt was a victim of a child's curiosity, but later a wonder of medical science. He is the only athlete to have won the Rose Bowl Player of the Game award twice, even though he has just one eye.

"I was five at the time it happened, playing with a bunch of kids in an alley behind my aunt and uncle's house," he says. "We were lighting firecrackers and dropping them down this Coke bottle, blowing rocks off the top of the bottle. The bottle exploded and a piece of flying glass hit me in the left eye, leaving only about five percent vision. I can make out shadows, but that's about all."

While a nation of opthamologists watched with curiosity and awe, Schloredt intercepted seven passes in one season, was an all-America quarterback, and directed the University of Washington to consecutive Rose Bowl victories in 1960 and '61. The Huskies not only buried Wisconsin, 44–8, in 1960, but scored more points and had the biggest victory margin by any West Coast team, in the history of the Rose Bowl. The following January, the once-again underdog Huskies stunned the nation's number one team, Minnesota, 17–7. As final proof that the eye wasn't a handicap, Schloredt dated the Rose Bowl queen.

"The way the medical profession is today, if the accident happened now, the eye probably could have been saved," said Schloredt. "The glass cut the lens and the cornea, but not the retina. Today you can get lens and cornea transplants. Not back then. Scar tissue formed over the eye, and that was it." He is grateful for one thing. "The fact that it happened so early, allowed me to compensate," he pointed out. "If it had happened later, like when I was thirteen or fourteen, it would have been a different story. But I grew up with it. The eye never was a handicap, even though eye doctors were absolutely amazed that I could play quarterback. Most of the people around me made more of a to-do about the eye than I did. But for me, one eye is like a natural thing."

Schloredt, talks in an easy, plain-speaking manner. He doesn't waste words—especially on himself—and the words he chooses are from the common man's dictionary. However, he shouldn't be allowed to minimize his extraordinary achievement of excelling above athletes with twice his vision. Try during the course of one day, or one hour, to lead a normal life with one eye closed. Try reading a newspaper, playing tennis or golf. Your perspective is entirely different. Schloredt overcame this difficulty by drawing from another source of vision, the mind's eye. "I learned to judge distance by the size of the person, but don't ask me how I did it," he replied when asked how he was able to throw the football effectively. "I also turned my head a lot. I played basketball as well as football in high school, and I wasn't bothered in either sport by the 'blind' side. By turning my head a lot from side to side, things just went normally."

Exactly. No coach of Schloredt's ever had to revise a game plan or leave out certain plays to compensate for a one-eyed quarterback. "We never varied anything," said Jim Owens, Schloredt's coach at Washington. "I can't remember a single play where Bob could have done it better with two eyes. He could hit the short pass or hit a guy in stride fifty yards downfield, and he could throw on the run. You should see some of our films. He was a fine, all-around competitor. He ran hard—he was like a fourth running back—and he hit as hard on defense as anyone we had. Bob was the finest punter in the conference. He could have played almost anywhere. Put him at end, throw him the ball, and he'd catch it. He was a real leader, too."

Schloredt never brought attention to his handicap. He treated the whole thing as if it never happened. Most of his teammates and coaches often forgot that he had only one eye. "The rest of us weren't in awe of Schloredt's handicap. He was just one of the guys," said Ben Davidson, who then was a reserve tackle at Washington before later using Joe Namath and Len Dawson as punching bags. "Schloredt never placed himself above anyone else. He was tough. On defense he'd come up and drill someone— especially if someone had just drilled him. He broke his collarbone and came back to play in the Rose Bowl. We had an unusual team, with no stars or cliques. Just one big happy family. I saw this same situation only one other time, with the Green Bay Packers in 1961. We had a lot of fine players at Washington. Someone on the team had to be a star and Schloredt was elected."

Schloredt wasn't interested in self-glorification, and seems embarrassed about his past accomplishments even now, in his new life along the rolling surf of Waikiki. "I was the Associated Press' all-America quarterback as a junior. I guess some Associated Press writer in Seattle got me on the team," he said. "It was a complete surprise. We didn't have any one individual who won all the games by himself." One thing does please Schloredt about the past, however. "We kind of turned things around. Husky fans will tell you that to this day. Before we played Wisconsin, the Big Ten beat the

Pac-8 practically every year in the Rose Bowl. Then we won two in a row. It has gotten to the point now where the Big Ten is happy to win one," he said.

Schloredt spent his early years in northern Wyoming. He lived in Buffalo, which isn't far from Saddlestring and Ucross in Johnson County. He also lived in Sundance and Moorcroft, a short drive from Aladdin and Beulah in Crook Country. It was in Moorcroft that he lost the vision of his left eye. His father was a grade school teacher and coach. "He encouraged me in sports right from the start and never gave me the idea that I had something wrong," said Schloredt. The family moved to Oregon and settled in the Portland suburb of Gresham.

Darrell Royal was the coach at Washington for one year, 1955, before moving on to the University of Texas. Royal began recruiting Schloredt after his junior year at Gresham High School and continued to phone the youngster later from Austin, Texas.

Schloredt narrowed the choices to Oregon and Washington. He was impressed with Washington's new coach, Owens, then thirty years old. "Jim had a fine appearance," said Schloredt. "He was about 6'5" in height, and athletic looking."

Owens was equally impressed with Schloredt. "He was the finest athlete in the state of Oregon," said Owens. "To tell you the truth, I didn't even know he had one eye at the time we recruited him."

Owens' rebuilding process took three years. The Huskies were 3–6–1 in 1957 and 3–7 in 1958, Schloredt's sophomore year. That same season, a 12–7 loss to Ohio State proved to Owens and his players that things were on the move. "Ohio State was number one in the nation, and here were we playing before 85,000 at Columbus," Schloredt remembered. "They blocked a punt late in the game to get the winning touchdown. We had nine sophomores and two seniors starting. That game showed we had a pretty good ball team, if we could keep it together. Of the seven games we lost, only two were by more than one touchdown. We just made a lot of rookie mistakes."

Schloredt's first varsity start was against the Buckeyes—at fullback. "I was 6'0", 198 pounds in college, which is big for a quarterback. I was more like a fullback who could throw the ball." Schloredt played mostly quarterback later on that season and set a school record with a 71-yard punt against Oregon State, a mark which lasted until Don Feleay punted 73 yards in 1975.

The Huskies were ready to catch fire in 1959, although the rest of the newly named Athletic Association of Western Universities (AAWU) had no idea what was coming. "We were picked about second from the bottom before that season," said Schloredt. "But we had lots of confidence. We had a couple of wins at the start and things started snowballing."

The Huskies mushed through Colorado, 21–12; Idaho, 23–0; Utah, 51–6, and Stanford, 10–0, before losing their only game that year, 22–15, to USC.

"Those were the days when you had to play both ways," said Schloredt. "If you started a quarter, you could only come out one time that quarter. We were ahead, but had played our first team most of the way and Jim put in the second unit. Right away,

Jerry Traynham of USC ran 42 yards to our 15. We brought the first unit back in there, but they got across in about seven or eight plays for the winning touchdown. We were on their 15 when time ran out. USC lost two games after that, while we kept getting better. I really believed after the USC game that everyone on our team knew no team could stop us from then on."

No team did, as Washington won an important game the following week, edging undefeated Oregon, 13–12, as Schloredt made a game-saving pass interception. The Huskies then dumped UCLA, 23–7; California, 20–0, and Washington State, 20–0, to finish with a 9–1 record, its best since 1925, and win the AAWU championship.

Schloredt passed for 733 yards and five touchdowns, and ran for 225 yards and nine more touchdowns. Seven interceptions tied him with teammate George Fleming for the Pacific Coast lead. He was named to the Associated Press' all-America backfield of Heisman Trophy winner Billy Cannon of LSU, Charley Flowers of Mississippi, and Jim Motty of Arkansas.

One of the tackles on that 1959 team was Dan Lanphear of Wisconsin, which had just won its first undisputed Big Ten championship since 1912. The Badgers were not a dominant team in 1959, but the Big Ten was somewhat jumbled, and they were able to win the title with a 7–2 record. Wisconsin's quarterback was Dale Hackbart, later a "hatchet man" defensive back with the Minnesota Vikings. His backup was Jim Bakken, the St. Louis Cardinals' kicker. Hackbart was a big, punishing runner, who inflicted more punishment than he received, when he decided to run. He was the difference in a number of close games, as the Badgers defeated Stanford, 16–14, and Marquette, 44–6, lost to Purdue, 21–0, struggled past Iowa, 26–15; Ohio State, 12–3; Michigan, 19–10; and Northwestern, 24–19; submitted to Illinois, 9–6, and then clinched the Rose Bowl berth by nudging Minnesota, 11–7.

Although Washington had the more impressive record, giving up sixty-five points in nine games, the Big Ten was the stronger of the conferences at the time, and number six ranked Wisconsin was made a six-point favorite over number eight Washington.

"Some people had them favored by fourteen to twenty points, though," said Schloredt. "We were very confident going into the game, after watching their films. We felt we had the better team. They were bigger than we were, but we were quicker and knew we could control the line of scrimmage. We thought we could throw the ball, too. We weren't very shy, so we didn't try to feel them out. We wanted to put some points on the board right away, and that's exactly what we did."

The Huskies had an option-type attack. "We called a lot of passing plays, but wound up running seventy-five percent of the time," said Schloredt. With Schloredt at the controls, Washington marched 48 yards not long after the game began, and halfback Don McKeta ran the final 6 for the touchdown.

Fleming, like Schloredt a fine all-purpose player, then kicked a 44-yard field goal, for a Rose Bowl record. Fleming came right back with a 53-yard punt return for a touchdown, and Washington had a 17–0 lead after one quarter. "The turning point was when Fleming kicked the field goal to give us a 10–0 lead," Owens said after the game. "That put us in control, and Wisconsin began to press."

Wisconsin gained a measure of hope when halfback Tom Wiesner slipped into the end zone from four yards out, and Hackbart's two-point conversion pass to Allen Schoonover brought the Badgers to 17–8.

Schloredt quickly regained the momentum for Washington with a 23-yard touchdown pass to Lee Folkins, who made a fantastic diving catch. "It was one of the nicer catches in Rose Bowl history," said Schloredt. "It happened just before halftime, and we went into the dressing room jazzed up. We came right back out and did the same thing in the second half."

Ray Jackson, a slashing fullback, scored from two yards and Schloredt from three. Reserve quarterback Bob Hivner's 3-yard pass to Don Millick completed the slaughter.

"Washington was just more aggressive than we were—much more aggressive," said Wisconsin coach Milt Bruhn of the lighter Huskies. Schloredt rushed for eighty-one

Washington stars Bob Schloredt (No. 15) and George Fleming after their 44-8 win over Wisconsin in the 1960 Rose Bowl. The pair reurned to beat Minnesota 17-7 in the 1961 game. Schloredt was a one-eyed quarterback and Fleming the Huskies' placekicker.

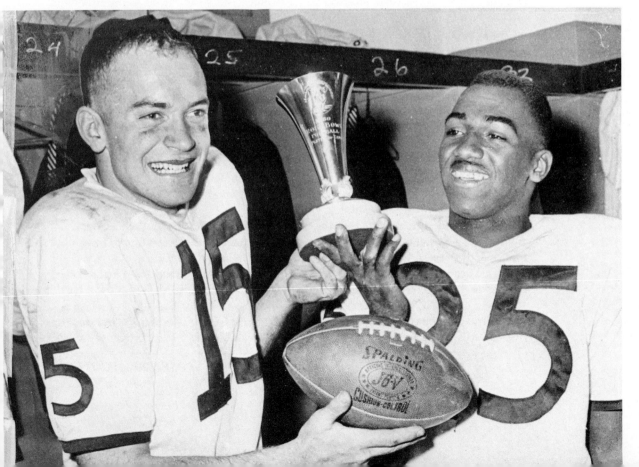

yards and Jackson for sixty-one as Washington pounded through the Badgers for 215 yards on the ground. Schloredt threw only seven passes, completing four for 102 yards. Hackbart carried only five times for twenty-one yards. Forced into a passing situation early, he completed but eleven of twenty-five passes for 145 yards. Fleming, besides his record field goal, set another Rose Bowl mark with three punt returns for 122 yards and kicked six straight conversions (Washington passed for its seventh). Fleming's fifteen points earned him co-Player of the Game honors with Schloredt.

"It was like a Cinderella story for us that first year," recalled Schloredt. "Everything we touched turned to gold." However, it was a copper-plated year, and career at Washington, for Ben Davidson. "I didn't play any football until junior college," he said. "Washington recruited me on my size and potential, and I wound up playing one minute in each of the Rose Bowls. I only started two games in two years at Washington —one time as a junior when the coach got mad at the first string, and another time as a senior when someone got hurt. I'd come into camp at 260 at the start of the year, but would be down to 235—and third or fourth string—by the end. The reason was I never got enough to eat. They only gave you one sandwich for lunch."

Jim Owens had taken Washington to the Rose Bowl for the first time since 1944. "Before the Wisconsin game," said Davidson, "Jim Murray wrote that we didn't have a chance against the Big Ten. Then we won. Right after the game he began calling us the Purple Gang. For years afterwards, he would write, 'The Purple Gang is coming to town,' whenever Washington played in Los Angeles. I guess he was trying to make up for that one article."

Washington also had an impact on the West Coast. "The Pacific-8 didn't have a reputation for hard-nosed football like the Big Ten, up until that time," Schloredt pointed out. "After our two Rose Bowl victories, you saw more Pac-8 teams becoming hard-nosed in their style of play."

Owens became a magic figure in the Pacific Northwest. One story was that he bought a home across Lake Washington, which is adjacent to the Washington campus, so he could walk to work. Owens was thought of with reverence, but not to that extreme. "You respected Jim a lot," said Schloredt. "He had some fine coaches, and he let them coach while he did a super job of motivating the team. He was a tough disciplinarian. We won a lot of games in the fourth quarter, because we were the best conditioned team on the coast."

Schloredt's picture appeared on the cover of *Sports Illustrated* as well as the usual supply of pre-season football magazines in 1960. But an injury forced him to miss more than half that season, while a number of bruised Husky linemen sat out as long or longer. Washington toyed with College of Pacific, 55–6, and Idaho, 41–12, to kick off the season, then received its only defeat that fall at home against Joe Bellino and Navy, 15–14.

"Bellino didn't have a Bellino day," said Schloredt. "The only thing Joe did was run twelve yards to set up their winning field goal. Greg Mather kicked it from 31 yards, which is ten yards more than he ever kicked one, and we lost with fourteen seconds left." Washington had the ball on the Navy 8 with time for one more play at the end of the first half. Owens gambled against a certain field goal by Fleming, which proved costly as Schloredt was nailed a yard from the end zone. "That defeat kept us from being the national champion," Schloredt said.

Washington rebounded to handle Stanford, 29–10, then lost Schloredt for the remainder of the regular season in the following week's 10–8 win over UCLA. "I was on defense and hit one of the UCLA receivers who was about to catch the ball," he said. "I landed on my left collarbone, breaking it." Schloredt took himself out of the running for the Heisman Trophy, won by Bellino. Schloredt was in a cast for only two weeks and four days, and swallowed large doses of calcium and phosphorous. He then began a weight training program. He was a man in a hurry. "I had all the confidence in the world that we would get back to the Rose Bowl," he explained.

It wouldn't be easy. Washington throttled California, 27–7, and USC, 34–0, but had to survive three one-point victories—30–29 over Oregon State, 7–6 over Oregon, and 8–7 over Washington State. "Defense and conditioning were the differences in most of our games those two years," declared Schloredt. "In all those games we won by a point, we had to come from behind in the fourth quarter."

In the early Sixties, a team that was voted number one at the end of the regular season, remained number one regardless of what happened during the bowl games. There were no poll revisions as there are now. The national championship trophy Owens wanted was sitting in the office of Murray Warmath, the Minnesota coach,

The Gophers were physically overpowering, a team of Samsons. They didn't bother with finesse. Instead they hammered at their opponents who resembled a fighter helpless against the ropes, who eventually can't take anymore and, drained of ability and strength, slips beaten to the canvas. Minnesota had a 220-pound fullback, Roger Hagberg, and a rollout quarterback, Sandy Stephens, who was almost as big and would emerge as an all-America the following year. But the biggest and meanest Gopher was guard Tom Brown, not only an all-America in 1960, but the winner of the Outland Award—a lineman's equivalent of the Heisman Trophy. Minnesota had decked Nebraska, 26–14; Indiana, 42–0; Northwestern, 7–0; Illinois, 21–10; Michigan, 10–0; Kansas State, 48–7; Iowa, 27–10; and Wisconsin, 26–7; the week after they were upset by Purdue, 23–14. Owens wasn't worried. Even though he had lost the national championship, there was always the lure of beating the national champion.

Nevertheless, Minnesota was made a seven-point pick over the sixth-ranked Huskies. "We weren't as confident before Minnesota as we had been before Wisconsin," Schloredt admitted. "Wisconsin had won some games on big plays. But Minnesota looked like it had earned what it had gotten. The Gophers had worn out teams physically by manhandling them. Brown just manhandled centers. We saw on the films that he would line up at middle guard and knock the center straight backwards, screwing up the backfield patterns."

Washington had an all-America center, Roy McKasson, who was the same height as Brown, 6'0", but considerably lighter at 205 pounds to Brown's 243. "We worked on several ways to block Brown," said Schloredt. "Instead of firing out and taking Brown head on, Roy would miss him with the shoulder and get his belly wrapped around Brown's legs. Roy never really knocked him back, but he got in his way real well." For insurance, Washington had another way to attack the Gopher great. "We had a couple of designed sweeps, or what looked like sweeps," Schloredt elaborated. "I'd fake the pitchout and Tom would take off in the direction our backs were heading. I'd run right up the middle where he had been. I had one run of 21 yards and another of 31."

Once again the Huskies bolted to a 17–0 lead, although this time it took them the better part of one half. Fleming's field goal of 44 yards made it 3–0. Schloredt later sent halfback Brent Wooten in motion, faked a handoff into the line, and flipped a pass to Wooten all alone in the flat to complete a 4-yard touchdown play. Five minutes later, Schloredt broke through the middle on one of his sizeable sneaks then culminated the drive of 67 yards by squirming the final yard over left guard. At halftime, it was completely one-sided. Washington was well ahead in first downs, ten to two, and in total yardage, 158–61. Owens decided on a conservative plan of attack in the second half.

"We had the seventeen-point lead and didn't think anyone could march on us or score seventeen points against us," said Schloredt. "So we took the risky plays out of our offense. We didn't chance throwing an interception and left it up to our defense. We also had a good punting game, really covered well on punts. I had two punts roll dead inside their 10."

Washington gave the Gophers a golden opportunity, fumbling the ball away at its 36. Minnesota reached the 18, then Stephens rolled out on an option play and pitched to halfback Bill Munsey, who streaked into the end zone. Jim Rogers' PAT kick whittled Washington's lead down to 17–7, and that's where the scoring stopped. Minnesota easily dominated the second half in first downs, twelve to one, and in yardage, 192–35, but Owens' plan had worked. Jackson and Schloredt each rushed for 60 yards, Schloredt averaging 12 yards a carry. He threw but six passes, completing two, and punted seven times for a 41-yard average. He also tackled hard on defense, refusing to favor the shoulder. This time he was Player of the Game by himself.

"The whippets of Washington ran off and hid from Minnesota's mastiffs," led off Red Smith in his account of the game. "The swift Washington backs raced over, past and around the meaty monsters of the Midwest, who seemed to be moving in hip boots. . . . Best of all was Schloredt, who operated with cool class, doing little as a passer, but running boldly on rollouts and sneaks up the middle." Smith concluded, "It goes without saying that the entertainment was suitably festooned with neon roses over the stadium entrance, capering bands, shapely baton-wreckers in brief and glistery swatches of gold and silver, civic boosters in immaculate stuffed shirts, and a Tournament of Roses queen. Nowhere else is higher education served more handsomely."

The Tournament of Roses queen was Carol Washburn, who met Schloredt before the game. "We went out for awhile after the Rose Bowl," he said. "People really made a to-do about it, too." Six days after the game, he signed to play with the British Columbia Lions of the Canadian Football League (CFL). Schloredt had been drafted fifteenth by the Chicago Bears and also had talked with the Dallas Texans (later the Kansas City Chiefs) of the AFL. "American teams weren't paying all that good then, but the Canadians were, so I played two years with the Lions. Tom Brown was my roommate," he said. "I did most of the quarterbacking my first year. Joe Kapp came the next year, and so I was a defensive back. I was all set to sign for a third year, when Coach Owens offered me a chance to work for him. I didn't want to make the pros a career, anyway."

Schloredt was an assistant coach under Owens for eleven years, 1963–73. Washington returned to the Rose Bowl during Schloredt's first year back, but lost to Illinois, 17–7, the same score by which the Huskies had beaten Minnesota three years earlier. This would be Washington's last Rose Bowl team under Owens, who remained as head coach through 1974.

Schloredt, thirty-eight, and a divorced father of two, has lived in Honolulu for three years. He originally left the mainland to become offensive coordinator of the Hawaiians of the World Football League. After the league went bankrupt, Schloredt stayed on Oahu as corporate sales manager of the Ilikai Hotel.

"Life's not too tough over here," he said, with perfect vision.

THE MOST
INCREDIBLE GAME

Dusk already had settled on the Rose Bowl as Ron VanderKelen looked up at the scoreboard through the glare of the stadium lights. USC had scored its sixth touchdown and now was trampling Wisconsin, 42–14, in the fourth quarter. The only thing which could spare the Badgers from further abuse, it seemed, was the clock, but fourteen minutes remained in the game. Just let us get out of this thing alive, the Badger players were thinking. Well, not every Badger. "In one corner of my mind I was thinking the game was out of reach," said VanderKelen. "In another corner I was thinking that miracles do happen."

The only miracle in this case was that USC was able to withstand what was about to happen next. VanderKelen, in the most incredible passing performance in the long history of the Rose Bowl, in what would be rated as the event's most incredible game, revived the lifeless Badgers and brought them to within 42–37 of the disbelieving Trojans, before the final gun mercifully spared USC. "That game," said white-haired John McKay, rolling a long, thin cigar around in his mouth, "is one of the reasons I'm no longer a red-head."

That game, on January 1, 1963, had a number of paradoxes. It marked the turn-around of the USC football program. It was McKay's first winning season at the school, as USC finished with an 11–0 record, and the national collegiate championship. Two more unbeaten seasons, four more Rose Bowl victories, and three more national championships would follow for the Trojan Horse during McKay's sixteen years as head coach.

Wisconsin, which had been to the Rose Bowl three times in eleven years, hasn't smelled the roses since. With three defeats in their only trips ever to Pasadena, the

Badgers languish among the have-nots of the Big Ten. Yet, the hero of that 1963 game emerged from the losing team.

"Everywhere I go, people still talk about that game," said VanderKelen. "The only thing I wish is that we would have had two or three more plays that day, and a chance to score again. Whether we would have won or not is something you can debate until

Wisconsin quarterback Ron VanderKelen, who authored the greatest passing performance in Rose Bowl history, although his club fell short, losing 42-37 in the gloaming to USC.

you die. You just don't know. We'll never get the chance to prove it, one way or another."

VanderKelen completed thirty-three of forty-eight passes for 401 yards. His fifty-seven plays accounted for 406 yards of total offense. These statistics remain Rose Bowl records.

"It was the greatest performance by a quarterback against USC while I was there," declared McKay, who in 1976 became the head coach of the Tampa Bay Buccaneers of the NFL. However, VanderKelen's greatest personal triumph may not have been his performance in the game, but that he even played in the game.

VanderKelen was nothing more than an obscure quarterback before his final season at Wisconsin. He had played ninety seconds as a sophomore, as a defensive back. Wisconsin went to the Rose Bowl that year, with Dale Hackbart at quarterback, and Jim Bakken, eventually the St. Louis Cardinals' place-kicker, as his backup. "I was third or fourth string," said VanderKelen. He then missed his junior season because of a knee operation, and was academically ineligible the following fall.

Because of the knee surgery, VanderKelen was awarded a year of eligibility. He made up his grades and turned out for spring practice. But he was just a face in the crowd.

"I was one of seven quarterbacks," he remembered. "With my being a senior and the team not expected to be very good, the coaches were not looking to me. They were expecting one of the sophomores to come through. Then they'd start building for the following year. Nobody had ever heard of me. Everybody was talking and writing about the young quarterbacks. I thought I was good enough to play, and knew this would be my last chance. The only thing I was hoping for is that the coaching staff would give me a chance."

The younger quarterbacks, it turned out, needed time to develop. VanderKelen's one advantage was experience. He did become the number one quarterback, but didn't feel all that secure. "I'm assuming the coaches were thinking that if I didn't do well, they could pull me out and get one of the younger guys in there. Fortunately, we started out on the right foot."

The Badgers destroyed New Mexico State, 69–13, in their 1962 season opener. It was a demonstration of offensive power, that not only surprised the Midwest media but Coach Milt Bruhn and the Badgers. "Everyone thought before the season that we would have an average team at best. We were picked for fifth or sixth in the Big Ten," said VanderKelen. "The players and coaches thought we were better than average. But you never really know." Wisconsin gained more believers by rolling over Indiana, 30–6; Notre Dame, 17–8; and Iowa, 42–14. Ohio State shattered the Badgers' momentum with a 14–7 defeat. "We just made a lot of errors against Ohio State," said Vander-Kelen, "like fumbles and dropped passes by wide-open receivers. Things like that. We played them a close game as it was, but we made more mistakes, and they won."

The loss infuriated the Badgers, who then knocked off Michigan, 34–12; Northwestern, 37–6; Illinois, 35–6; and Minnesota, 14–9 to capture the Big Ten championship with an 8–1 record.

"The game which sparked us, and made us realize that we had one heckuva team, was against Northwestern," said VanderKelen. "They were ranked number one in the country at the time, and everyone was writing that there wasn't a team around that could touch them. We really caught them in Madison. We weren't even ranked in the top ten until we beat them, but we moved up pretty fast after that."

VanderKelen was named the Big Ten's Most Valuable Player, for his rags-to-riches season. Wisconsin was ranked second in the country behind USC, which had cut out its own success story from Cinderella cloth.

McKay was an assistant coach at the University of Oregon when USC selected him as head coach in 1960. The Trojans were 4–6 and 4–5–1, during his first two seasons. "When I took over, USC had only one winning season in three years," said McKay. "They had recruited people who weren't fast enough to play winning football. I inherited ninety-one people on scholarship, and sixty-seven never lettered. We went out and recruited faster and better people in Willie Brown, Pete Beathard, Bill Nelsen, Hal Bedsole, and Damon Bame, all of whom became stars."

Washington was coming off consecutive Rose Bowl victories, and was favored in the West again, before the 1962 season. USC, which hadn't been to the Rose Bowl in eight years, figured to finish third or fourth. "We knew we had much more talent than we had the first two years," said McKay. "Even though we had losing records those years, the scores were close. We just weren't very fast, and so had to play conservatively. We were faster in 1962. We could see that we were a great team."

It didn't take the Trojans long to convince others. They defeated Duke, 14–7; Southern Methodist, 33–3; Iowa, 7–0; California, 32–6; and Illinois, 28–16, before tangling with Washington in a battle of supremacy. The Trojans won, 14–0, and then flattened Stanford, 39–14; Navy, 13–6; UCLA, 14–3; and Notre Dame, 25–0.

After the final game, Trojan fullback Ben Wilson faced the USC rooting section and said, "If anyone doesn't think we're number one, he can come down here and fight me." No one took him up on the offer, not even the wire services, which agreed that USC indeed was the best in the land.

McKay was named Coach of the Year. "In those days the Big Ten was shoving it down our throats, and really lording it over us," he said. "We were committed to their not beating us."

"USC and Wisconsin had the best defensive teams in the country," McKay pointed out. "We had given up fifty-five points in ten games, and they had given up eighty-seven in nine. But after looking at their movies and seeing that they played man-to-man defense, we felt we could score on them pretty good."

VanderKelen had made news in the Midwest, but he was practically unknown to the average West Coast fan. The primary reason was that the all-America quarterback and Heisman Trophy winner that year was Terry Baker of Oregon State.

But VanderKelen's talents weren't lost on McKay. "Wisconsin's offense was predicated on the backs coming out on pass patterns, which most people weren't doing in those days," said McKay. "Ron ran their offense extremely well, and was willing to take what the defenses would give him. In other words, he didn't force the ball. He'd send Pat Richter over the middle, and if Richter wasn't open then he'd throw underneath to Lou Holland, coming out of the backfield, and let him run with it."

VanderKelen said Wisconsin had a basic game plan. "We didn't go after any one individual, because USC was so strong over-all. We were going to do what we did best, throw the ball and run a lot of options, and rely on our defense to stop them when necessary. And we didn't do anything differently in the game, except throw more when we got behind."

Even though the Trojans were undefeated and the Badgers had one defeat, Wisconsin was made a three-point favorite, which didn't strike VanderKelen as unusual. "We didn't think anyone could beat us," he said. The Badgers, in truth, were favored because the Big Ten still was regarded as a superior football conference to the Athletic Association of Western Universities.

USC was ready, not only with talent, but theatrics. After holding Wisconsin on the opening series, the men of Troy moved deep into Badger territory, on the running of Wilson and Beathard. USC lined up at the 13, for an apparent field goal. Beathard, the holder, received the center snap, stood up, and fired a touchdown pass to Ron Butcher on a tackle-eligible play.

VanderKelen came right back with an 18-yard pass to fullback Ralph Kurek, at the USC 23. The crew-cut 6'1", 172-pound quarterback then ran to the 13, and completed the first of many passes that day to Richter at the 1, setting up Kurek's end-zone smash.

USC moved ahead 14–7 as all-America linebacker Bame snared the first of three VanderKelen interceptions—which tied a Rose Bowl record—and returned it 25 yards to the Badger 30. Brown, the Trojans' leading rusher and best all-around athlete, carried for 12 on the next play. Wilson took care of the rest, pounding to the 7, and eventually the final yard.

Wisconsin believed a quick whistle, in the second quarter, deprived it of a fumble recovery at the Trojan 30. On the next play, Bill Nelsen, substituting for Beathard, threw a 45-yard pass to Brown at the Wisconsin 25. Halfback Ron Heller, a doubtful participant before the game because of a knee injury, used three Trojan blocks on the ensuing play, and streaked into the end zone. The Trojans led at halftime, 21–7, having scored more points in one half than Wisconsin had given up, in one game, all season.

Bedsole and VanderKelen almost got into a fight in front of the Wisconsin bench in the second quarter. "I was out of bounds by five yards when Hal, who was playing defensive end, pushed me over the bench," said VanderKelen. "It was a minor thing, and I never held it against Hal. In fact, we were teammates later on with the Minnesota Vikings and we laughed and joked about the game a lot." There was little joking on the sidelines, however, as VanderKelen shoved back, and Bedsole was lucky to make it unscathed through the angry Badger players and back on the field.

"At halftime," joked McKay, "I told the team we would run a slant pass at the start of the third quarter, and if their linebacker did what I thought he would do, Bedsole would run for a touchdown. And he would run by our bench, so if there was another altercation, he would be among friends."

On USC's first offensive play, Beathard threw a short pass to Bedsole who, practically as McKay had diagrammed, raced down the sidelines on a 57-yard scoring play.

VanderKelen retaliated with passes of 18 and 13 yards to Richter, and Wisconsin

USC quarterback Pete Beathard who shared Player of the Game honors with VanderKelen.

was at the USC 26. At the 17, VanderKelen couldn't find a receiver and took off for the end zone. Brown met him on the goal line in a jarring collision, and VanderKelen somehow managed to avoid a concussion and get a touchdown at the same time. "It was a difference of my stopping on the two or going in," he said. "I closed my eyes, put my head down, and lucked out."

Wisconsin had closed to within 28–14, but in no way was it back in the football game. Not yet, anyway. Beathard completed third-down passes of 29 yards to Brown and 9 to Bedsole to reach the Badger 24. Once more on third down, this time from the 23, Beathard threw for the end zone. Bedsole, an all-America that year and who still holds the Trojan career record for touchdown receptions (twenty), made a fantastic leaping reception, despite losing a shoe and throwing out his shoulder on the play.

USC was now operating at a fever pitch. Everything the Trojans touched turned into a touchdown. Tom Lupo intercepted a VanderKelen pass at the Wisconsin 35 and chugged to the 14, as the game swung into the fourth quarter. Two plays later, end Fred Hill caught a 13-yard toss from Beathard for the quarterback's fourth touchdown pass of the game—another Rose Bowl record. Although VanderKelen is remembered as the star of that forty-ninth Rose Bowl game, Beathard completed eight of twelve passes, for 190 yards. In other words, one out of every two passes Beathard completed was for a score. Beathard and VanderKelen were named co-Players of the Game.

After Lupo kicked his sixth straight conversion, USC led 42–14. A third of the 98,698 fans started for the exits. With the Trojans ahead by twenty-eight points, the crowd placed little stock in miracles. They were concerned with a more-realistic phenomenon, trying to avoid one of those classic Southern California freeway jams.

And it was getting dark. The start of the game had been delayed fifteen minutes, and the beginning of the second half was set back ten minutes, as the USC and Wisconsin marching bands staged their own confrontation.

In addition, referee Jim Cain, who would become known after the game as "the man in the white cap," was using the playing field as a stage. His gestures for clipping and holding had all the dramatic flair of Barrymore playing Hamlet. And so he would repeat them, four to a call. It seemed obvious to all that Cain was performing for the television cameras.

VanderKelen threw twenty-one of his forty-eight passes in the fourth quarter, meaning the clock would stop with each incompletion (there weren't too many) or every time a Badger caught a pass and stepped out of bounds. The result of all of these delays was that the game lasted a record three-and-a-half hours, and was finished under lights.

"I wasn't really worried at that point from the standpoint of our lead (42–14), because the same things they would try in the fourth quarter we had been successful in stopping earlier," said McKay. "But I was worried for another reason. We had run out of tackles. Gary Kirner had an accident in his hotel room and tore a couple of fingers, and we kept it a secret before the game. Then another of our tackles, Marv

Marinovich, was ejected for swinging at some guy he missed. That was terrible. I told Marinovich when he came out of the game that if he was going to get thrown out, at least hit him. Mike Gale, who plays behind Marinovich, had a broken neck. We had guards playing tackle in the second half."

The Trojans could have played Truman Capote and Bella Abzug at tackles for three quarters and not been hurt. Over that period, USC was unstoppable. In the fourth quarter, Wisconsin was not only unstoppable, but inexplicable.

"The basic feeling on our team was that the game was over with, but let's at least go out and look respectable," said VanderKelen. "At that time, it was a runaway, and the whole game could have been a shambles. It could have been 60–14. We got together and decided to get a touchdown or two, and see what happened."

VanderKelen's fantastic final quarter was made possible, in large part by Richter, the other all-America end that season. The Badgers' punter, 6'5", 230 pounds, wound up with eleven catches for still another Rose Bowl record. His 163 yards in receptions fell a yard shy of the Rose Bowl mark, held by Alabama's Don Hutson.

"Pat was absolutely a super college receiver," said VanderKelen. "He was so big that he would jump in front of the defensive backs, who are usually small, and block them out. Pat was an easy target to find, and he always seemed to find the open spot. Whenever I was in trouble, I looked for Pat, and he was there."

VanderKelen began Wisconsin's memorable comeback with a 13-yard pass to Richter at USC's 48. The quarterback then connected on a 15-yard throw to Carl Silvestri, and a 12-yard pass to Holland. From the 13, Holland found an opening in the Trojan line and darted into the end zone, with 11:40 remaining to play. USC 42–21.

"After that first touchdown, it became a little easier for us," said VanderKelen.

"I still didn't think we could lose," said McKay, "unless we did something silly—which we did."

Wilson fumbled on USC's next series, and Wisconsin's Elmars Ezerins pounced on the ball at the Trojan 29. VanderKelen quickly hit Richter at the 10, and then threw a 4-yard touchdown pass to Gary Kroner, with 8:32 left. USC 42–28.

"We had started to gain momentum," said VanderKelen, "and you could just feel that everyone believed we could win that game."

USC marched to Wisconsin's 33, turning the ball over on fourth down. VanderKelen caught fire again, completing passes of 15, 25 and 16 yards, all to Richter, as the Badgers reached the USC 4 yard line.

"I don't think there is anyone in the world who could explain what was happening," said VanderKelen. "It was one of those mysterious things where everything clicks and you get hot. It seems like there wasn't anything I could do wrong. I bumped into an official one time while scrambling, and still completed the pass. USC players were all around me on another play. Two of them tackled me, and as I fell to the ground, I threw a pass sidearm to one of our men. Maybe out of every two hundred passes like that, you could get one ball near a guy. Here, I completed it!"

THE MOST INCREDIBLE GAME

Only this time, the Badgers did not score, as Brown got in front of another Vander-Kelen pass to Richter and intercepted in the end zone. That one play, as it turned out, saved a Trojan victory. "I knew if I could get close to Richter, I would have a chance," recalls Brown. "So I moved close to him and Ron found me instead of him."

USC center Larry Sagouspe then showed a strong arm from his 25 by snapping the ball over punter Ernie Jones' head and into the end zone, where the frantic Jones reached it before Wisconsin. However, the Badgers had a safety, with 2:40 left. USC 42–30.

The Trojans had a free kick, but Bill Smith returned it 21 yards to the USC 43. It was so dark that you could barely make out the numbers of VanderKelen (15) and Richter (88).

"To be honest with you, I didn't even know it was dark," said VanderKelen. "We were down, trying to get some points back. We didn't even know what was happening." USC knew it would be VanderKelen to Richter on almost every down, but still couldn't prevent this amazing two-man air circus. Following a 6-yard VanderKelen pass to Holland, Richter flew up the field once more and cut across the middle, and Vander-Kelen threw him an 18-yard pass to the USC 19.

"We couldn't get them slowed down at all," McKay remembered. "VanderKelen made some amazing completions, but Richter made some impossible catches, too. Richter came across the middle and reached behind him to stab a pass that you wouldn't have expected even a receiver as good as he was to have caught. But he caught it." On the following play, Richter went across the middle again, and VanderKelen drilled him with a touchdown pass, with just over a minute to play. USC 42–37.

USC desperately protected the ball on its next possession. Jones barely got off the punt to Holland at the Wisconsin 40. Holland fumbled, but Wisconsin's Jim Schenk recovered. As VanderKelen hurried his offense up to the line of scrimmage for one last chance, the gun sounded. Each Badger reacted like he had been shot in the heart. Some slumped to the turf. Instead of a Frank Merriwell finish, the script had been authored by O. Henry.

"I remember standing out there on the field, not knowing what had happened," said VanderKelen. "It seemed so unfair that we didn't have one more chance. It was such a letdown. Our locker room was quiet when I walked into it. Everyone was sad, down. Then all of a sudden, someone—I can't remember if it was the governor or the president of the university—walked in and told us what we had accomplished. That made us a little more excited. We had looked at it as a defeat. Then the impact of how great a game it had been hit us, and also what a great day it was for our school and our state."

A sportswriter entering the two dressing rooms at that point might have been confused. There was as much laughter and back-slapping on the Wisconsin side as one would have expected in a winning locker room. "What I wouldn't give for one minute more," said a beaming coach Bruhn. "The clock simply ran out on us. I'm real proud of our kids and the way they stayed in there."

Although USC captured the victory, the level of excitement wasn't what you might expect in the winning locker room at the Rose Bowl. "There was an 'Oh, boy, thank God it's over' kind of attitude with our team," said McKay. "But we were happy. That game made sure we were the national champions, which hadn't happened in thirty-some years at USC. Our players knew what they had accomplished. At least I told them so, as soon as I could get to them."

Associated Press quoted McKay following that game as saying, "We're still number one and they're number two. They are a good team, but they'd finish about sixth in our league." McKay denies that he ever made such a statement. "What happened was that Woody Hayes had made a statement about USC before I got there. He reputedly said that our school wouldn't finish fourth or fifth in the Big Ten," he said. "What I said was, 'I assure you that Wisconsin would finish better than fourth or fifth in our league.' That's all I said. I did feel that we were much the superior team to Wisconsin. But I have to give a lot of credit to coach Bruhn and Wisconsin. A lot of teams would have collapsed under this kind of situation. Wisconsin hung in there tough, and darn near came back to beat us."

McKay was speaking in a San Francisco hotel room. Ironically, the date was January 1, 1977. He would be doing the TV color at the East-West Shrine Game the next day at Stanford, and had just watched USC defeat Michigan, 14–6, in the Rose Bowl on his hotel room television set. "Many times I've run out on that field and said to myself, 'I wish I were in Wyoming, watching it on TV.' So here I sat in a hotel room by myself. I really enjoyed it. USC dominated them, but I thought they would anyway. Michigan never could pass. When I was the USC coach, they couldn't pass. Terrible!"

Now thirty-eight, VanderKelen envisions the day when Wisconsin will return to Pasadena. "Ohio State and Michigan still are the class of the conference, but other schools have closed the gap," he said. "Maybe in three or four years it will be a much closer conference."

VanderKelen believes that what was accomplished on January 1, 1963, has nothing to do with the final score. "No matter what the score is, you can always come back," he stressed, reaching for words and collecting some of Rockne's. "Any player worth his salt is one who never gives up, who keeps on fighting. That game proved if you want to, you can come back and gain respectability."

And with one minute more, who knows what else?

MEN WHO
MOVED MOUNTAINS

Gary Beban remembers his first sight of that mountainous Michigan State team and the uncomfortable feeling that the football field suddenly had tilted. UCLA was opening the 1965 season at East Lansing with Beban, a sophomore, starting at quarterback. "We came out on the field for the pre-game warmups," he said. "I was nervous enough as it was, then Michigan State came out. I said to someone, 'My God, they're awfully big.' Byron Nelson, our tight end, turned to look at them and said, 'Oh, my God, they haven't even put on their pads yet!' They were huge. I kept thinking, 'Is this college football?'"

Michigan State bullied UCLA that day, 13–3, and continued undefeated through the regular season. "Totally undefeated," stressed Beban. "When they came out for the Rose Bowl, they were being called the greatest team in Big Ten history. In some articles, it was written that they were the finest college team ever put together." Waiting, hesitantly, in Pasadena for a rematch was UCLA. "On paper there was no way we should have been within three touchdowns of them," declared Beban. What followed was the equivalent of Henry Armstrong knocking out Joe Louis or Nate Archibald stuffing over Kareem Abdul-Jabbar. The Liliputian Bruins achieved one of the great upsets in Rose Bowl and college football history by shocking the Brobdingnagian Spartans, 14–12, on January 1, 1966.

Michigan State not only was number one in the polls at the time, but number one on defense, number one in potential first-round pro draft picks (Bubba Smith, George Webster, Gene Washington, Clint Jones), and number one in lumps administered.

"We knew we had achieved a great victory, but I don't think anyone enjoyed it for a few days," said Beban. "I can't ever remember a game, except the USC game of 1967, where I was so physically beaten up. I didn't do anything the day after the Rose Bowl.

I didn't even get out of bed. I could hardly move." Neither could Dallas Grider and Bobby Stiles, who finally brought the Michigan State monster to its knees, just in time to save this classic victory. Stiles was named MVP. He had to be revived to accept it.

Beban became the "Great One," as he was known on the UCLA campus. He directed the Bruins to their first Rose Bowl triumph, after five previous failures. He developed into the school's first all-America quarterback and its only Heisman Trophy winner. "The Heisman wasn't a one-year performance," he said. "I don't think anyone in the country in 1967 played better than O. J. Simpson. But I don't think anyone in the country had a better year than I did in 1965, when Mike Garrett won the Heisman. So, to me, the Heisman reflected three years of always being in the chips, and making UCLA a power again in football."

In his mind, none of Beban's accomplishments ever surpassed that one afternoon in Pasadena. "Football was a bonus for me," Beban declared. "It was important for my dad that I make it at a big-time university. My parents sacrificed vacations when I was young so I could play Little League baseball. My dad was there to watch me start at quarterback against Michigan State. And we won. I achieved everything I wanted out of football in that Rose Bowl game."

Gary Beban was the only child of a shipping clerk who worked on the San Francisco docks. The youngster was a single-wing tailback at Sequoia High School in Redwood City, California, five miles north of Stanford University. "It came down to Stanford, California and UCLA," he said of his college preferences. "I didn't want to go to school out of state, and I didn't want to go to school so close to home, so it was UCLA." Coach Bill Barnes was fired during Beban's freshman year, and Tommy Prothro of Oregon State took over. Prothro had taken Oregon State to the Rose Bowl the year before, losing convincingly to Michigan, 34–7. He was back at Pasadena the next year, but with another school. If this isn't some sort of personal record, how about the trivia item that Prothro and Pete Elliott are the only individuals to have participated in a Rose Bowl as a player, assistant coach, and head coach. Prothro played on the Duke team that lost to Oregon State, 20–16, in 1942, the only Rose Bowl game not played in Pasadena. Later, he was an assistant coach for Red Sanders' UCLA Rose Bowl teams in the Fifties, before moving on to Oregon State.

"You could see the changes overnight," said Beban of Prothro's takeover. "You knew it wasn't going to be a democracy. There was one boss and you would do it his way or not play. That first spring practice was the toughest I ever went through." It was basically a sophomore-junior UCLA squad that flew to Michigan State as Beban made his varsity debut. "It was a close game really," he pointed out. "A break here or there and we could have won. We had a 65-yard touchdown pass called back, and they scored near the end to make it 13–3. Tommy admitted after the game that Michigan State was a better team than he had thought. Nobody knew going into that season that Michigan State was going to be the team they turned out to be. They were like us, sort of a darkhorse."

UCLA quarterback Gary Beban chats on the sidelines with his coach, Tommy Prothro, as the Bruins upset Michigan State 14-12.

The Spartans were loaded with talent. They ran past Penn State, 23–0; Illinois, 22–12; Michigan, 24–7; Ohio State, 32–7; Purdue, 14–10; Northwestern, 49–7; Iowa, 35–0; Indiana, 27–13; and Notre Dame, 12–3. Quarterback Steve Juday received all-America recognition. His backup, Jimmy Raye, eventually would be a star in his own right. Jones and Dwight Lee were swift halfbacks, and Bob Apisa a rugged fullback, who figured in the key play of the Rose Bowl. Barefoot kicker-punter Dick Kenney and Apisa were from Hawaii. Michigan State had the United Nations playing the right side of its line—Boris Dimitroff, John Karpinski and Joe Przybycki. Wide receiver Gene Washington had exceptional speed—he was the Big Ten hurdles champion as well. Defensively, the Spartans were even more awesome. Bubba Smith was a 292-pound defensive end who made quarterbacks twitch with fear, while the Spartans' rooting section chanted, "Kill, Bubba, Kill." Harold Lucas represented more brute strength in the front four, while George Webster was becoming one of the best college linebackers of all time. Safety Jess Phillips had attended Pollard High School in Beaumont, Texas, with Bubba, where both played for Bubba's father, W. R. Smith.

The proud—and fortunate—coach of all this talent was Duffy Daugherty, the little, gray-haired leprechaun who was faster with a joke than his coaching whistle. Did the Spartans take the Bruins too lightly that second time around? "No one takes a bowl game lightly," cautioned Prothro. "But an underdog team has a psychological advantage in that kind of game."

The Bruins lost only one other time that autumn, a 37–34 scoring marathon at Tennessee in the final regular-season game. In between, UCLA subdued Penn State, 24–22; Syracuse, 24–14; tied Missouri, 14–14; then defeated California, 56–3; Air Force, 10–0; Washington, 28–24; Stanford, 30–13; and USC, 20–16, to wrest the Rose Bowl invitation from the Trojans.

"Coming out of our first four games 2–1–1 gave us the feeling we might be a pretty good football team," said Beban. "We were very young, but we were very cocky." The Bruins had good reason. In AP's final regular-season poll, Michigan State was number one, Missouri number six, Tennessee number seven and USC number eight. So the number five Bruins had played four of the nation's top eight teams. "We had the toughest schedule in the country, yet we finished 7–2–1," said Beban. After they played the number one team a second time, they would be 8–2–1.

The Bruins had similar confidence in their head coach. "Tommy always seemed to have a trick or two in his attache case that worked in games where we needed a little extra," said Beban. A perfect example would be the 1965 game against Washington. The Huskies jumped out into a 14–0 lead, but Beban, in perhaps his most spectacular performance, ran 40 and 65 yards for touchdowns and threw a 55-yard touchdown pass to Dick Witcher to seal the 28–24 victory. "That pass was a sleeper play that started a fierce rivalry between the two schools," said Beban.

"Tommy noticed in the films that the Washington players would stay in the defensive huddle for a long time, with their heads down. So we ran this play to the left side, and everyone kind of piled up. Witcher just lay there while the Washington players quickly got up and ran back into the huddle. Witcher never came back to the huddle. We lined up quickly, and I threw him the long bomb for the touchdown. Their coach, Jim Owens, thought it was a trick play, and he never forgot it. But Prothro always was thinking, and what he did was within the rules. We had an awful lot of respect for the man, and his mind."

The UCLA players, while they believed in Prothro, never grew close to him. "He was very aloof, and there was a degree of fright about him, but he never lied to you," said Beban. "Before a game, he would tell us, 'You're the better team, and if you don't win today it's because you aren't mentally ready to play football.' We were a substantial underdog to USC my first year. In the pre-game talk, Tommy said, 'You players, as a group, could play your best game ever today and you still might not win. But let's go out there and give it our best.'" Prothro's subtle, truthful approach worked as UCLA won by four.

"Tommy also had a dry wit," Beban recalled. "Before a game with Stanford, he said, 'I would very much like to read off the reasons why I would like to beat Stanford.' He had this sheet of paper in his hand, and as he let it go, it rolled all the way to the floor. It was funny, but at the same time he got his point across."

Beban gives Prothro the full credit for the Rose Bowl upset. "It was a coaching victory," said the Bruins' all-time total offense leader. "Tommy felt there were ways to stay in the game, but only by using a balanced offense. We used the pass only to keep them off-balance. We also put two wide receivers on the same side of the field for the first time that season. It worked. We maintained the football a good portion of the game."

Prothro studied the Michigan State game films with the eye of a microbiologist, looking for tendencies that might help the Bruins. "Tommy noticed that Clint Jones would put one foot back a half-step every time he was about to run to the right side," said Beban. "Our linebackers picked it up right away. Our defense had a fabulous game, partly because we had Michigan State so well scouted." Prothro alluded to this by saying the UCLA defense "guessed well in short-yardage situations."

Offensively, the Bruins were equally prepared. "We felt we had to keep Bubba Smith out of our backfield," Prothro continued, "so instead of bringing a back out in motion to block on him, we set the back close to the line of scrimmage, for that purpose. We also directed our offense away from George Webster. Michigan State never was in the game, until the end when they completed a couple of long passes."

Beban is convinced the Spartans made a mistake by "verbally humiliating" the Bruins before the game. "We got to the Rose Bowl, dumped our stuff in the locker room, then went out to check the field, trying to get rid of some of the nerves," said the quarterback. "Up until then we felt a certain degree of awe towards Michigan State, and were concerned about not getting humiliated and blown out of the park. They were out on the field as we arrived and shouted loud enough for us to hear, things like 'We're going to show the surfer boys how to play football.' That was one of the turning points of the game, and we hadn't even put on our uniforms yet. We were such a small team that we had to play on our psyche. Bobby Stiles and Mo Freedman, one of our centers, went around pumping everyone up. They were really mad. By the time we hit the field, we were as high as any team I've ever played on."

Even before that incident, Prothro sensed that something great was about to happen. "I told my father before the game that Michigan State had better be every bit as good as they're supposed to be, because I knew we were emotionally ready," he said. Once again, Prothro truthfully assessed the situation as he faced his already inspired players. "There is no way you can be losers today," he said. "All we can do is come out winners. No matter what the final score is, even if you win and it's close, you can make college football history."

If the Rose Bowl's public address system had been connected to the Bruin locker room at that precise moment, the laughter of the 100,500 in attendance would have reverberated off the San Gabriel Mountains. It mattered little, as the Bruins were saving the last laugh for themselves.

Beban gave an indication of what was to happen by galloping for 27 yards on the game's first offensive play. The Bruins bogged down, but regained possession as Stiles intercepted Juday's pass at the UCLA 15, and returned it 42 yards to the Spartans' 43. The Bruins then received an important break, as Don Japinga received Larry Cox' punt and was hit hard by Byron Nelson. Japinga went one way and the football the other as UCLA's John Erquiaga recovered at the Michigan State 6. Beban took it across in two plays, sneaking over from a yard out. Kurt Zimmerman converted and UCLA led 7–0 just into the second quarter.

Zimmerman came right back with an onside kick. Michigan State was caught completely off-guard, and Grider pounced on the hopping football at the Spartans' 42. Mel Farr sliced through tackle for 21 yards, and Beban, following a five-yard UCLA penalty, threw for 27 yards to end Kurt Altenberg, at the 1. Beban scored his second touchdown on the next play, and Zimmerman made it 14–0.

"We had the attitude that no matter how big or small the opponent, we could out-quick them," said Beban. "We did things with anticipation and speed. We felt in our own minds that we were quick as anyone who ever lived. I'm sure we bothered Michigan State this way."

The Spartans were both bothered and bewildered. UCLA defensive end Jim Colletto recovered a Juday fumble at the Bruins' 19, and then intercepted a Juday pass at the UCLA 42, to personally stop two second-quarter drives by Michigan State.

Yet the Spartans were by no means clamped by UCLA. Jones may have been stopped on sweeps to the right, but he darted between the tackles for 113 yards in twenty carries, as the Spartans traveled 204 yards by land. Jones cut loose on a 20-yard run that later set up an unsuccessful 23-yard field goal attempt by the shoeless Kenney, who stubbed his toe, and the ball. Surprising UCLA left the field at halftime with a two-touchdown lead.

UCLA gave up 314 yards of offense to the Spartans that afternoon, compared to its own total of 212. But UCLA proved strong in key situations. Three times in the second half, it stopped the Spartans on fourth down and a yard needed for a first down. Stiles made the key tackle on one of those stops and intercepted his second pass, again on a Juday attempt, in the third quarter. UCLA moved to within striking distance again as Beban completed a 35-yard, tackle-eligible pass to Larry Slagle—more Prothro trickery—and a 17-yard throw to Nelson at the Spartan 12.

"If we had scored right then, it would have been 21–0 and the game would have been broken wide open," said Beban. "But I made the all-time faux pas. I rolled out on the next play and, as the films would later show, everyone was open. But I just dropped the ball. I don't ever remember having done that before or after. I just dropped it, then kicked it, and Bubba and the boys recovered back on our 27. That really hurt." UCLA had another chance to increase the distance between itself and Michigan State, but Zimmerman missed a 44-yard field goal attempt in the fourth quarter.

UCLA could suppress the Spartans' explosiveness only so long. Michigan State finally erupted, covering eighty yards in just two plays for its first touchdown. Washington broke free behind the UCLA secondary to catch Juday's 42-yard pass, at the Bruins' 38. Raye replaced Juday and rolled right, reaching the 32 before pitching to the trailing back, Apisa, who continued down the sidelines into the end zone. Juday, a holder on conversions, took the center snap and jumped up, looking for a receiver and two points. Jerry Klein deflected his pass, and UCLA led 14–6 with 6:13 remaining in the game.

"From the middle of the third quarter on, it was really a Michigan State game," Beban admitted. "We were starting to wear down and they had some awfully good football players. After being beaten and bruised, you lose some of your speed. By then, both our offense and defense were tired."

The Spartans suddenly were reinvigorated. Bubba Smith crashed through to partially block Cox' punt, which traveled only 16 yards to the Spartans' 49. Juday was dropped for a 7-yard loss by Terry Donahue (eventually UCLA's head coach) on the first play, but on fourth and seventeen Raye and Washington teamed on a 21-yard completion to the UCLA 37. Washington caught another 9-yard reception and Lee two passes for fifteen yards to bring about fourth and one at the 1. The Spartans didn't fail this time, as Juday squeezed across with thirty-one seconds left to make it 14–12.

No matter how close the game is, Prothro had told his Bruins, by winning you'll make football history. Now it came down to one play.

"A tie would have seemed like a loss to us because we had played so hard," said Beban. "Tommy told Grider, 'Watch for the option and Apisa coming around because they're going with the Bull.' Prothro had the Bruin defense overload to the right. Once again, Prothro had scouted the Spartans perfectly. The Bull, Apisa, took the pitchout and headed for the flag. Grider moved in his path and made contact. But it would take more than one man, and the 5' 9", 175-pound, cornerback Stiles was that man. He threw himself with such force at Apisa that Stiles was knocked unconscious. Apisa finally surrendered, just shy of the goal line.

"Bobby sacrificed his life," summarized Beban, "and we had what we thought was the biggest upset ever." Slagle covered the onside kick for UCLA, then Beban dropped to the ground with the football tucked under his belly as time expired. Prothro hadn't lied.

"We could have given up when we were behind by two touchdowns with seven minutes to play," said Daugherty in the aftermath of the upset, his normally whimsical Irish grin now a dour expression. "But we gave it a real good effort, and I'd say only lost by just inches. In that first half, we probably made more mistakes than at any time this season. However, a lot of our mistakes were forced by UCLA. They played a fine defensive game and took away from us a lot of the things we generally do well." In the final poll, Michigan State dropped from first to second, as Alabama moved up from fourth to claim the national championship. Arkansas finished third, and UCLA moved up a notch to fourth. Nebraska, Missouri, Tennessee, Louisiana State, Notre Dame, and USC completed the Top Ten. The poll notwithstanding, since the Bruins had beaten number one, they had it fixed in their brains that they were numero uno.

UCLA defensive back Bob Stiles who made the game-saving tackle in the 1966 contest. He was knocked cold making the play.

Michigan State had mostly juniors on that team, but would not make it back to the Rose Bowl the next January because of the Big Ten's no-repeat rule. MSU played the famous 10–10 tie with Notre Dame the following year, before disappearing from the college football spotlight.

After that, schools like Texas and Oklahoma began admitting more black athletes, preventing Michigan State from raiding the predominantly black schools along the Texas gulfport. Michigan State ran into problems with the NCAA as well, as Ohio State and Michigan turned the Big Ten into the Big Two.

Beban was a sophomore and Farr a junior, but UCLA failed to return to the Rose Bowl in 1967, "even though we were as good that season as at any time during my three years at UCLA," Beban pointed out. The quarterback broke his ankle against Stanford, the week before UCLA defeated USC, 14–7, with Norman Dow as the Bruin quarterback. UCLA was 9–1, but 3–1 in the conference to USC's 4–1. The Trojans, following the defeat to UCLA, were voted the Pac-8's Rose Bowl representative because of a better conference percentage. However, they were humiliated the following Saturday by Notre Dame, 51–0, and lost to Purdue, 14–13, at Pasadena.

"We were number one in the country and USC number two when we played each other my senior year," said Beban of another college football classic. "The city, state, and national championships were on the line. Our Rose Bowl win over Michigan State was exciting, but this was more so because of all the factors. We also had two players going for the Heisman Trophy. It was an incredible, wide-open game. They had long runs for touchdowns, we had long bombs for touchdowns. O. J. ran 69 yards for one score, but his 14-yard run for a touchdown was even more incredible because he ran through so many people, and made a number of cuts within a short distance to get there." Simpson and Beban were spectacular as USC won, 21–20, and then defeated Indiana, 14–3, in the 1968 Rose Bowl to clinch the national title.

Beban scored thirty-five touchdowns and amassed 5,358 yards in total offense during his three years, both still UCLA records. He became the only Bruin in history to have his number (16) retired. The Los Angeles Rams drafted him early in the second round (their first pick), but couldn't sign him and traded his rights to the Washington Redskins.

"Just by walking on a field, Beban can pick up a team," said Redskins' coach Otto Graham. "He's a winner." Beban spent three years with Washington, only because he had a three-year, no-cut contract estimated at $200,000 a year. "I didn't want to play any position but quarterback," he said.

"Vince Lombardi replaced Graham as coach and asked me if I would play wide receiver my second year for the good of the team. I told him I would if I could get a shot at quarterback the next year. He agreed to that. I played my heart out for the man, working behind Charley Taylor—far behind—as Taylor never was injured. At the end of the season, Lombardi told me he appreciated what I had done, and for me to come back the next year ready to play quarterback. I came back, but he didn't."

The Redskins released Beban in November of his third season. He had a tryout the following summer with the Denver Broncos, who were not interested in Beban as a quarterback. "Lou Saban asked me if I would play free safety. I told him I wouldn't and I got my walking papers from the Broncos too," said Beban. "My attitude was the same as the kid who wanted all his life to be a lawyer, went to law school, but couldn't pass the bar exam. Does he become a bailiff just to stay in the court room? I didn't want to play another position just to stay in the game. I was a quarterback.

"I didn't leave football disappointed. By that time, I had other things in life I wanted to do," said Beban. "Football had been good to me and I was good to it. It was a fair trade."

EVERY UNDERDOG
HAS HIS DAY

The wonderful, child-like world of Disney has brought laughter to hundreds of millions, but not Woody Hayes, the Grumpy of college football. A perfect example is the 1971 Rose Bowl game, which began as have most Rose Bowls of recent memory, at Disneyland, where for the benefit of wire service photographers, opposing players pose with one another, the Tournament of Roses queen, and Disney characters. This annual event is the unofficial kickoff to the events leading up to the New Year's Day game, and the intended atmosphere is one of fun and relaxation.

But this isn't what Dr. Don Bunce remembers. "The Ohio State players came marching down Main Street in their military style, very stern and rigid," said the former Stanford quarterback. "We were running all around, eating cotton candy, having a good time. Jim Kauffman, one of our defensive backs, was doing cartwheels and wearing his Mickey Mouse ears, and taking pictures of Ohio State players. Woody Hayes only let his players stay a short while, while we had most of the afternoon there. It was such a contrast of philosophies. I just wish I had a videotape of that day."

Bunce didn't play for Stanford against Ohio State in that 1971 game; he was being red-shirted. He wanted to save his final season of athletic eligibility for a good reason —he was a senior at Stanford the same time as Jim Plunkett. Bunce was on the sidelines, however, as Plunkett drilled the Buckeyes full of holes, and the Cardinals scored a major upset, 27–17. Stanford returned to the Rose Bowl the following year, with Bunce as the regular quarterback. This time the opponent was Michigan, whose coach, Bo Schembechler, was about as interested in shaking hands with Goofy and watching his players dance with the Aristocats as Hayes. "Michigan was about the same as Ohio State, although I don't remember them marching," said Bunce. "But Hayes and Schembechler wouldn't let their players do anything. In fact, Schembechler took his players to Bakersfield to get away from the extracurricular activities." The effect is about the same as going to Altoona to prepare for a game in Pittsburgh. Michigan, as Ohio State, was a heavy favorite, but Stanford won again, 13–12. Generals Hayes and Schembechler and their aides-de-camp wondered afterwards "just who is John Ralston and what kind of a football program is he running?"

Ralston seemed like the Disney of football coaches. He smiled like the Cheshire cat, and scooted around football fields like the Mad Hatter. Ralston's two-minute offense drill, during which his assistants would stand back as he hurriedly moved the football, counted down the seconds out loud, and blew the whistle, was like something out of the Looking Glass.

Ralston had graduated from three different Dale Carnegie courses with a Ph.D in positive thinking. His speaking manner had some of the stuffiness of Foghorn Leghorn and swagger of Yosemite Sam. Ralston loved to shake your hand, slap your back, and first-name you to death. It all seemed affected, but you found, in time, that he was consistent in this personality, whether or not it was his to begin with. Because of this unusual man, you wouldn't expect his players to march to a military tune. Ralston tried it once, and it was like war.

"John changed tremendously from when I first got to Stanford," said Plunkett. "He was a Woody Hayes kind of guy, from the old school. John wouldn't allow long hair or beards. There were rumors about his getting fired. As the years progressed, his attitude changed enormously, towards the players and in his own philosophy. He became much more liberal and flexible in both his attitude and coaching manner. I think this helped him establish better rapport with the players, and helped him win more."

As Ralston's personality relaxed over the years, so did his Stanford football teams. The Cardinals would beat an Arkansas or USC one week, then lose to San Jose State or Washington State the next.

"This was Stanford's reputation," said Plunkett. "We tied UCLA, 20–20, my junior year, in a game we should have won. We dropped a touchdown pass and had a field goal blocked. Walking to the dressing room afterwards, some hippie-type guy, obviously inebriated, came up to me and said, 'It's not you guys, it's Stanford.' People really believed that."

Ohio State and Michigan learned otherwise. The two Big 10 schools went into the Rose Bowl undefeated, while Stanford had three defeats each season. Stanford came out 2–0.

The Cardinals' one advantage in both games was a passing attack. "Ohio State and Michigan don't get to see a Jim Plunkett or a Don Bunce," declared Ralston. "We knew we had the equalizers in our passing games." Plunkett and Bunce each brought Stanford from behind, in the fourth quarter, with fantastic passing performances. Their exploits are even more interesting when you consider that Bunce's college career almost wasted away because of Plunkett, and that Plunkett's own rags-to-recognition story perhaps is symbolic of the Heisman Trophy, which he received in 1970.

Plunkett's parents were legally blind from the time he was born, the third and last child. His father worked as a waiter and also a news vendor in a San Jose, California, post office. From the time he was at James Lick High School, Plunkett was helping support the family as a newspaper boy, grocery clerk, and gas station attendant. James William Plunkett Sr. died before Jim received the Heisman. His mother continues to live in San Jose, dependent upon Jim and his two older sisters.

"Jim has all the pride and determination in the world. I knew that from the first time I saw him, at a high school wrestling match," said Ralston. "This guy was trying to pin him, but Jim ultimately turned him over and pinned him." The Stanford coach would also recognize, in time, that Plunkett had a strong passing arm. "One of the strongest ever to play the game," Ralston emphasized. Plunkett narrowed his college choices to Santa Clara, adjacent to San Jose, and Stanford, twenty miles north. "Jim wanted to stay close to home because of his mother's blindness. Recruiting him was easy," said Ralston. Certainly. Santa Clara couldn't offer the Rose Bowl.

There was a moment of fear before Plunkett enrolled at Stanford. A cancerous-like growth appeared on his right shoulder. It was benign. Plunkett prefers not to discuss this near-tragedy, or the difficult period of his growing up, even with close friends.

"Jim never talked too much about his family life," said Stanford teammate and roommate Jack Lasater. "He never made a big issue about the hard life he had." Not only was Plunkett's face chiseled out of stone, like that of a proud Indian warrior, but so was his amazing character. Ralston knew he had a special athlete and person and revised his offensive philosophy to accommodate Plunkett's skills.

"John was coaching a sprint-out attack when I got to Stanford," said Plunkett. "I just wasn't that type, so John adapted a pro-type passing attack to me, and had coaches like Jack Christiansen and Mike White to install it."

Ralston had two senior quarterbacks when Plunkett was a sophomore, and so red-shirted him. That same year, Bunce entered Stanford as a freshman. Plunkett and Bunce turned out for their first year of varsity football in 1968. Plunkett was first string from the beginning, a pattern Bunce could never break. "It was a very difficult situation," Ralston remembered, "because Don always felt that he was better than Jim."

Plunkett was a sensation from the beginning. He threw fourteen touchdown passes his first year, and twenty as a junior. Over that same period, Bunce, who was friends with Plunkett and lived in the same fraternity house, threw only six-three passes, seven for touchdowns.

Plunkett injured his ribs in the first half of a game against Washington, during his sophomore year. Bunce came in with the score tied, 7–7, and proceeded to run for one touchdown and throw for three—including an 80-yard bomb to Gene Washington— as Stanford won, 35–20. Bunce was back on the bench the next week.

"There was no question it was frustrating," he said. "The whole thing was compounded by the fact that when I got a chance to play sporadically, things went well. I couldn't rationalize in my mind why I wasn't playing. Ralston wanted to keep me interested and enthusiastic about the program, and I can see what a tough job it was for him. I never thought of leaving Stanford, but I thought of getting away. During the last part of my junior year, I attended one of Stanford's European campuses in Florence, Italy. Actually I was there from March through the summer, and it was an important time in my life, because it gave me a chance to get out of my isolated football environment and experience a whole different world. Diana also was going to Stanford. She came over in May and we were married in Athens, in a little church on a hill overlooking the Acropolis."

Ralston had "numerous sessions" with Bunce about red-shirting his senior year. Stanford was promoting Plunkett for Heisman Trophy consideration, and the head coach knew Bunce could have the job all to himself in another year's time.

"I told Don that if Jim got hurt before the fifth game against USC, we would activate him," said Ralston. "If Jim was injured any time after that, then we would go with either one of two other quarterbacks, Jesse Freitas or Mike Boryla."

Bunce finally agreed, but not entirely through Ralston's coaxing. "By my senior year I had decided to go to medical school, and being away from football would give me a chance to take some classes I would need," he said. Meanwhile, another kind of agreement was being reached. "After our junior season," said Plunkett, "a group of us —Jack Schultz, Jack Lasater, Ron Kadziel and myself—made a little pact that we were going to come back and win the Pac-8 and go to the Rose Bowl." Not much was made of this vow, possibly because the term "Vow Boys" had been used at Stanford in the mid-1930s. But the more contemporary prophesy also proved true.

Actually, Stanford hadn't missed the Rose Bowl by much the previous two years, but field goals by Ron Ayala gave USC 27–24 and 26–24 victories and sent the Trojans instead. After the second defeat to the Trojans on a last-second Ayala field goal, Bob Murphy, then Stanford's sports information director, said, "Stanford is going to ask USC to retire Ayala's uniform—with Ayala in it."

Plunkett knew the 1970 team had the weapons to support its secret pledge. "We were explosive, we could score from anywhere," he said. "We were so confident, that no matter how many points were scored against us, we knew we could outscore our opponent." Stanford opened impressively, defeating Arkansas, 34–28, at Fayetteville, then knocked off San Jose State, 34–3, and Oregon, 33–10.

The Cardinals' fourth opponent was winless Purdue at Stanford. "The whole week of the Purdue game, everything was directed towards USC the following week," said Plunkett. "Whenever we'd have a wind sprint, Mike White (later head coach at California) would shout, 'This is for USC.' Everyone, including the coaching staff, was looking past Purdue. It showed, because Purdue kicked our butts."

The Boilermakers stomped on Stanford, 26–14, but the Cardinals ripped back for their first victory in thirteen years over USC, 24–14. Stanford then defeated Washington State, 63–16; UCLA, 9–7; Oregon State, 48–10; and Washington, 29–22; to clinch the Pac-8 championship. Then true to Stanford's up-and-down tendencies, it finished the season by losing to Air Force, 31–14, and California, 22–14.

"There was kind of an emotional letdown after we won the conference championship," said Plunkett. "The coaches let up on us in practice, and the guys weren't working that hard." Nevertheless, Plunkett had set an NCAA total offense record of 7,887 yards, and was voted the consensus all-America quarterback, as well as becoming the first Stanford player ever to win the Heisman Trophy.

Meanwhile, in Columbus, Ohio, there was no let-up. Woody Hayes' fantastic sophomores of 1968—Jack Tatum, Rex Kern, John Brockington, Jim Stillwagon, etc. —were now seniors. They were 10–0 and the national champions their first year, defeating USC and O. J. Simpson, 27–16, in the 1969 Rose Bowl. The Buckeyes finished 8–1 as juniors, losing their last game to Michigan, 24–14. This was during the time of the Big 10's no-repeat rule. Michigan was going to Pasadena, regardless of whether they won or lost against Ohio State. "Enthusiasm prevailed in that game," said Buckeye cornerback Tim Anderson.

Ohio State began the 1970 season by incinerating Texas A&M, 56–13. Falling in order next were Duke, 34–10; Michigan State, 29–0; Minnesota, 28–8; Illinois, 48–29; Northwestern, 24–10; Wisconsin, 24–7; Purdue, 10–7; and Michigan, 20–9. The Buckeyes now were 27–1 over three years. "We're not worried about Stanford," said Brockington, sipping on a soft drink after the victory over Michigan.

And Stanford was not worried about Ohio State. "I felt confident," said Ralston, who seldom felt otherwise. "I didn't think Ohio State was the kind of team we could beat in a best three-out-of-five shot. But in a one-game, all-out, two-hour basis, I thought we had an excellent opportunity. Not only because we had a great passer, but because we didn't have any problems in figuring out their defense. They had the 'rover' (Tatum) who went to the far side of the field. They used the 'Slant Arkansas' out of a 5–2 set, and we knew that the quarterback draw was the perfect play for this kind of defense. We knew where their people would drop on pass coverages. Ohio State was a disciplined team, but we knew where we could take advantages."

Ralston hadn't forgotten the defeats to Air Force and California. "He was terribly upset about them," said Plunkett. "The coaches hadn't been tough on us after we clinched the Rose Bowl bid. But he really worked our tails off before Pasadena, in the rain and the mud. It was the hardest we worked all year. Some of the players thought we were working too hard and not getting enough free time. Some of them were really unhappy, so we called a team meeting. Schultz, Kadziel and myself went to see Coach Ralston. He told us he had certain commitments in his heart, a philosophy he had to stick by. He did let up some, giving us a later curfew, and the use of some Rose Bowl cars made available to Stanford. But he was determined to win this game."

Ralston admitted that he did "relax a couple of things, but not the standards on the practice field. I suppose you could adopt the philosophy that you go to a game of this type and have a good time, that the game itself was not of paramount importance. Our philosophy was that the game was everything. We still had a good time."

The Ohio State players, comparing their lifestyle to Stanford's during this same period, thought the Cardinals must be partying it up. "We read that Stanford was staying out at night, just like USC the first time we went to the Rose Bowl," said Anderson. "The Rose Bowl is the classic of all the games. It means a lot to those who get the opportunity to play in the game. We were excited the first time, as sophomores, but the workload was such that we didn't want to go through it like that again. Actually, we voted that we didn't want to go as seniors, but we were talked into it." The heavy hand of Woody Hayes prevailed. He was successful in changing his players' minds, but not their attitudes.

"Coach Hayes runs a camp so tightly," said Anderson, "our players were bickering among themselves before the game. Being in Pasadena for three weeks and not being able to take part in any of the activities, had an effect on our team. It took the edge off the game." And there was little choice but to accept it.

"You can't argue with the guy (Hayes) because he's a winner," Anderson pointed out. "He has to change his own mind." Anderson said the Buckeyes' unhappiness had nothing to do with Hayes as a human being. "He is a great man, like a father to most of the guys on the team. I could call him right now, and he'd stop what he was doing and we'd have a very nice conversation. He's very interested in his players even after they're gone. But we were practicing twice a day for close to two weeks before the Rose Bowl. That's why we weren't interested in going out there a second time and being . . . stagnant."

Ohio State, ranked second in the country (behind Texas) to Stanford's twelfth, was a constant nine-point favorite for the game. Some oddsmakers, recognizing that the Buckeyes had first-team all-Americans in defensive backs Tatum, Anderson, and Mike Sensibaugh, middle guard Stillwagon, fullback Brockington and tight end Jan White, favored Ohio State by as much as twenty-one points. The Buckeye secondary, which also included Harry Howard, was formidable, but so was the Stanford passing game of quarterback Plunkett and his receivers, Randy Vataha, Demea Washington and tight end Bob Moore.

Ralston also had a few surprises planned. On Stanford's first offensive play, Eric Cross ran 41 yards on a flanker reverse to the Buckeyes' 18, as Ohio State was fooled completely. "Because of the intensity of a game of this type, the defensive team usually is going all out on the first play," said Ralston. "We thought with a misdirection play right off the bat, if it broke right, we had a chance for a big gain." A five-yard penalty on the next play nullified a touchdown pass from Plunkett to Moore, but Plunkett came back with the first of several quarterback draws—Stanford hadn't used one all season —for 13 yards to the 9, where a piling-on penalty moved the ball to the 4-yard line. Jackie Brown scored from that point. Steve Horowitz kicked a 37-yard field goal on Stanford's next series and the Cardinals were ahead, 10–0.

"Any time we felt we needed to turn something on, we could do it," said Buckeye Anderson, of Stanford's quick lead. Hayes had a few tricks, too. Split end Bruce Jankowski raced 37 yards with a Kern handoff on the first offensive play, following the field goal. Kern then broke loose for 23 yards to set up Brockington's 1-yard smash. Ohio State came right back with another Brockington score from a yard away. Stanford fumbled away an opportunity at the Buckeyes' 7. The half ended with Ohio State leading, 14–10.

"I'll never forget our center, John Sande, at halftime," said Ralston. "We wanted to use the quarterback draw, which requires that the center block their nose guard whichever way he's slanting. Stillwagon was the nose guard, and I hadn't seen him make a bad play in about 16,000 feet of film. We thought we might have to double Stillwagon with a guard in order to help Sande. I asked John how he was doing. He said, 'Coach, I can handle him myself.' And he was doing it too, I'll tell you that." Horowitz started the third quarter with a Rose Bowl record 48-yard field goal, but Fred Schram retaliated from 32 yards away and the Buckeyes led, 17–13. Then came the pivotal play of the game.

Ohio State hammered on the ground to the Stanford 20. It was fourth and one. "They lined up for the next play, and Coach Ralston could see that Brockington was 'cheating'

Stanford quarterback Jim Plunkett with his coach, John Ralston, during Stanford's amazing 27-17 upset of Ohio State in 1971.

towards the line," said Plunkett. "But before they could get the play off, the third quarter ended. Ralston called the right defense in case they lined up that way again. That's exactly what they did, and we stopped them." Kadziel, who asked for a shot at linebacker before the season because he couldn't beat out Moore at tight end, hit Brockington a yard behind the line, and the fullback barely made it back to the line of scrimmage.

"The old coach didn't make that play," cautioned Ralston. "If the tight end blocks Kadziel, school's out. But Kadziel went underneath the tight end to pop Brockington straight up. Then before you could snap your fingers, six other players hit Brockington. It was a great singular effort by Kadziel, and the turning point of the game."

Stanford took over, and Plunkett ran the quarterback draw for 10 yards, and completed five straight passes for 69 yards on the ensuing series. The last completion was what Hayes labeled the "mad dog" pass after the game.

"We were third and fifteen, and in the huddle I told Bob Moore to stay in and block," said Plunkett. "But just after we broke, I told Bob nonchalantly, 'You better go out.' I was pressured, and had almost run out of bounds, when I spotted Bob. He went up between two guys and somehow came down with the ball at the two." Brown then scored his second touchdown, from a yard out, and Stanford had the lead, again, 20–17.

Anderson could sense danger. "I thought we had the superior team offensively and defensively, even though we hadn't seen a passer like Plunkett," he said. "But if you don't watch it, a good team can be right back in your face, and it's a fight to the finish. I suppose we looked like Goliath to them. They had all the enthusiasm in the world and their enthusiasm surpassed everything."

The Cardinals were more than enthusiastic by now; they were possessed. Strong safety Schultz dropped Leo Hayden for a 2-yard loss at the Buckeyes' 19. Kadziel blocked a Kern pass. Kern threw again, but Schultz intercepted 25 yards away from a Stanford insurance touchdown. Plunkett got it on passes of 11 and 10 yards to Vataha, and Stanford had its first Rose Bowl victory in thirty years.

"The last game you play leaves that taste in your mouth," said Anderson. "We had a bad taste in our mouths after a great career."

For Plunkett, the taste was as sweet as wine. "Ever since I saw my first Rose Bowl game on TV, when Ron VanderKelen almost beat USC, I wanted to be there and win," he said. "The victory over Ohio State ended a lot of frustration for Stanford and our players. I really believed we out-prepared them. I can't ever remember a more jubilant time in my life."

Plunkett had completed twenty of thirty passes for 265 yards and was named Player of the Game. Notre Dame knocked off Texas that same day in the Cotton Bowl, 24–11. With Ohio State also having lost, third-ranked Nebraska, which beat Louisiana State in the Orange Bowl, 17–12, was named the national champion in the Associated Press' final poll. Ohio State fell to fifth, and Stanford advanced to eighth.

A grim Woody Hayes heads for the other side of the field.

Stanford star Randy Vataha.

Watching in person among the 103,839 at Pasadena that day was John Mazur, then the new head coach of the Boston (now New England) Patriots, who had the first pick in the upcoming NFL draft. "Before the bowl games, we were uncertain whom we would take," said Mazur. "But after I saw the way that Plunkett brought Stanford back —you could just see him lifting his team up—there was no question in my mind that it would be Plunkett."

Happy, but slightly confused, in the wild Stanford locker room after the game was Don Bunce. "During the practices before the Rose Bowl," he said, "I was 'Rex Kern' running the Ohio State plays against our defense. I was half in it, half not, knowing I wasn't going to play. Ralston had me suit up for the game, for the experience of being there. I remember being down on the field and what a strange feeling it was for me."

Bunce, blond and fair in stark contrast to Plunkett's swarthiness, grew up in Menlo Park, California, and lived practically next door to the Stanford campus. Although not wealthy, the six Bunce children lived comfortably off their engineer father's earnings. Six houses away lived John Ralston.

"Don had personal visits from John McKay of USC, Tommy Prothro of UCLA, and Ray Willsey of California the final week before the letters of intent were due," said Ralston. "We didn't know until the end that Don would come to Stanford."

Bunce had been watching Stanford games all his life and never thought he would go anywhere else. "My decision did become somewhat harder when McKay and Prothro took my parents out for dinner and talked of the Rose Bowl," he said. "But I felt it would be more valuable for me to start a tradition, instead of carrying on a tradition of going to the Rose Bowl. What I saw at Stanford was a program on the way up. I also thought we had a very good chance of going to the Rose Bowl."

Bunce was a better natural athlete than Plunkett. "Don was a great runner," said Ralston. "He would be a perfect quarterback for the Veer and Wishbone offenses you see today. But he was a good dropback passer, and so we didn't have to change our offense after Jim left. Don didn't have Plunkett's arm, but he had a quick delivery and was accurate. Both had a burning desire to succeed."

The transition from Plunkett to Bunce in no way changed Stanford's penchant for winning against the stronger teams and losing to the lesser lights. "We kept stubbing our toes in the little games, and I blame myself," said Ralston. "I didn't set a high enough goal. Coming back from the Rose Bowl, we should have talked about a national championship."

The Cardinals put away Missouri, 19–0; Army, 38–3; and Oregon, 38–17; then failed to score a touchdown against underdog Duke in a 9–3 defeat. Stanford rebounded to defeat Washington, 17–6; and USC, 33–18; then lost to lowly Washington State, 24–23. The Cardinals got off the floor again to outlast Oregon State, 31–24; and UCLA, 20–9; before being shocked by San Jose State, 13–12, as Cardinal kicking specialist Rod Garcia missed five field goals.

The Cardinals came back to defeat California, barely, 14–9, and to find themselves, somewhat ruffled, in the Rose Bowl.

Bunce, nevertheless, had a brilliant year, with 2,513 yards of total offense, second best mark in the country. But the Cardinals' great strength that year was defense, beginning with the "Thunder Chickens."

Plunkett's Rose Bowl club had scored 343 points, while yielding 206 over twelve games. Bunce's team wasn't quite as explosive on offense, 261, but was much better on defense, 135, and showed it against Michigan in the 1972 Rose Bowl.

The Wolverines scored almost at will in 1971; their 421 points were the most at Michigan since 1905. Dana Coin's fifty-four points after touchdowns established an NCAA record. Billy Taylor's 3,072 yards rushing set a Michigan career mark. The Wolverines had allowed only seventy points in eleven games, to rank fourth in NCAA defense. They had four first team all-Americas—Taylor, guard Reggie McKenzie, linebacker Mike Taylor, and safety Tom Darden—to Stanford's two—middle linebacker Jeff Siemon and defensive lineman Pete Lazetich, the creator of the "Thunder Chickens."

Two years earlier, USC had a defensive line known as the "Wild Bunch." Lazetich, looking for recognition for Stanford's front four, remembered the name of a motorcycle gang in his home town of Billings, Montana. Thus, the "Thunder Chickens" rode into college football that year, made up of Lazetich, Greg Sampson, Larry Butler, and Pierre Perreault.

Michigan had run over eleven straight opponents, humiliating teams such as Virginia, 56–0; UCLA, 38–0; Navy, 46–0; Indiana, 61–7; and Iowa, 63–7; before season-ending narrow wins over Purdue, 20–17, and Ohio State, 10–7. The fourth-ranked Wolverines were a twelve-point favorite over the sixteenth-ranked Cardinals.

"We felt Michigan was every bit as strong as Ohio State the year before," said Ralston. But, again, the Stanford coach wasn't worried. "Michigan and Ohio State play the same defense. Both were predictable in their pass coverages. The fact that we had already played Ohio State gave our coaches a chance to say, 'Whatever we did against Ohio State should work against Michigan.' The two schools were almost similar on offense, too, which helped us on defense."

Bunce felt Stanford had gained another advantage. "There's no question that the media helped give us a psychological edge for the Rose Bowl," he said. "They played up the fact that we were a hang-loose bunch of guys who were at the Rose Bowl to enjoy ourselves. We met with Ralston several times during practice and asked if we could take more part in our conditioning and strategy, and enjoy the Rose Bowl. By that, I mean not having to work so hard that we couldn't enjoy the Rose Bowl experience. He thought initially that we were looking more for fun than hard work. But that wasn't it at all. We just wanted to have some input. I'm sure the Michigan players were aware of what was going on, and noticed the definite contrasts in philosophies of the two schools."

However, Bunce knew the Cardinals were in for a Pier Six brawl. "There was no question that Michigan had superior athletes. We couldn't attack them running the ball, like their Big Ten opponents. We were a gambling, take-chances type of team. We were even encouraged this way by the Stanford band, which does some crazy, wild things. We knew we had to throw the ball to win, take a lot of chances, and try some trick plays. A good example was the fake punt."

Neither team could gain an advantage for three quarters, after which the score was 3–3 on field goals of 30 yards by Coin and 42 by Garcia. Fullback Fritz Seyferth powered over from a yard out early in the fourth quarter, and Michigan led, 10–3. Then Ralston reached into his apparently bottomless bag of tricks, and out came the fake punt.

Stanford had a fourth and 10 at its 33-yard line. Fullback Reggie Sanderson, lined up as a blocker in front of punter Steve Murray, received the center snap and passed it through the legs of halfback Jackie Brown, in front of him. Brown faked a reverse and took off running around right end. Michigan, dipsey-dooed to death, didn't catch up to him until thirty-one yards later, at its 36.

Bunce then completed a third down, 12-yard pass to tight end Bill Scott at the 24, from where Brown streaked through a big opening at right end and sped into the end

Stanford quarterback Don Bunce, named Player of the Game in his team's upset of Michigan in 1972.

zone, to make it 10–10. This was his third touchdown in back-to-back Rose Bowls.

Bunce heard several Michigan players yell, 'Watch out for the fake punt,' as Stanford lined up. Ralston said one of his players heard a Michigan player scream, 'It's a fake reverse,' as the play was unraveling. Ralston had gotten the play from Ron Earhardt, the North Dakota State coach, and had used it once during Plunkett's final year. Schembechler was looking for a fake punt too. "We ran against it all week," he said.

The theatrics were just beginning. Coin tried a field goal from 46 yards away, but the kick was short and wide. Sophomore James Ferguson caught the ball in the end zone. Stanford had a blocking wall set up to the right, but Ferguson decided to run straight ahead. He was just a few yards in front of the goal line, when he realized he had made a mistake. He tried to reverse his tracks to the right, but Ed Shuttlesworth slammed into him a yard from the goal and drove him back into the end zone. It was ruled a safety, and Michigan led, 12–10, with 3:18 remaining.

"It was a controversial play, because James definitely was tackled in front of the goal line and knocked into the end zone," said Ralston. "We had called for a field goal return. Only when we had practiced the play, James would catch the ball in front of the goalposts. But the ball was kicked so far to his left, that he became confused. We just hadn't practiced the play enough."

Stanford couldn't afford another mistake. "Now we had to kick, hold them to three downs, and drive into scoring position," said Ralston. Bo Rather returned Garcia's kick to Michigan's 45. The Wolverines needed only one first down, perhaps two, to seal the victory. A job for the "Thunder Chickens."

Shuttlesworth and Glenn Doughty hit up the middle, each for two yards. Third and six. Taylor found a small gap at right tackle, but cornerback Charles McCloud stopped him after 3 yards. Michigan had to punt, and Stanford had the football at its 22 with 1:48 left.

"I had planned to say something to the team as I walked into the huddle—a little pep talk—but I looked at everyone and they all had this look of determination," said Bunce. "There was no question in my mind that we were going to score." Bunce was about to extract himself permanently from Plunkett's immense shadow. "All of the plays on that last drive were audibles we had worked on for the Rose Bowl," he said. "They were basic curl patterns, which involved the backs as well, so I had at least five possibilities on every play. Our receivers were running about thirteen yards downfield and curling inside. Michigan was expecting us to go deep, so this opened the middle wide up."

Bunce's first pass was for 13 yards to Scott, and the quarterback followed quickly with a 16-yard completion to flanker John Winesberry at the Michigan 49. A Stanford penalty on the next play moved the ball back to the Cardinals' 46. Bunce came right back with an 11-yard pass to split end Miles Moore at the Michigan 43.

"I was so tired by then," said Bunce, "that I was stumbling over my feet as I dropped back." Bunce dumped off a short pass to fullback Sanderson, who turned it into a 14-yard gain. Bunce's fifth straight completion of the drive went to Winesberry for 12 yards at the Wolverines' 17. Sanderson struggled through the middle to the 14 before Stanford signalled for its second-to-last time out with twenty-two seconds left. Stanford was in excellent field goal range. Garcia paced the sidelines, looking up at the clock.

"Against San Jose State, I had gone to Rod after each missed field goal and told him to relax," said Ralston. "Greg Sampson came up to me at the Rose Bowl and said, 'Coach, don't say anything to Rod.'" Stanford ran one more play, Brown gaining nothing, and used its last time out with sixteen seconds remaining. Garcia trotted on the field.

"I said a little prayer," recalled Ralston.

"I watched the kick, peeking through my fingers," said Bunce.

Garcia swung into the football soccer-style and his kick, from Murray's hold, curved over the middle of the crossbar with 0:12 showing on the clock. Pandemonium broke loose in front of the Stanford bench. Ralston and his underdog Cardinals had done it again. Michigan threw an incomplete pass at the end to make it official: Stanford 13, Michigan 12.

"Stanford deserved to win," said Schembechler. "They had the best offense we've played against this year."

Garcia said he wasn't nervous before his pressure kick. "I was pretty confident since I'd already gotten one off well," he said. "I'd have preferred a touchdown because it would have been easier on me. But I thought it would end up with me having to kick a field goal."

Bunce had completed 24 of 44 passes for 290 yards. Just as Plunkett, he was named Player of the Game. "It was poetic justice that we won," Bunce philosophizes even now. "The whole thing was kind of like a storybook setting." Michigan looked upon the whole thing as a horror tale. The Wolverines dropped to sixth in the final poll as Stanford moved up to tenth.

Those stunning, consecutive Rose Bowl victories caught the attention of the Denver Broncos, who named Ralston as their new general manager-head coach. "I had thought about the pros the year before," he said, "but we had a solid group coming back at Stanford and I wanted to duplicate the Rose Bowl experience. The only way I could ever get the same feeling now would be to win the Super Bowl." Ralston was talking by phone from Denver, after completing a 9–5 record in 1976, the best record in the Broncos' history. But his general managership then was stripped away by the Denver ownership. Angered, Ralston resigned as head coach in early 1977.

Plunkett was an immediate sensation in the NFL and was named Rookie of the Year in 1971, after throwing nineteen touchdown passes. He requested, and was traded to, the San Francisco 49ers before the 1976 season. What was hailed as a glorious home-

Placekicker Rod Garcia, whose 31-yard field goal with 12 seconds to play gave Stanford a 13-12 win.

coming—Stanford and San Jose are within an hour's drive from San Francisco—turned into something far less during Plunkett's first year with the 49ers. His passing never looked worse, and he was lifted from games twice.

The 49er charter was en route to New Orleans for the final game of the 1976 season as Plunkett spoke happily about Stanford and the Rose Bowl. "Winning that game meant more to me than winning the Heisman Trophy," he said. It was much less painful to look back into the past, because Plunkett would not play at all in New Orleans. He had been benched in favor of a rookie, Scott Bull. "I've come back before,

---

EVERY UNDERDOG HAS HIS DAY   211

and I know I can do it again," said Plunkett. All the pride and determination in the world, Ralston had said.

Bunce was drafted twelfth by the Washington Redskins. "But I was George Allen's fourth pick," said Bunce of the notorious trader. "Allen told me that I had a good chance of making the club, and that he would play me during the exhibitions. But if I wanted to play for him, it would involve a four or five-year apprenticeship. Diana and I fell in love with Vancouver." Fast. Bunce spent a year with the British Columbia Lions, alternating at quarterback with Don Moorhead. "It was part of my contract that I attend the University of British Columbia Medical School, but some people became upset when this was made known. Their feeling was that a Canadian medical school was training me, and I would never practice medicine in Canada," Bunce said. After a year of professional football, Bunce enrolled fulltime at the Stanford Medical School. His wife became a reporter for *Sunset* Magazine, a western living monthly published in Menlo Park. Dr. Don Bunce graduated in June, 1977, and immediately started his internship towards a career in orthopedics.

"You caught me at a perfect time," he said. "I was scheduled to do a hip, which is like a day-long procedure, but the operation was just cancelled." Athletics remain a part of his life. "I'm very interested in sports medicine as a career. Athletes make nice patients, because they're so motivated about getting back to perfect health." It's not inconceivable that Dr. Don Bunce someday may become Stanford's team physician. "It would be great if it happened," he said.

LUCK + TALENT = MONEY

Anthony Davis has moved in on Easy Street. In 1977, at the unbelievably young age of twenty-five, he owned a $200,000 home, $100,000 waterfront condominium, nine automobiles (including two Rolls-Royces and several collectors' items), land in California and Texas, and five closets of fashionable clothing. This wealth was not inherited, but accumulated through an incredible stroke of good fortune—the signing of three separate million-dollar contracts in three different football leagues in the span of eighteen months. Davis is financially ahead, by leaps and bounds, when others his age are only thinking of getting ahead. In fact, retired executives from our country's biggest corporations, a number of whom as youths heeded their mothers' advice and followed in the footsteps of Henry Ford and not Red Grange, are not living as handsomely as Anthony Davis.

"Secure for life? I'm almost there. If something came up where it was push to shove, I wouldn't just crumble," said Davis. "Nobody in football has done what I have done financially, for being such a young ball player. It would take someone like O. J. Simpson seven or eight years to have what I have. I'm one of the luckiest young athletes walking."

Only Anthony Davis doesn't walk much anymore. He rides. His home is in Villa Park, ten minutes from Newport Beach, California, and two hours from his condominium in Pacific Palisades, near Malibu, a retreat for artists and actors. Davis mixes with these types between football seasons, since he is also a fashion model and Hollywood bit player. "When do you want to do the interview?" Davis said by phone from one of his Rolls-Royces, speaking long distance from somewhere on a Southern California freeway. "I'll be home in about forty minutes." The good life is his, and the natural assumption would be that even a size ten Tampa Bay football helmet would be too small for Davis' expanding head.

"Not really, and you know why?" said Davis, back home in Villa Park, speaking above the barking of his three Doberman pinschers. "I've been shot at three times and stabbed once. I know what it is not to have anything and then to have something. Damn, I could be six feet under." Davis was raised in Pacoima (population 40,000), twenty-five miles north of Los Angeles in the San Fernando Valley. "Pacoima is stone ghetto, a baby Watts," Davis emphasized. "We had two riots when I went to San Fernando High School. One day, I was walking through the crowd and the confusion when a guy with a big blade stabbed me. Luckily, I saw him coming down with it and he only caught my forearm, about an inch deep. Another time, someone came at me with a trash can. I blocked him and the next thing I knew, I heard this shot. I turned around and the bullet had hit the wall behind me. The guy took off. I've had nightmares since about that incident. I've been shot at two other times, once on a canyon road and another time at a drive-in, but never hit. There are kids I grew up with who are in jail, on dope, or dead. I don't like it when people tell me, 'A. D., you're ego-tripping.' People talk about awards, the Heisman Trophy. It didn't bother me when Archie Griffin won the Heisman Trophy. Getting to USC was the Heisman Trophy for me."

Davis' father left home when Anthony was twelve, leaving his mother to care for two boys and three girls. "I've raised myself since I was sixteen," said Anthony. "I upholstered cars on weekends and boxed groceries at a market, to help out my mother, while playing ball and going to high school. I mean, if you had told people in my area ten years ago that Anthony Davis would be where he is today, they'd have said you were crazy, man. I was the smallest kid in the neighborhood. But I already had my goals made out when I was fifteen. I wanted to go to a major university, to graduate, and to become a professional ball player."

Someone once said, in describing an undersized NFL star, that "it's not the size of the dog in the fight, but the size of the fight in the dog." This could easily describe Davis, who was talked into turning out for varsity football, as a 5'6", 135-pound, high school sophomore. "I was more interested in baseball, but the football coach knew I had a strong arm and thought I could be a quarterback. I only turned out because I thought it would be a kick to be on the varsity," he remembered. "Our regular quarterback, Harvey Snead, was hurt early in the season, and they called on me, a tenth-grader. I carried my team to the playoffs."

That started the football, and Davis' gridiron career, rolling. He was an outstanding high school quarterback, but his skills were more evident as a runner than a passer, and USC wanted him as a tailback. And since USC is a citadel for tailbacks, how could Davis say no?

"A. D. had the hardest time adjusting at first," said John McKay, then the Trojans' head coach. "He was fumbling the ball for a long time"

Davis recalls that painful conversion process his first year. "Instead of being a quarterback handing off, I was now taking handoffs from quarterbacks. I had never taken one in high school. I didn't even think I would play as a sophomore. If you asked me as a freshman, I thought I would, if anything, play professional baseball, not football." Davis twice was drafted by the Baltimore Orioles and once by the Minnesota Twins, and might have chosen baseball except for the coming of spring in his freshman year. "We put A.D. through a tough spring practice, probably the toughest I ever had at USC," said McKay. "He was absolutely phenomenal. He didn't make any long runs, but he showed he could take the beating. I don't think there ever was any question that he was the best runner. But Rod McNeill was the starting tailback going into the 1972 season, and we didn't want to change things. Then McNeill went down, and we started Davis."

That wasn't until the ninth game of the season, against Washington State. Up until that point, Davis had played strictly as a substitute. But the week before, on a rainy day at the University of Oregon, he came on in the third quarter after a scoreless first half. He scored on 48 and 55 yard runs, and finished with 206 yards rushing. USC won 18–0.

After the Oregon game, Davis had carried 105 times for 562 yards and eight touchdowns—as a reserve. He rushed for 195 yards and three more touchdowns against Washington State, but the best was yet to come.

Notre Dame and USC have staged some of the country's best college football intersectional games since the days of Knute Rockne and Howard Jones. Anthony Davis put on the greatest one-man performance in the history of this rivalry, when he scored six touchdowns on December 2, 1972. He opened the game with a 97 yard kickoff return, then scored on runs of 1 and 5 yards, to give USC a 19–10 halftime lead. Davis' fourth touchdown was a 4-yard burst, but Notre Dame soon narrowed the Trojans' lead to 25–23. Davis then broke off another kickoff return of 96 yards to finish the Irish, adding his sixth touchdown on an 8-yard run. USC won going away, 45–23. "I have three accelerations," Davis told an astounded press after the game. "One acceleration is when I get the ball, one when I get to the line, and one when I get to the open. But never in my wildest dreams did I anticipate a game like this."

Davis rushed for 1,191 yards and scored nineteen touchdowns that year, to become the only USC sophomore ever to gain 1,000 yards. Even more phenomenally, 629 of those yards and eleven of the touchdowns came in his last four games, including the Rose Bowl.

"A. D. has a thing about running with the football, kind of like Tony Dorsett," said McKay. "He runs like Dorsett. A. D. always did a good job against Notre Dame. He's not too big, but he's quick, and this kind of player bothers Notre Dame." Davis, now grown to 5′ 9″, 190 pounds, set a school record with his thirty-six points against the Irish. "That game plus my first game against Oregon and our 55–24 win over Notre Dame my senior year, are the games I remember most from college," said Davis.

By the time this once too-small high school quarterback was finished at USC, he would be the all-time Trojan leading rusher, ahead of such standouts as Mort Kaer (the school's first all-America, in 1926), Russ Saunders, Orv Mohler, Frank Gifford, Mike Garrett, O. J. Simpson (who only played two years), Clarence Davis, and Ricky Bell. Davis' career totals of 784 carries, 3,724 yards, fifty-two touchdowns, and three 1,000-yard seasons set school and conference records. His six kickoff returns for touchdowns established an NCAA record. He was an all-America in 1974, and a runner-up in the Heisman Trophy balloting to Griffin that year.

The 1972 Trojans "had the best offensive people I have ever played with—college or pro," said Davis. More than that, the 1972 USC team may have been the greatest team to play in a Rose Bowl, and college football as well. "I believe it was the greatest college team that was ever put together," said McKay. "It had all the facets you need to have a great football team." Like talent and depth.

The quarterbacks were Mike Rae and Pat Haden; Davis and Sam Cunningham were the running backs; Lynn Swann, Edesel Garrison and John McKay Jr. the wide receivers; and Charles Young the tight end. Pete Adams, Booker Brown and Steve Riley were offensive linemen; John Grant, James Sims, Jeff Winans, and Dale Mitchell defensive linemen; Richard Wood and Charles Anthony linebackers; and Charles Phillips, Artimus Parker, and Marvin Cobb defensive backs.

Young, Adams, Cunningham, Grant, and Wood made at least one first-team all-America. All of the above, plus backup tight end Jim Obradovich, fullback Manfred Moore, and tailback McNeill, later played professional football.

"Over the years, USC had been accused of not having much depth. But we had talent coming out of our ears in 1972," said McKay. "No one even made it close. Stanford got the closest (30–21), but they scored right at the end." USC scored 467 points in twelve games, or 38.9 a game. They allowed 134 points, or 11.1 per game. That figure probably would have been even lower, except for USC's dominant offense. The Trojans often scored quickly and in great numbers, after which McKay pulled his regulars. Several opponents picked up touchdowns at the ends of games, matching their regulars against USC's reserves.

The Trojans marched over Arkansas, 31–10; Oregon State, 51–6; Illinois, 55–20; Michigan State, 51–6; Stanford, 30–21; California, 42–14; Washington, 34–7; Oregon, 18–0; Washington State, 44–3; UCLA, 24–7; and Notre Dame, 45–23.

"You can't find an attack like the one we had," said Davis. "There was no way you could key on us. We exploded on teams. From the physical and yardage standpoints, we didn't have a close game. Not only was it a confident team, but the guys felt for one another. We lived together, socialized together . . . a real closeness. We didn't have just one leader. Everyone was a leader. Remember, USC was coming off two losing seasons, and the coaches were looking for leadership. They got it from a lot of guys."

Actually, the Trojans were 6–4–1 in both 1970 and 1971. At USC these are considered "losing" seasons. There was no way the Trojans could lose in 1972, and they didn't. Quarterback Rae set a USC single-season total offense record, of 2,001 yards.

"Rae passed for a good many yards (1,754) that year. We had two great quarterbacks in Rae and Haden, and great receivers," said McKay. "We always threw a lot more than people guessed. It's just that our tailbacks got so much publicity, that people forgot."

When Davis became a starter, the Trojan powerhouse was complete. He not only added points, but pizzazz. "One day, after a practice before the UCLA game, I did this knee dance and told one of our coaches, Wayne Fontes, that I would do it in the game. He started laughing," said Davis. "Well, I scored against the Bruins, and actually slipped to my knees in the end zone. I did the dance, even though I had forgotten about it. I walked into the sports information office the following Monday and the guys in there told me, 'A. D., you can't stop that dance now. It's nation-wide.' "

While USC was building an 11–0 record and a number one ranking, Ohio State had captured its fourth Big Ten championship in five years, with a 9–1 mark. The Buckeyes' one defeat was to Michigan State, 19–12.

An unheard of freshman, named Archie Griffin, had set a school record of 239 yards rushing against North Carolina, in his first varsity start. Fullback Harold "Champ" Henson led the nation in scoring with 120 points. Linebackers Randy Gradishar and Rick Middleton, cornerback Neal Colzie, tackles John Hicks and Kurt Schumacher, and Griffin eventually would be first-round NFL draft choices.

The Buckeyes, however, were pushed at times in defeating Iowa, 21–0; North Carolina, 29–14; California, 35–18; Illinois, 26–7; Indiana, 44–7; Wisconsin, 28–20; Minnesota, 27–19; Northwestern, 27–14; and Michigan, 14–11. Michigan's coach Bo Schembechler was in excellent position to defeat the Buckeyes, but, strangely, elected to go for a first down twice on fourth and short yardage inside the Buckeyes' 10-yard line, and failed each time. Two field goals would have sent the Wolverines to Pasadena in 1973, instead of the Buckeyes.

"We were talented, but Ohio State had a tremendous amount of talent themselves in some awfully fine football players," said McKay. "We thought we could run the ball on them, even though we were told we wouldn't be able to. But we felt at USC that if you couldn't run, you couldn't win. And we ran on them. We controlled the game. It was never very close." Not quite. For a little more than a half it was very close.

Charles Phillips recovered a first-quarter Griffin fumble at the Ohio State 38, and Davis' 19-yard run set up Rae's 10-yard touchdown pass to Swann. Rae's conversion kick made it 7–0. The Buckeyes' Brian Baschnagel returned the ensuing kickoff 39 yards, to his 44. Eight plays later, Randy Keith scored on a 1-yard plunge, and Blair Conway's PAT try made it 7–7 at halftime.

"You can't take two teams as good as we were and not expect a physical, hard-fought game," said Davis of the halftime tie. "Ohio State was worried about my six touchdowns against Notre Dame, and kicked away from me the whole game. We started breaking them down in the third quarter."

Ohio State started the second half by kicking short to Cunningham at the 28, and he returned it to his 43. Rae passed for 12 and 23 yards to Swann, and 14 yards to John McKay Jr., and USC was at the Ohio State 6-yard line. Cunningham dived over the pile from the 2, and USC led 14–7.

Conway's field goal from 21 yards narrowed the score to 14–10. Again the Buckeyes kicked short in order to avoid Davis, and USC had excellent field position at its 44. Rae threw a 24 yard pass to Swann on first down, moving the Trojans to the Buckeyes' 20. The dam was about to break.

"I broke through right tackle, even though the play was designed to hit outside," said Davis. "I just saw the hole and wiggled through. I was really running for a first down, but I saw the end zone and something came over me." Gradishar had a chance

USC running back Anthony Davis.

to stop Davis, but A. D. slipped free and escaped Colzie's goal-line tackle to make it 21–10.

Greg Hare's pass for Tim Holycross was deflected by USC's Eddie Johnson, and Phillips intercepted at his 20, returning 48 yards to the Buckeye 32. Davis shot through left guard for 19 yards, and Rae passed to Charles Young for 10 more. Cunningham, a 230-pound fullback, with fantastic human lift-off, hurtled over the Buckeyes from a yard out, and it was now 28–10. "It's pretty hard to stop 230 pounds coming down," said Davis.

The Trojans scored on their next two possessions, each time Cunningham carrying —or leaping—the final yards to set a modern Rose Bowl record of four touchdowns. (Neil Snow of Michigan had five in the 1902 game.)

John Bledsoe scored on a 5-yard run with forty-six seconds left, but Ohio State had been demolished, 42–17, before the largest crowd (106,869) in Rose Bowl history.

Ohio State coach Woody Hayes, like McKay, said USC was the greatest team he had ever seen, "because of their enormous balance. You can run on them some, but then they passed us out of the park."

The forty-two points were the most given up by an Ohio State team since Hayes became head coach in 1951. Ohio State moved the ball, largely on the ground, for 285 of its 366 yards. Griffin had ninety-five yards, in twenty carries. However, USC amassed 451 yards.

Cunningham was named Player of the Game, but USC had numerous stars. Davis rushed for 157 yards on twenty-three carries. Rae was fantastic, completing eighteen of twenty-five passes for 229 yards.

"Watching Ohio State on film," said Young, the 6' 4", 238-pound tight end, "all they could do is run. We didn't have just one attack. I caught six passes, Lynn caught six (for 108 yards). A. D. and Sam ran. Bring on Miami!" The Dolphins were about to win their first Super Bowl championship. It didn't matter to Young and the unbeatable Trojans. They were ready for anybody!

The 1973 Rose Bowl triumph clinched McKay's third unbeaten season at USC, and his third national championship. He added a fourth national title in 1974, a record for a college football coach.

Things did not go quite so well for Davis in the intervening months, after his fantastic sophomore year. Named the winner of the W. J. Voit Memorial Award, as the Pacific Coast's outstanding college player in 1972, Davis fell asleep at the wheel of a sports car in the wee hours of January 13, 1973, and crashed into a light pole. He partially severed his left Achilles tendon and punctured his right knee cap, besides cutting and bruising his chin, arms, and legs.

Davis was in surgery for ninety minutes, and a cast was placed on his left leg. He told the press later that he had been at a party, and was driving his brother's date home in his brother's car. "I just dozed off, and I can't remember the impact," he told the

John McKay, whose
Trojan teams have played
in eight Rose Bowls,
winning in 1963, '66, '70,
'73, and '75. They lost
in 1967, '69, and '74.

press two days later. Counted on to help the Trojans in baseball that spring, he appeared in only sixteen games after a late start, batting .346, as USC won the NCAA championship.

"I saw people turn their backs on me after the accident. They were the same people who had just been telling me I was the greatest," said Davis. "That's how life is. When you're up, you're up—when you're down, you're down. I had to prove some things to people and myself. So I kept moving and motivating."

Davis worked extremely hard in the off-season to prepare for his junior season, and came back "stronger than when I was a sophomore." He rushed for 1,112 yards and scored fifteen touchdowns, but began to hear accusations instead of accolades.

"People said I was through," he recalled, somewhat bitterly. "I just didn't have the same people around me. Manfred Moore is a good football player, but you can't ask a 185-pound fullback to block like a 230-pounder (Cunningham). Jim Obradovich is a good tight end, but you can't ask him to play like Charles Young, an all-America, and an all-pro his first year in the NFL."

If the difference wasn't noticeable to the Trojan fans, it certainly was to McKay and Hayes in the 1974 Rose Bowl game. The Trojans were 9–1–1 before Pasadena and the Buckeyes 9–0–1. Ohio State received the Big Ten's invitation after it tied Michigan, 10–10, to share the conference championship. Schembechler screamed in protest, but the decision remained. Ohio State, not hurt as much by graduation from 1972 as USC, and having improved its quarterbacking with Cornelius Greene, annihilated USC, 42–21, to gain revenge from the previous Rose Bowl.

Davis took solace by appearing in fifty-seven games for the Trojan baseball team in 1974, hitting six home runs, driving in forty-five runs, stealing thirteen bases and batting .273 as USC won its fourth straight NCAA championship. Davis later starred for a United States collegiate team, that toured through Japan. He closed out his USC football career with 1,421 yards rushing and eighteen touchdowns as a senior. Once again it was Ohio State and USC in the 1975 Rose Bowl and Davis had 67 yards rushing by halftime. An injury kept him from playing the second half, but USC pulled out the victory, 18–17, on Shelton Diggs' diving catch of Haden's two-point conversion pass.

"You are a helluva football player," an Ohio State assistant coach told Davis after the game. "You've been great for three years. I'm sorry that you got hurt." Davis thanked him, and after he had left, complained about Ohio State's "hitting me late."

Davis didn't play baseball his senior year. He was about to become the youngest member of pro football's bourgeoisie. The World Football League (WFL) came on the scene in 1974 and, with Harry Houdini as its commissioner, disappeared midway through the 1975 season, a get-rich quick experiment that turned into a get-lost-fast disaster. But during its short existence, "Wiffle," as the league was sometimes called, paid out astronomical sums of money to National Football League (NFL), or "Niffle," players, as well as college seniors, such as Anthony Davis.

The Southern California Sun gambled a bankroll on Davis—reportedly a five-year, two-million dollar contract—much to the consternation of the NFL New York Jets, who had drafted him in the second round. A. D. remembering his ghetto days in Pacoima, signed with the Sun on May 21, 1975. A Jets' spokesman said his team had made every effort to sign Davis, but knew it was overmatched. "It wasn't a matter of $20,000 or $50,000, but rather a sum around one million," said the spokesman.

Leaning against his new $38,000 Rolls-Royce, Davis said, "My roots are here, my home is here, my friends and my family, and my fans are here. The best situation was for me to stay here."

Davis' agent, Mike Trope, said the silver-blue Rolls was a "small part" of a "very substantial" bonus guaranteed his client by the Suns' principal owner, millionaire businessman Sam Battistone. "The front money of this contract was more substantial than the entire Jets' offer," added Trope. "If this club went under after one year, Anthony could go to New York with more money than he would have made in three years with the Jets."

Trope, then twenty-three, had graduated magna cum laude with a degree in history from USC in 1973, but by that time was full-speed into the sports agent business. His first client was Johnny Rodgers of Nebraska, the 1972 Heisman Trophy winner, who signed a multi-million dollar package with Montreal of the Canadian Football League. Trope also negotiated the WFL and NFL contracts of UCLA running backs James McAlister and Kermit Johnson, and USC tackle Booker Brown, and the NFL contract of California running back Chuck Muncie, before representing running backs Tony Dorsett of Pittsburgh, the 1976 Heisman winner, and Ricky Bell of USC.

Trope was asked by United Press International how he had become so successful an agent at a young age. "I believe in laying my cards on the table, and apparently that works," he replied. "That plus the fact that my track record has been good, and players want to do business with someone who is going to make the best deal for them. I'm a good strategist and a good negotiator. Actually, the lifespan of an agent is very short. The average agent lasts one and a half years, and there's a reason. I don't get involved with investing and managing monies. That's where other agents have gone wrong. That's where the player turns around and sues his agent."

Of the WFL's nouveau riche, no one player earned his money more than Anthony Davis, in 1975. He rushed for an even 1,200 yards (5.0 average per carry) and sixteen touchdowns, caught forty passes for 381 yards and a touchdown, threw a 51-yard touchdown pass, and returned a kickoff 80 yards for a score.

He was far and away the leading rusher and scorer when "Wiffle" waffled and went under, after the twelfth game of the twenty-game season. Even while the league was collapsing amidst unpaid bills and unfulfilled promises, Trope was at work again and secured for Davis another five-year, multi-million dollar contract with the Toronto Argonauts of the Canadian League.

The whole thing only depressed Sam Cvijanovich. Sam a short, stubby middle linebacker who had lasted less than a week with the San Francisco 49ers, hooked up with the Argonauts and was named CFL Rookie of the Year in 1974. Unhappy with the Argos' contract offer for 1975, Cvijanovich played out his option at a ten percent cut, meaning his salary came to $12,600, or roughly what Davis would earn in about one half of a football game. Cvijanovich said he couldn't have afforded to play for Toronto in 1975, had not the parents of teammate Ernie Carnegie provided free room and board. Cvijanovich was looking for a contract "in the high twenties," while the Argonauts' final offer was $24,000. "I have nothing against the guy," said Cvijanovich, referring to Davis, "but when they sign someone for a million dollars and then you look at the kind of money we're talking about, such a small sum, it makes you wonder. They throw money around like that and then tell you they can't give you an extra thousand dollars. It makes you feel left out."

Davis felt exactly the same way after watching the Toronto premiere of the movie "Two-Minute Warning." Davis had majored in speech with a drama minor at USC. "I was cast in 'Two-Minute Warning' because I was Anthony Davis the actor, not the football player," he said. The movie was filmed in the Los Angeles Coliseum, where Davis had his greatest moments as a USC football player. He played a member of an ineffective SWAT (Special Weapons and Tactics) squad, but uttered only one word, "Yo," during the movie. "I had a much larger speaking role, which I understand was kept in the version of that movie shown in foreign countries. I wasn't happy the way my part turned out."

Davis was even less happy with the Argonauts, after reporting for the 1976 season. Toronto finished last in the Eastern Conference, and Davis rushed 104 times for 417 yards (4.0). He complained in the press that he wasn't being used enough. Coach Russ Jackson countered that Davis wasn't giving his best. "I was mistreated in Canada along with my teammates," Davis said. "We were cheated because we didn't have qualified people coaching us. We took criticism for things that weren't our fault." Only Davis was able to correct his situation in a way that his teammates couldn't: he simply bought up his Argonauts' contract.

In the interim, John McKay had moved on from USC to become the head coach of the NFL Tampa Bay Buccaneers. One of McKay's first acts was to acquire the NFL negotiating rights to Davis from the Jets. On November 16, 1976, Davis picked up a pen and signed again.

"It's like going back to school," said Davis after renewing his relationship with McKay. "The man knows me and I know him, not just as coach and player, but as people. I don't want to say that I'll break O. J. Simpson's, or Jim Brown's, or Gale Sayers' rushing records. I just want to get a piece of the rock, to be one of the best running backs in the NFL. I know I'm going to get my bumps and bruises at Tampa for awhile, but my main goal as a player is to be a 'team man' and do the best I can to help make a winning situation. My main goal as a person is to keep a solid mind and to keep peace of mind."

Davis does this, he says, with a less glamorous life than one might expect from one so young, with so much in the bank. "People think I'm flamboyant with my cars and the way I dress," he said. "I'm a conservative person really. My clothes are not wild, but basically conservative. Remember, I'm a fashion model. When I dress, I like to feel like a solid component. People wonder why I have all those cars. What they don't realize is that I have some rare cars which are worth three to four times more than when they were built. Cadillac built 500 Fleetwoods in 1941, and I have two of them. I was offered $20,000 for one, but turned it down. I'm a very disciplined person in the off-season. I train with my dogs. Actually, I'm a very picky person."

Davis said he entered USC at 5' 8½", but in 1977 was 5' 10". He never has worried about his size, and wasn't worried entering the NFL. "Archie Griffin is 5' 9", but he's a 1,000-yard type runner," said Davis. "But a running back has to be like a machine. You can't cut him on and off and expect him to gain a thousand yards. Size has nothing to do with it. A guy 6' 2" can't do more than a guy 5' 10" built well."

THE 1977 GAME

The old coach, the famous old coach, a legend in his own time and that sort of thing, sat there at the piano bar of the Huntington Sheraton, your friendly hallowed headquarters hotel, and smiled as the skilled piano bar lady plunged into the musical comedy hit of the day, a song about female chests and bottoms from "A Chorus Line." He was having one heckuva time, and the young woman seated alongside with her husband wondered who this old gentleman was, who kept putting his hand on her knee.

The Rose Bowl in 1977.

One of the papers said at least 30,000 people had come West from Michigan to see this one. The Wolverines hadn't been to Pasadena in five years and there was a rush on plane reservations. A fellow crouched over the bar at the Huntington was pushing one hundred fifty dollar game tickets—ten times their original cost. He was sanguine, finally. Ohio State had been to the bowl with such repetitive frequency that scalping had become a back-burner art. How many people from Columbus could afford to travel West, year after year after year? But now there was fresh meat, fresh money, and mobs in maize and blue accessories, set to hail the victors valiant. Also, there were fresh hordes of media, because eight days after the Rose Bowl game between the Wolves and USC that new kid on the block, the Super Bowl, would be unfurled for the first time here in the big ballpark in Pasadena. Many writers and broadcasters would be covering a double-header.

Early on, several of the reportorial swarm noticed an obvious January parlay: USC and the Oakland Raiders. Hadn't Trojan coach John Robinson and Raider coach John Madden been great and good friends since the fifth grade at Our Lady of Perpetual

Help, just down the peninsula from San Francisco? Hadn't Robinson worked for Madden as an assistant coach in Oakland, before succeeding the impossibly successful John McKay at USC? Hadn't Robinson and Madden dreamed about back-to-back moments of glory here under the uncovered big top?

The joint jubilation would be only fitting for the poets of the sporting press. All one had had to do was take the Trojans and six, take the Raiders and give (to the Minnesota Vikings) maybe about five. It would all work out.

John Robinson had played for Oregon in the last fifteen seconds of the 1958 Rose Bowl. And now he had come back home—to USC, not Pasadena. In 1972–74 Robinson had been McKay's offensive coordinator at Troy, then shuffled up north to work for Madden. When McKay himself went to the professionals, the man who revered him returned, at age 41, to become head coach, and immediately lost his opening game to Missouri. Ten victories later he had all-America tailback Ricky Bell, improved quarterback Vince Evans, and a jackrabbit freshman runner, named Charles White, in the Rose Bowl. Not so coincidentally, he had USC rated by pollsters as the nation's number three team—behind Pittsburgh and Michigan.

Pitt was to play Georgia, in the Sugar Bowl, earlier in the day. If the top-ranked Panthers lost, it seemed obvious the winner of the Wolverine-Trojan game would end up with the number one designation, in the final poll. Robinson felt the Pitt outcome should be discarded out of hand, that the two best teams in the land were playing in Pasadena. His Michigan counterpart, Glenn E. Schembechler, whom they called Bo, firmly agreed.

Bo had been here twice before, twice a loser. His first Michigan team was dumped 10–3 by USC in 1970, in a game Schembechler missed because of an eleventh hour heart attack. Two years later, the rain ruined the Wolves' practice sessions, and Stanford prevailed in a 13–12 upset thriller. The Wolves had not been back since; Bo's old Buckeye boss, Woody Hayes, had turned the game into an annual round-trip. On the ground, of course.

The 1976 regular season began with the Wolverines rated number one, in the early polls. Had they not stumbled to Purdue in their ninth game, the Wolves would have come to Pasadena still rated the best, Pitt notwithstanding. But Hayes and Ohio State had been thrashed in the regular season finale, and there was succor in that. Now the "new" Bo would have his day, his first New Year's grandeur in Pasadena.

Those closest to him called Bo "new" because his demeanor had lightened following open heart surgery, in May of 1976. "He's just learned to appreciate life," said his biographer, Detroit columnist Joe Falls. "He's honest. He's funny. He's actually become a performer." He now stops working at 10, not 2. He was 47, and apparently finally aware life consisted of more than X's and O's. Why, in the days before the game, he was even joking with writers.

What, a newsman asked, would Bo do if he had to interview Woody Hayes. "By God, I'd make him sit still until I was through with him."

Schembechler had been much like Hayes for most of his coaching career. Bo had played for Woody at offensive tackle, at Miami of Ohio, later was a graduate assistant for Woody, and then was an assistant coach for Woody. After he took the Michigan job, it seemed that Bo could beat anybody in the Big Ten, except Woody.

The Schembechler teams, then, were not unlike the Hayes teams: passing was an afterthought. Build a powerful ground game, and set up the run with a run. Control the ball, and the clock, by moving on the ground, play after play after play. Wear down the opposing defense, by making it stay on the field. And, build a formidable defense. But most of all, stick it to 'em with the run.

In the 1976 season, the Wolves had truly stuck it to 'em. Their offense was awesome, at least on paper: first in the country in total offense, with 448.1 yards average per game; first in the country in rushing, with 362.5 yards average; first in the country in scoring, with 38.7 points; first in the country in rushing yards per carry, with 6.03; first in the country in total offense yards per play, with 6.49; *and* first in the country in yards per attempted pass, with 9.49.

What you had to understand on this pleasant New Year's in Pasadena was that

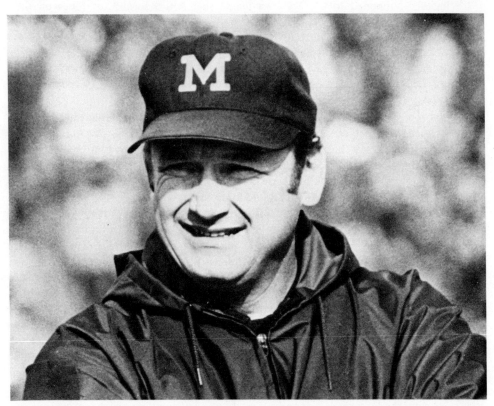

Michigan coach Bo Schembechler has had three teams in the Rose Bowl, all losers.

although the Wolverine passes may have averaged more than nine yards, they threw only nine passes a game. Only nine! In their bowl-clinching season finale victory over Ohio State, 22–0, at Columbus, Michigan quarterback Rick Leach threw only six times —and completed none. Leach, a left-handed, slightly bowlegged, highly intelligent sophomore and a perfect Schembechler protege, bristled when asked about this seeming lack of an aerial game. It had nothing to do with his passing ability, Leach said. It was merely the way Michigan played the game. If you did not have to pass to excell offensively, why bother?

This philosophy had filled the stadiums at Columbus and Ann Arbor, week after week, year after year. "It's not very exciting to watch a bunch of 6-yard runs, play after play," one Michigan fan observed to a visitor at the Huntington, "but as long as they win that way, you keep coming back to watch."

What happened to the Wolves at Rose Bowl 1977 certainly would not keep future crowds away from the Ann Arbor stadium. But the action here in Pasadena brought into rather resounding focus the balance of Michigan's offense, Michigan's coaching philosophy and, in the Wolverine wake, the thoroughness of Big Ten tactical football.

"Whatever happened to the Big Ten teams that could scratch matches on their beards?" wrote *Los Angeles Times* syndicated columnist Jim Murray. "What has happened? Aren't the coal mines working anymore? The steel mills shut down, are they? Who's doing the plowing back there? Surely, not these nice little fellows they keep sending out. These guys belong in the Ivy League, not the Big Ten. . . ."

For the want of a pass, a battle was lost. And a reputation with it.

Schembechler was talking to media locusts a few days before the besmirching: "It is a misconception for you writers out here to say that there is no passing in the Big Ten today. I would say that Michigan State passed for more than two hundred yards a game (under the influence of a coach fresh from San Jose, California, one Darryl Rogers). They pass a lot. So do several of the other teams. But it's a misconception because you guys always see Michigan and Ohio State, who are strong running teams, physical teams. But there are other teams in our league who pass. Now when we come out here to play you people, we don't see passing teams. You wouldn't call UCLA a year ago (which upset Woody in the Bowl) a passing team. You wouldn't call Southern California this year a passing team. The strength of their team is the power of their running attack, with a great back like Ricky Bell. In this league, the two best teams run the ball first. In our league, the two best teams run the ball first. That's how they get here. You don't get here with a pure passing attack very often."

F. Lee Bailey outlining his case to the jury in an opening statement. Subsequent testimony would prove this statement to be a sound, honest, sincere rationale.

Elsewhere in his remarks that day, Bo hedged. USC, he said, is a "better running team than anyone we've played, and they do have passing ability. Any team that gets 1700 yards passing, you've got to figure is a pretty good passing team. If you overcommit toward stopping their running game, you can get hurt by their passing. They have the balance that everyone would like to have."

Even Michigan.

Going into the game, USC's Bell needed to gain only fifty-two yards to become the all-time career rusher in the Pac-8. Those additional yards would make him the ruler of a running class, which included the names of Anthony Davis, O. J. Simpson, and Mike Garrett.

Before the 1976 season began, Bell was among the favorites to win the Heisman Trophy, as the athlete adjudged to be the finest collegian in the land. But back East, Pitt's Tony Dorsett caught fire, and Bell, who had been indestructible when he led the nation in rushing the year before, was hobbled by a hip pointer and sprained ankle. He sat out eight quarters in three different games, and played one full game in under-par condition. He finished second to Dorsett (as USC finished second to Pitt). And he did not complete the Rose Bowl.

Ricky carried immediately after Leach fumbled away the game-opening drive at the Trojan 42. Bell hit left tackle for 4, then left end for 2, then rested as his quarterback, Vince Evans, tossed a first down pass. But Bell was not finished: 4 through left tackle, 6 in a sweep to the left. And out. On that final sweep, Bell ran into two Michigan tacklers and staggered off the field in a sea of dizziness, with a mild concussion. He had 16 yards in four carries, and that would be all; a disappointing end to a season so filled with promise.

Rick was not the only all-America ground gainer in the game. The Wolves had their guy, too—sturdy Rob Lytle, who had averaged nearly seven yards a carry in 1976, and held most of the Michigan rushing records. He had scored thirteen touchdowns in the just-concluded season, and now would dive in from the 1 for the first TD in Pasadena, in 1977. The Wolves had moved fifty yards in twelve plays for the score; Lytle carried on eight of those plays, for 30 yards.

But Bob Wood's conversion attempt was blocked by Walt Underwood, and USC thus was able to take the lead shortly before the end of the half, 7–6, on Evans' little 1-yard rollout, on a fourth down play, and the PAT by Glen Walker, 24, perhaps the first former assistant prison supervisor (during his Army stint at Fort Leavenworth) ever to play in a Rose Bowl game. Or, at least the first in 1977.

Bell's caddy, the freshman White, 18, had been as impressive in the Trojan 80-yard touchdown march as Lytle looked in the Wolverine scoring drive. He was following in the footsteps of another San Fernando Valley football star, Anthony Davis. And now he was to fulfill the legacy of A. D. at USC. "He's like Davis," said Coach Robinson. "He improves each week. He never makes the same mistake twice."

White said afterwards that he was "scared" at having to replace Bell on such a prestigious occasion. "But only the first time I carried the ball," Charles said. "After I got hit, I settled down."

On the USC go-ahead drive, Charles carried on eight of the twelve Trojan plays, for 35 yards. His running under that pressure—and through the nation's tenth ranked defensive team—was admirable. But the big play in the drive was a 20-yard pass by Evans, to wide receiver Shelton Diggs. At day's end, Diggs had caught eight passes for 98 yards, an individual effort surpassing the entire Michigan passing game.

The numbers at halftime provided the tipoff. Michigan had a rush-pass yardage imbalance of 125–12; USC's figures were 104–62. Certainly, the game was close, only 7–6 Trojans, but Leach's feeble attempts at passing in that first half would be a harbinger.

The southpaw sophomore had thrown once (incomplete) in the first quarter. He did not throw again until the waning moments of the second period—at a time when it seemed more judicious merely to run out the clock around the Wolverine 30. Schembechler and/or Leach had picked a peculiar time not to carry out their program of disdaining the forward pass. Rick did hit one for 12 yards, but missed on a couple of others. At halftime he was one for four. Storm warning.

In the scoreless third quarter, the Trojans set their defense to stop the obvious: the run. Lytle had gained 60 yards in the first half and netted only nine in the final thirty minutes. It was as though the Trojans were daring Leach to throw. He did, three times (with one completion), in the third quarter.

USC blew a chance to score early in the quarter after Lytle fumbled on his own 9: White fumbled right back on the next play.

In the final quarter's first minutes, Leach twice tried to sustain a drive with passes. Once he was forced to run instead and lost two. The second time he was sacked and lost ten. The Wolves immediately had to punt to the USC 42, and Trojans came downfield on the running of Mosi Tatupu (30 yards in two carries, on the drive) and White (21 yards in five rushes, the last for a 7-yard TD), and the passing of Evans (a 27 yarder to Randy Simmrin).

As the game progressed, Evans became the story. He was named the afternoon's outstanding player—the seventeenth Trojan to win that accolade at the Rose Bowl, the ninth USC quarterback so honored. One year earlier there was doubt if Evans would even be USC's regular quarterback in 1976.

After the 1975 season—after a season in which Vincent Tobias Evans had a sickly thirty-one percent pass completion non-record, after a season in which he threw four times as many interceptions as touchdowns, after a season in which he threw fourteen consecutive incompletions in the biggie against UCLA—USC fans whipped out a new bumper sticker reading: "Save USC Football. Shoot Vince Evans."

He had come to Troy via Greensboro, North Carolina, and Los Angeles City College. The offenses he had conducted there did not require him to throw forward passes with great frequency or to operate a Power-I formation. In high school, in fact, Vince had been the tailback in a single-wing. Evans was thus uneasy when he assumed the quarterback's job at USC; this uneasiness translated into passing uncertainty. Finally, in a late 1975 game, he was benched by the Trojans. There was talk of moving him to a flanker spot. But then there was the coming of Robinson, which meant the arrival of assistant coach Paul Hackett, who had schooled quarterbacks Steve Bartkowski and Joe Roth at the University of California, up in Berkeley.

"Hackett did not coddle Evans," wrote John Underwood in *Sports Illustrated.* "In the weeks and months that followed, he tempered daily doses of expertise and encouragement with the solemn facts of life at the top. 'If you screw up, you're out,' he told Evans."

Evans did not screw up.

In the opener, in the loss to upstart Missouri, which also beat Ohio State and Nebraska in 1976, Evans was ten for eighteen. Two games later, in a victory over Michigan's conqueror, Purdue, Vince hit thirteen of sixteen, and probably wondered whatever had become of the writer who in 1975 said, "Evans couldn't throw a football into the Grand Canyon, while standing at the rim."

In the Bowl-clinching battle against UCLA, Vince passed only thirteen times (seven completions), and ran fourteen.

He wound up at Pasadena with fourteen completions in twenty attempts, and 181 passing yards.

"He is very much underestimated," said Schembechler, without saying who was responsible for the underestimation. "I think if you really look at it," continued Bo at the post-mortem, "it came down to Evans. He is so strong, he can roll one way and throw back with strength and accuracy the other way. He made the plays."

Wolverine defensive tackle Greg Morton, twice all-Big Ten and an exemplary sacker, had chased Vince—or tried to—much of the afternoon. "It was like there was grease on him," said Morton. "he's just so quick."

Vince allowed as how it was a nice way to end his collegiate career. "It was a boyhood dream," he said, "to play at USC and play in the Rose Bowl. I'll treasure this moment the rest of my life."

His Michigan counterpart, Leach, had little to treasure. Almost, though.

After SC had made it 14–6, there remained three minutes and three seconds to play. Now—without any question—it was time to pass.

From his own 33 on first down, Rick hit Jim Smith for 32 yards. The Wolves were on the Trojan 35; there was time for a TD and two-point conversion. Time for a face-saving tie.

Leach threw to Gene Johnson for twelve, but his next pass went incomplete. A quarterback keeper moved the ball to the USC 17. Leach aimed for Curt Stephenson on the sideline, and overthrew. Fourth down. Leach targeted Lytle in the end zone. And overthrew badly. Rick's passing stats for the game: four of twelve for 76 yards.

"I think if I'd thrown more during the year, I could have been more effective today,"

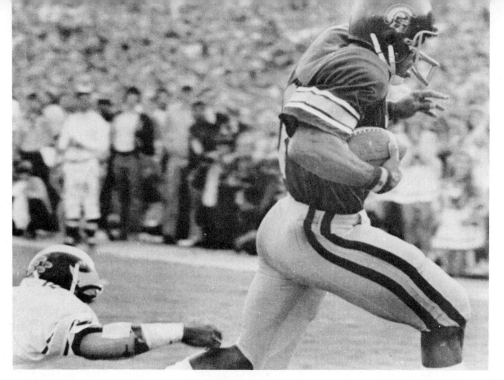

USC quarterback Vince Evans, named Player of the Game, rushes for yardage during the Trojans' 14-6 win over Michigan.

said Leach. "But all year long our offensive line did such a great job that we never needed to pass."

Charles White finished with only thirty-three less rushing yards than the entire Michigan ground attack (122–155). The Trojan defense had held Michigan to 217 yards below the Wolves' per game average.

"I don't know where we ranked in defense this past season," said a USC publicist. "I know we weren't in the top fifteen. We're down there somewhere in the NCAA computer."

Coach Robinson called the game the most exciting and physical he'd ever seen. "I believe we wore them down," he said. "We simply tried to run at them and mix it up with passes."

The right mix.

Schembechler said the Trojans should be ranked number one. Less than one week after the game he was ready to hire an assistant coach to help Michigan develop a passing attack. "I don't think there's any question that we have to improve our passing," he said.

Rose Bowl 1977 gave the Pac-8 seven wins in its last eight Pasadena gatherings with the Big Ten. In those eight games, five different West Coast quarterbacks had been named the day's outstanding player.

One certainly couldn't accuse the Big Ten of throwing the Rose Bowl.

TOURNAMENT FACTS

YEAR	PRESIDENT	GRAND MARSHAL	QUEEN	THEME	SWEEPSTAKES WINNER
1890	Prof. Charles F. Holder	Dr. Francis F. Rowland			Charles Daggett Rig
1891	B. Marshall Wolkyns				George H. Rogers Carriage
1892	Frank C. Bolt	Dr. Francis F. Rowland			W. C. Stewart's Pony and Cart
1893	Frank C. Bolt				Raymond Hotel
1894	Charles Daggett	Dr. Francis F. Rowland			Columbia Hill Tennis Club
1895	Charles Daggett	Dr. H. H. Sherk			The Spalding House
1896	Edwin Stearns	Edwin Stearns			Knights of the Maccabees
1897	Edwin Stearns	Edwin Stearns			Taylor's Choral Society
1898	Martin H. Weight	Martin H. Weight			YMCA
1899	Martin H. Weight	Martin H. Weight			Pasadena High School
1900	Herman Hertel	Charles Daggett			Pasadena Chamber of Commerce
1901	F. B. Weatherby	Charles Daggett			Wilson School
1902	James B. Wagner	†C. C. Reynolds			Pasadena Hook and Ladder Co.
1903	Charles Coleman	C. C. Reynolds			Hotel Green
1904	Charles Daggett	Dr. Francis F. Rowland			Hotel Maryland
1905	Charles Daggett	Dr. Francis F. Rowland	Hallie Woods		Ocean Park
1906	Edwin D. Neff	John B. Miller	Elsie Armitage		Pasadena High School

Chariot racing at the 1907 Tournament of Roses. There was no football that day, but there was competition in tent-pegging and bronco busting.

YEAR	PRESIDENT	GRAND MARSHAL	QUEEN	THEME	SWEEPSTAKES WINNER
1907	Edward T. Off	Dr. H. P. Skillen	Joan H. Woodbury		Pasadena High School
1908	George P. Cary	Dr. H. P. Skillen	May Sutton		Redondo
1909	George P. Cary	Walter S. Wright			Pasadena Realty Board
1910	George P. Cary	Dr. Francis F. Rowland			Hotel Maryland
1911	Frank G. Hogan	Dr. Ralph Skillen	Ruth Palmer		Azusa
1912	Edward T. Off	E. H. Groenendyke			Pasadena High School
1913	Edward T. Off	Leigh Guyer	Jean P. French		Los Angeles Chamber of Commerce
1914	R. D. Davis	Charles Daggett	Mabel Seibert		Mrs. Anita Baldwin McClaughry
1915	John B. Coulston	M. S. Pashgian			Los Angeles Chamber of Commerce
1916	Lewis H. Turner	Dr. Francis F. Rowland			Santa Monica
1917	D. M. Linnard	Dr. C. D. Lockwood			Eagle Rock
1918	B. O. Kendall	Dr. Z. T. Malaby		Patriotism	South Pasadena
1919	B. O. Kendall	Frank Hunter		Victory Tournament	Long Beach
1920	William L. Leishman	Frank G. Hogan			Glendale
1921	William L. Leishman	W. A. Boucher			Glendale
1922	John J. Mitchell	Harold Landreth			Portland (Oregon)
1923	John J. Mitchell	H. L. Gianetti	May McAvoy		Glendale
1924	W. F. Creller	Col. George S. Parker			†Glendale
1925	W. F. Creller	Lewis H. Turner	Margaret Scoville		Angelus Temple
1926	Harry M. Ticknor	Col. L. J. Mygatt	Fay Lanphier		Long Beach
1927	Harry M. Ticknor	Dr. C. D. Lockwood		Songs in Flowers	Beverly Hills
1928	Harry M. Ticknor	John McDonald	Harriet Sterling	States and Nations in Flowers	Beverly Hills
1929	Leslie B. Henry	Marco Hellman		Poems in Flowers	Glendale
1930	C. Hal Reynolds	James Rolph	Holly Halsted	Festival Days in Flowers	Beverly Hills
1931	C. Hal Reynolds	Gen. C. S. Farnsworth	Mary Lou Waddell	Dreams in Flowers	Glendale
1932	D. E. McDaneld	William May Garland	Myrta Olmsted	Nations and Games in Flowers	San Marino
1933	D. E. McDaneld	Mary Pickford	Dorothy Edwards	Fairyland: Fairy Tales in Flowers	Glendale
1934	George S. Parker	Adm. William S. Sims	Treva Scott	Tales of the Seven Seas	Long Beach
1935	C. Elmer Anderson	Harold Lloyd	Muriel Cowan	Golden Legends	Santa Barbara
1936	C. Elmer Anderson	James V. Allred	Barbara Nichols	History in Flowers	South Pasadena
1937	Cyril Bennett	Eugene Biscailuz	Nancy Bumpus	Romance in Flowers	Santa Barbara
1938	George S. Campbell	Leo Carrillo	Cheryl Walker	Playland Fantasies	Burbank City Schools
1939	Lathrop K. Leishman	Shirley Temple	Barbara Dougall	Golden Memories in Flowers	Burbank
1940	Harlan G. Loud	Edgar Bergen & Charlie	Margaret Huntley	Twentieth Century in Flowers	Santa Barbara
1941	J. W. McCall, Jr.	E. O. Nay	Sally Stanton	America in Flowers	Glendale
1942	Robert M. McCurdy	Kay Kayser	Dolores Brubach	The Americas	*
1943	James K. Ingham	Earl Warren	Mildred Miller	We're In to Win	*
1944	Frank M. Brooks	Alonzo Stagg	Naomi Riordan	Memories of the Past	*
1945	Max H. Turner	Herbert Hoover	Mary Rutte	Hold a Victory So Hardly Won	*
1946	Charles A. Strutt	Adm. William Halsey	Patricia Auman	Victory, Unity and Peace in Flowers	Long Beach
1947	William P. Welsh	Bob Hope	Norma Christopher	Holidays in Flowers	Glendale
1948	Louis R. Vincenti	Gen. Omar Bradley	Virginia Goodhue	Our Golden West	San Francisco
1949	Harold C. Schaffer	Perry Brown	Virginia Bower	Childhood Memories	Long Beach
1950	Drummond J. McCunn	Paul G. Hoffman	Marion Brown	Our American Heritage	Long Beach
1951	L. Clifford Kenworthy	Cpl. Robert S. Gray	Eleanor Payne	Joyful Living	Monterey Park
1952	Leon Kingsley	Medal of Honor Men	Nancy True Thorne	Dreams of the Future	Southern Calif. Floral Association
1953	William H. Nicholas	Richard M. Nixon	Leah Feland	Melodies in Flowers	Glendale
1954	Harry W. Hurry	Gen. William F. Dean	Barbara Schmidt	Famous Books in Flowers	Long Beach
1955	Elmer M. Wilson	Earl Warren	Marilyn Smuin	Familiar Sayings in Flowers	Long Beach
1956	Dr. Alfred L. Gerrie	Charles E. Wilson	Joan Culver	Pages From the Ages	Burbank
1957	John S. Davidson	Eddie Rickenbacker	Ann Mossberg	Famous Firsts in Flowers	Indio
1958	John H. Biggar, Jr.	Robert Gordon Sproul	Gertrude Wood	Daydreams in Flowers	Burbank
1959	Stanley K. Brown	E. L. "Bob" Bartlett	Pamela Prather	Adventures in Flowers	Glendale
1960	Raymond A. Dorn	Richard M. Nixon	Margarethe Bertelson	Tall Tales and True	Long Beach
1961	Arthur W. Althouse	William F. Quinn	Carole Washburn	Ballads in Blossoms	Burbank
1962	H. Burton Noble	Albert D. Rosellini	Martha Sissell	Around the World With Flowers	San Diego
1963	Stanley L. Hahn	Dr. William H. Pickering	Nancy Davis	Memorable Moments	Santa Monica
1964	Hilles M. Bedell	Dwight D. Eisenhower	Nancy Kneeland	Symbols of Freedom	Long Beach
1965	Walter R. Hoefflin, Jr.	Arnold Palmer	Dawn Baker	Headlines in Flowers	Lakewood
1966	J. Randolph Richards	Walt Disney	Carole Cota	It's a Small World	Montana
1967	Henry Kearns	Thanat Khoman	Barbara Hewitt	Travel Tales in Flowers	South Pasadena
1968	H. W. Bragg	Everett Dirksen	Linda Strother	Wonderful World of Adventure	Lakewood
1969	G. L. "Tige" Payne	Bob Hope	Pamela Anicich	A Time to Remember	City of Los Angeles
1970	G. Lewis Edwards	Charles Conrad, Jr.	Pamela Tedesco	Holidays Around The World	City of Los Angeles
		Alan L. Bean	Kathy Arnett	Thru The Eyes Of A Child	Georgia
		Richard F. Gordon, Jr.	Margo Lynn Johnson	The Joy of Music	Glendale
1971	A. Lewis Shingler	Rev. Billy Graham	Salli Noren	Movie Memories	Lakewood
1972	Virgil White	Lawrence Welk	Miranda Barone	Happiness Is . . .	St. Louis
1973	Otis Blasingham	John Wayne	Robin Carr	Heritage of America	Georgia
1974	Edward Wilson	Charles Schulz	Anne Martin	America, Let's Celebrate	CUNA (Credit Union)
1975	Paul G. Bryan	Hank Aaron	Diane Ramaker	The Good Life	Glendale
1976	Ralph Helpbringer	Kate Smith			
1977	Carl E. Wopschall	Roy Rogers & Dale Evans			

†First Official Designation   *No Parade

ROSEBOWL FOOTBALL

YEAR	WINNING TEAM		LOSING TEAM		WESTERN COACH	EASTERN COACH	PLAYER OF THE GAME
1890	Tilting at the Rings, Foot Races, Pony Races, Burro Races						
1891	Tilting at the Rings, Pony Races, Donkey Races, Foot Races						
1892	Tilting at the Rings, Pony Races, Donkey Races, Steeplechase, Bicycle Races						
1893	Novelty Horse Races, Donkey Races, Pony Races						
1894	Ranchman's Horse Races, Bicycle Races, Pony Races, Egg-and-Spoon Race, Donkey Race, Steeplechase						
1895	Crown City Cycle Club Races						
1896	Amateur Bicycle Races						
1897	Bicycle Races (Professional and Amateur)						
1898	Bicycle Races, Wheelbarrow Race, Sack Race, Obstacle Race						
1899	No Sports						
1900	Amateur Horse Races, Bronco Races, Egg-and-Spoon Race, Umbrella Race, Dressing Race, Lasso Contest						
1901	Polo (Riverside 4, Santa Barbara 1), Greased Pig Race, Greased Pole Climbing						
1902	Michigan	49	Stanford	0	Charley Fickert	Fielding Yost	Neil Snow (Michigan)
1903	Polo (Riverside 3, Southern California All-Stars 2)						
1904	Chariot Racing (1. Mac Wiggins; 2. Ed T. Off) Automobile Speed Exhibition, Egg-and-Spoon Race						
1905	Chariot Racing (1. P. B. Michel; 2. Mac Wiggins)						
1906	Chariot Racing (1. C. C. West; 2. Mac Wiggins), Polo Pony Races						
1907	Chariot Racing (1. P. B. Michel; 2. Mac Wiggins), Bronco Busting, Tent Pegging						
1908	Chariot Racing (1. C. C. West; 2. P. B. Michel)						
1909	Chariot Racing (1. C. C. West; 2. E. Hogaboom), Marathon Race Finish						
1910	Chariot Racing (1. Revel English; 2. E. J. Levengood), Balloon Ascension						
1911	Chariot Racing (1. C. E. Post; 2 E. J. Levengood)						
1912	Chariot Racing (1. Ed Cornell; 2. E. J. Levengood)						
1913	Chariot Racing (1. Mac Wiggins and Albert Persons), Ostrich Race, Cowboy Race						
1914	Chariot Racing (1. E. J. Levengood and Elmer Dooley), Track and Field Meet						
1915	Chariot Racing (1. E. J. Levengood and Frank Lathrop), Track and Field Meet						
1916	Washington State	14	Brown	0	W. H. "Lone Star" Dietz	E. N. Robinson	Carl Dietz (Washington State)
1917	Oregon	14	Pennsylvania	0	Hugo Bezdek	Bob Folwell	John Beckett (Oregon)
1918	Mare Island Marines	19	Camp Lewis	7	Hugo Bezdek	W. L. "Fox" Stanton	Hollis Huntington (Mare Island)
1919	Great Lakes Navy	17	Mare Island Marines	0	W. H. "Lone Star" Dietz	Lt. Clarence J. McReavy	George Halas (Great Lakes)
1920	Harvard	7	Oregon	6	Shy Huntington	Bob Fisher	Eddie Casey (Harvard)
1921	California	28	Ohio State	0	Andy Smith	J. W. Wilce	Harold "Brick" Muller (California)
1922	*California	0	*Washington & Jefferson	0	Andy Smith	"Greasy" Neale	Russ Stein (W. & J.)
1923	U.S.C.	14	Penn State	3	Elmer Henderson	Hugo Bezdek	Leo Calland (U.S.C.)
1924	*Washington	14	*Navy	14	Enoch Bagshaw	Bob Folwell	Ira McKee (Navy)
1925	Notre Dame	27	Stanford	10	"Pop" Warner	Knute Rockne	E. Layden (N.D.), E. Nevers (S)
1926	Alabama	20	Washington	19	Enoch Bagshaw	Wallace Wade	John Mack Brown (Alabama)
1927	*Stanford	7	*Alabama	7	"Pop" Warner	Wallace Wade	Fred Pichard (Alabama)
1928	Stanford	7	Pittsburgh	6	"Pop" Warner	"Jock" Sutherland	Cliff Hoffman (Stanford)
1929	Georgia Tech	8	California	7	"Nibs" Price	Bill Alexander	Bennie Lom (California)
1930	U.S.C.	47	Pittsburgh	14	Howard Jones	"Jock" Sutherland	Russ Saunders (U.S.C.)
1931	Alabama	24	Washington State	0	"Babe" Hollingberry	Wallace Wade	John Campbell (Alabama)
1932	U.S.C.	21	Tulane	12	Howard Jones	Bernie Bierman	Ernie Pinckert (U.S.C.)
1933	U.S.C.	35	Pittsburgh	0	Howard Jones	"Jock" Sutherland	Homer Griffith (U.S.C.)
1934	Columbia	7	Stanford	0	"Tiny" Thornhill	Lou Little	Cliff Montgomery (Columbia)
1935	Alabama	29	Stanford	13	"Tiny" Thornhill	Frank Thomas	"Dixie" Howell (Alabama)
1936	Stanford	7	Southern Methodist	0	"Tiny" Thornhill	"Matty" Bell	Jim Moscrip, Keith Topping (S)
1937	Pittsburgh	21	Washington	0	Jimmy Phelan	"Jock" Sutherland	Bill Daddio (Pittsburgh)
1938	California	13	Alabama	0	"Stub" Allison	Frank Thomas	Vic Bottari (California)
1939	U.S.C.	7	Duke	3	Howard Jones	Wallace Wade	Doyle Nave, Al Krueger (U.S.C.)
1940	U.S.C.	14	Tennessee	0	Howard Jones	Bob Neyland	Ambrose Schindler (U.S.C.)
1941	Stanford	21	Nebraska	13	Clark Shaughnessy	"Biff" Jones	Pete Kmetovic (Stanford)
1942	†Oregon State	20	Duke	16	"Lon" Stiner	Wallace Wade	Don Durdan (Oregon State)
1943	Georgia	9	U.C.L.A.	0	"Babe" Horrell	Wally Butts	Charley Trippi (Georgia)
1944	U.S.C.	29	Washington	0	"Jeff" Cravath	"Pest" Welch	Norman Verry (U.S.C.)
1945	U.S.C.	25	Tennessee	0	"Jeff" Cravath	John Barnhill	Jim Hardy (U.S.C.)
1946	Alabama	34	U.S.C.	14	"Jeff" Cravath	Frank Thomas	Harry Gilmer (Alabama)
1947	Illinois	45	U.C.L.A.	14	Bert La Brucherie	Ray Eliot	Julie Rykovich, Buddy Young (Ill.)
1948	Michigan	49	U.S.C.	0	"Jeff" Cravath	"Fritz" Crisler	Bob Chappius (Michigan)
1949	Northwestern	20	California	14	"Pappy" Waldorf	Bob Voigts	Frank Aschenbrenner (Northwes'n)
1950	Ohio State	17	California	14	"Pappy" Waldorf	Wes Fesler	Fred Morrison (Ohio State)
1951	Michigan	14	California	6	"Pappy" Waldorf	Ben Oosterbaan	Don Dufek (Michigan)
1952	Illinois	40	Stanford	7	"Chuck" Taylor	Ray Eliot	Bill Tate (Illinois)
1953	U.S.C.	7	Wisconsin	0	Jess Hill	"Ivy" Williamson	Rudy Bukich (U.S.C.)
1954	Michigan State	28	U.C.L.A.	20	"Red" Sanders	"Biggie" Munn	Billy Wells (Michigan State)
1955	Ohio State	20	U.S.C.	7	Jess Hill	"Woody" Hayes	Dave Leggett (Ohio State)
1956	Michigan State	17	U.C.L.A.	14	"Red" Sanders	"Duffy" Daugherty	Walt Kowalczyk (Michigan State)
1957	Iowa	35	Oregon State	19	Tommy Prothro	Forest Evashevski	Kenneth Ploen (Iowa)
1958	Ohio State	10	Oregon	7	Len Casanova	"Woody" Hayes	Jack Crabtree (Oregon)
1959	Iowa	38	California	12	Pete Elliott	Forest Evashevski	Bob Jeter (Iowa)

TOURNAMENT FACTS

YEAR	WINNING TEAM		LOSING TEAM		WESTERN COACH	EASTERN COACH	PLAYER OF THE GAME
1960	Washington	44	Wisconsin	8	Jim Owens	Milt Bruhn	Bob Schloredt, G. Fleming (Wash.)
1961	Washington	17	Minnesota	7	Jim Owens	Murray Warmath	Bob Schloredt (Washington)
1962	Minnesota	21	U.C.L.A.	3	Bill Barnes	Murray Warmath	Sandy Stevens (Minnesota)
1963	U.S.C.	42	Wisconsin	37	John McKay	Milt Bruhn	Vanderkelen (W.), Beathard (U.S.C.)
1964	Illinois	17	Washington	7	Jim Owens	Pete Elliott	Jim Grabowski (Ill.)
1965	Michigan	34	Oregon State	7	Tommy Prothro	Chalmeirs "Bump" Elliott	Mel Anthony (Michigan)
1966	U.C.L.A.	14	Michigan State	12	Tommy Prothro	"Duffy" Daugherty	Bob Stiles (U.C.L.A.)
1967	Purdue	14	U.S.C.	13	John McKay	Jack Mollenkopf	John Charles (Purdue)
1968	U.S.C.	14	Indiana	3	John McKay	John Pont	O. J. Simpson (U.S.C.)
1969	Ohio State	27	U.S.C.	16	John McKay	Woody Hayes	Rex Kern (Ohio)
1970	U.S.C.	10	Michigan	3	John McKay	Glenn Schembechler	Bob Chandler (U.S.C.)
1971	Stanford	27	Ohio State	17	John Ralston	Woody Hayes	Jim Plunkett (Stanford)
1972	Stanford	13	Michigan	12	John Ralston	Glenn Schembechler	Don Bunce (Stanford)
1973	U.S.C.	42	Ohio State	17	John McKay	Woody Hayes	Sam Cunningham (U.S.C.)
1974	Ohio State	42	U.S.C.	21	John McKay	Woody Hayes	Cornelius Green (Ohio)
1975	U.S.C.	18	Ohio State	17	John McKay	Woody Hayes	Pat Haden (U.S.C.) & John McKay Jr. (U.S.C.)
1976	U.C.L.A.	23	Ohio State	10	Dick Vermeil	Woody Hayes	John Sciarra (U.C.L.A.)
1977	U.S.C.	14	Michigan	6	John Robinson	Glenn Schembechler	Vince Evans (U.S.C.)

*Tie Games
†Played at Duke University, Durham, N.C.

ROSEBOWL FOOTBALL

THE LINE SCORES

1902

(Four-quarter system not adopted until 1910)

Michigan	17	32——49
Stanford	0	0—— 0

*Michigan scoring: Touchdowns, Snow (5), Redden (2), Herrnstein. PAT,
Sweeley (4). Field goal, Sweeley
*(Touchdowns counted as five points, field goals as five, and conversions as one.)

1916

Brown	0	0	0	0—— 0
Washington State	0	0	7	7——14

Washington State scoring: Touchdowns, Boone, Dietz. PAT, Durham (2).

1917

Oregon	0	0	7	7——14
Pennsylvania	0	0	0	0—— 0

Oregon scoring: Touchdowns, Tegert, S. Huntington. PAT, S. Huntington (2).

1918

Mare Island Marines	0	9	0	10——19
Camp Lewis Army	0	7	0	0—— 7

Mare Island scoring: Touchdowns, Brown, Huntington. PAT, Ambrose. Field goals, Ambrose (2).

Camp Lewis scoring: Touchdown, Romney. PAT, McKay.

1919

Great Lakes Navy	3	7	7	0——17
Mare Island Marines	0	0	0	0—— 0

Great Lakes scoring: Touchdowns, Reeves, Halas. PAT, Blacklock (2). Field goal, Driscoll.

1920

Harvard	0	7	0	0——7
Oregon	0	6	0	0——6

Harvard scoring: Touchdowns, Church. PAT, Horween.
Oregon scoring: Field goals, Steers, Manerud.

1921

California	7	14	0	7——28
Ohio State	0	0	0	0—— 0

California scoring: Touchdowns, Sprott (2), Stephens, Deeds.
PAT, Toomey (3), Erb.

1922

California	0	0	0	0——0
Washington and Jefferson	0	0	0	0——0

1923

USC	0	7	7	0——14
Penn State	3	0	0	0—— 3

USC scoring: Touchdowns, Campbell, Baker. PAT, Hawkins (2).
Penn State scoring: Field goal, Palm.

1924

Navy	0	14	0	0——14
Washington	0	7	0	7——14

Navy scoring: Collen, McKee. PAT, McKee (2).
Washington scoring: Touchdowns, Wilson, Bryan. PAT, Sherman (2).

1925

Notre Dame	0	13	7	7——27
Stanford	3	0	7	0——10

Notre Dame scoring: Touchdowns, Layden (3), Huntsinger. PAT, Crowley (3).
Stanford scoring: Touchdowns, T. Shipkey. PAT, Cuddeback. Field goal, Cuddeback.

1926

Alabama	0	0	20	0——20
Washington	6	6	0	7——19

Alabama scoring: Touchdowns, Hubert, J. M. Brown (2). PAT, Buckler (2).
Washington scoring: Touchdowns, Patton, Cole, Guttormsen. PAT, Cook.

1927

Alabama	0	0	0	7——7
Stanford	7	0	0	0——7

Alabama scoring: Touchdown, Johnson. PAT, Caldwell.
Stanford scoring: Touchdown, Walker. PAT, Bogue.

1928

Stanford	0	0	7	0——7
Pittsburgh	0	0	6	0——6

Stanford scoring: Touchdown, Wilton. PAT, Hoffman.
Pittsburgh scoring: Touchdown, Hagan.

1929

Georgia Tech	0	2	6	0——8
California	0	0	0	7——7

Georgia Tech scoring: Touchdown, Thomason. Safety, Maree blocks Lom's punt, rolls out of end zone.
California scoring: Touchdown, Phillips. PAT, Barr.

1930

USC	13	13	14	7——47
Pittsburgh	0	0	7	7——14

USC scoring: Touchdowns, Edelson (2), Duffield (2), Pinckert, Saunders, Wilcox. PAT, Shaver (2), Baker (2), Duffield.
Pittsburgh scoring: Touchdowns, Walinchus, Collins. PAT, Parkinson (2).

1931

Alabama	0	21	3	0——24
Washington State	0	0	0	0—— 0

Alabama scoring: Touchdowns, Campbell (2), Suther. PAT, Campbell (3). Field goal, Whitworth.

1932

USC	0	7	14	0——21
Tulane	0	0	6	6——12

USC scoring: Touchdowns, Sparling, Pinckert (2). PAT, Baker (3).
Tulane scoring: Touchdown, Haynes, Glover.

1933

USC	7	0	7	21——35
Pittsburgh	0	0	0	0— 0

USC scoring: Touchdown, Palmer, Griffith, Warburton (2), Barber. PAT, Smith (4), Lady.

USC reserve quarterback Cotton Warburton, who came into the game against Pitt in the fourth quarter of the 1933 game. He scored two touchdowns in the 35-0 Trojan victory.

1934

Columbia	0	7	0	0——7
Stanford	0	0	0	0——0

Columbia scoring: Touchdown, Barabas. PAT, Wilder.

1935

Alabama	0	22	0	7——29
Stanford	7	0	6	0——13

Alabama scoring: Touchdowns, Howell (2), Hutson (2). PAT, Smith (2). Field goal, Smith.
Stanford scoring: Touchdown, Grayson, Van Dellen. PAT, Moscrip.

1936

Stanford	7	0	0	0——7
Southern Methodist	0	0	0	0——0

Stanford scoring: Touchdown, Paulman. PAT, Moscrip.

1937

Pittsburgh	7	0	7	7——21
Washington	0	0	0	0— 0

Pittsburgh scoring: Touchdown, Patrick (2), Daddio. PAT, Daddio (3).

1938

California	0	7	6	0—13
Alabama	0	0	0	0— 0

California scoring: Touchdowns, Bottari (2). PAT, Chapman.

1939

USC	0	0	0	7—7
Duke	0	0	0	3—3

USC scoring: Touchdown, Krueger. PAT, Gaspar.
Duke scoring: Field goal, Ruffa.

1940

USC	0	7	0	7—14
Tennessee	0	0	0	0— 0

USC scoring: Touchdowns, Schindler, Krueger. PAT, J. Jones, Gaspar.

1941

Stanford	7	7	7	0—21
Nebraska	7	6	0	0—13

Stanford scoring: Touchdowns, Gallarneau (2), Kmetovic. PAT, Albert (3).
Nebraska scoring: Touchdowns, Francis, Zikmund. PAT, Francis.

1942

Oregon State	7	0	13	0—20
Duke	0	7	7	2—16

Oregon State scoring: Touchdowns, Durdan, Zelleck, Gray. PAT, Simas (2).
Duke scoring: Touchdowns, Lach, Siegfried. PAT, Gantt, Prothro. Safety, Durdan tackled in end zone by Karmazin.

1943

Georgia	0	0	0	9—9
UCLA	0	0	0	0—0

Georgia scoring: Touchdown, Sinkwich. PAT, Costa. Safety, Waterfield's punt blocked by Boyd, rolls out of end zone.

1944

USC	0	7	13	9—29
Washington	0	0	0	0— 0

USC scoring: Touchdowns, G. Callanan (2), Gray (2). PAT, Jamison (3). Safety, Planck blocks punt, Akins tackled in end zone.

1945

USC	6	6	0	13—25
Tennessee	0	0	0	0— 0

USC scoring: Touchdowns, J Callanan, Salata, J. Hardy, MacLachlan. PAT, West.

1946

Alabama	7	13	7	7—34
USC	0	0	0	14—14

Alabama scoring: Touchdowns, Self (2), Gilmer, Tew. Hodges, PAT, Morrow (4).
USC scoring: Touchdowns, Adelman, Clark. PAT, Lillywhite (2).

1947

Illinois	6	19	0	20—45
UCLA	7	7	0	0—14

Illinois scoring: Touchdowns, Rykovich, Young (2), Patterson, Moss, Steger, Green. PAT, Maechtle (3).
UCLA scoring: Touchdowns, Case, Hoisch. PAT, Case (2).

1948

Michigan	7	14	7	21—49
USC	0	0	0	0— 0

Michigan scoring: Touchdowns, Weisenburger (3), C. Elliott, Yerges, Derricote, Rifenburg. PAT, Brieske (7).

1949

Northwestern	7	6	0	7—20
California	7	0	7	0—14

Northwestern scoring: Touchdowns, Aschenbrenner (2), Murakowski. PAT, Farrar.
California scoring: Touchdowns, Jensen, Swaner. PAT, Cullom (2).

1950

Ohio State	0	0	14	3—17
California	0	7	7	0—14

Ohio State scoring: Touchdowns, Morrison, Krall. PAT, Hague (2). Field goal, Hague.
California scoring: Touchdowns, Monachino (2). PAT, Cullom (2).

1951

Michigan	0	0	0	14—14
California	0	6	0	0— 6

Michigan scoring: Touchdowns, Dufek (2). PAT, Allis (2).
California scoring: Touchdowns, Cummings.

1952

Illinois	6	0	7	27—40
Stanford	7	0	0	0— 7

Illinois scoring: Touchdowns, Tate (2), Karras, Bauchouras, Ryan, D. Stevens. PAT, Rebecca (4).
Stanford scoring: Touchdown, Hugasian. PAT, Kerkorian.

1953

USC	0	0	7	0—7
Wisconsin	0	0	0	0—0

USC scoring: Touchdown, Carmichael. PAT, Tsagalakis.

1954

Michigan State	0	7	14	7—28
UCLA	7	7	0	6—20

Michigan State scoring: Touchdowns, Wells (2), Bolden, Duckett. PAT, Slonac (4).
UCLA scoring: Touchdowns, Stits, Cameron, Loudd. PAT, Hermann (2).

1955

Ohio State	0	14	0	6—20
USC	0	7	0	0— 7

Ohio State scoring: Touchdowns, Leggett, Watkins, Harkrader. PAT, Weed, Watkins.
USC scoring: Touchdown, Dandoy. PAT, Tsagalakis.

1956

Michigan State	0	7	0	10—17
UCLA	7	0	0	7—14

Michigan State scoring: Touchdown, Peaks, Lewis. PAT, Planutis (2). Field goal, Kaiser.
UCLA scoring: Touchdowns, Davenport, Peters. PAT, Decker (2).

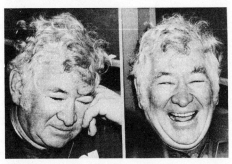

Michigan State coach Duffy Daugherty. In 1956 he beat UCLA 17-14; in '66 he lost to them 14-12.

1957

Iowa	14	7	7	7—35
Oregon State	0	6	6	7—19

Iowa scoring: Touchdown, Ploen, Hagler, Happel (2), Gibbons. PAT, Prescott (5).
Oregon State scoring: Touchdowns, Berry, Beamer, Hammack. PAT, Beamer.

1958

Ohio State	7	0	0	3—10
Oregon	0	7	0	0— 7

Ohio State scoring: Touchdown, Kremblas. PAT, Kremblas. Field goal, Sutherin.
Oregon scoring: Touchdown, Shanley. PAT, Morris.

1959

Iowa	7	13	12	6—38
California	0	0	6	6—12

Iowa scoring: Touchdowns, Fleming (2), Jeter, Langston, Duncan, Horn. PAT, Prescott (2).
California scoring: Touchdowns, Hart (2).

1960

Washington	17	7	7	13—44
Wisconsin	0	8	0	0— 8

Washington scoring: Touchdowns, McKeta, Fleming, Folkins, Jackson, Schloredt, Millick. PAT, Fleming (5). Field goal, Fleming.
Wisconsin scoring: Touchdowns, Wiesner. PAT, Schoonover (pass from Hackbart).

1961

Washington	3	14	0	0—17
Minnesota	0	0	7	0— 7

Washington scoring: Touchdowns, Wooten, Schloredt. PAT, Fleming (2). Field goal, Fleming.
Minnesota scoring: Touchdown, Munsey. PAT, Rogers.

1962

Minnesota	7	7	0	7—21
UCLA	3	0	0	0— 3

Minnesota scoring: Touchdowns, Stephens (2), Munsey. PAT, Loechler (3).
UCLA scoring: Field goal, B. Smith.

1963

USC	7	14	14	7—42
Wisconsin	7	0	7	23—37

USC scoring: Touchdowns, Bedsole (2), Butcher, Wilson, Heller, Hill. PAT, Lupo (6).
Wisconsin scoring: Touchdowns, Kurek, Kroner, Holland, VanderKelen, Richter. PAT, Kroner (5). Safety, Von Helmburg tackles punter Jones in end zone.

1964

Illinois	0	3	7	7—17
Washington	0	7	0	0— 7

Dick Butkus of Illinois makes a key pass interception against Washington in the 1964 game.

Illinois scoring: Touchdowns, Warren, Grabowski. PAT, Plankenhorn (2). Field goal, Plankenhorn.
Washington scoring: Touchdown, Kopay. PAT, Medved.

1965

| Michigan | 0 | 12 | 15 | 7—34 |
| Oregon State | 0 | 7 | 0 | 0— 7 |

Michigan scoring: Touchdowns, Anthony (3), Ward, Timberlake. PAT, Timberlake, Sygar, kicks; Timberlake run.
Oregon State scoring: Touchdown, McDougal. PAT, Clark.

1966

| UCLA | 0 | 14 | 0 | 0—14 |
| Michigan State | 0 | 0 | 0 | 12—12 |

UCLA scoring: Touchdowns, Beban (2). PAT, Zimmerman (2).
Michigan State scoring: Touchdowns, Apisa, Juday.

1967

| Purdue | 0 | 7 | 7 | 0—14 |
| USC | 0 | 7 | 0 | 6—13 |

Purdue scoring: Touchdowns, Williams (2). PAT, Griese (2).
USC scoring: Touchdowns, McCall, Sherman. PAT, Rossovich.

1968

| USC | 7 | 0 | 7 | 0—14 |
| Indiana | 0 | 3 | 0 | 0— 3 |

USC scoring: Touchdowns, Simpson (2). PAT, Aldridge (2).
Indiana scoring: Field goal, Kornowa.

1969

| Ohio State | 0 | 10 | 3 | 14—27 |
| USC | 0 | 10 | 0 | 6—16 |

Ohio State scoring: Touchdowns, Otis, Hayden, Gillian. PAT, Roman (3). Field goal, Roman (2).
USC scoring: Touchdowns, Simpson, Dickerson. PAT, Ayala. Field goal, Ayala.

1970

| USC | 3 | 0 | 7 | 0—10 |
| Michigan | 0 | 3 | 0 | 0— 3 |

USC scoring: Touchdown, Chandler. PAT, Ayala. Field goal, Ayala.
Michigan scoring: Field goal, Killian

A bird's-eye-view of the Rose Bowl in 1970. Capacity had reached 100,807.

1971

| Stanford | 10 | 0 | 3 | 14—27 |
| Ohio State | 0 | 14 | 3 | 0—17 |

Stanford scoring: Touchdowns, Brown (2), Vataha. PAT, Horowitz (3). Field goal, Horowitz (2).
Ohio State scoring: Touchdowns, Brockington (2). PAT, Schram (2). Field goal, Schram.

1972

| Stanford | 0 | 0 | 3 | 10—13 |
| Michigan | 0 | 3 | 0 | 9—12 |

Stanford scoring: Touchdown, Brown. PAT, Garcia. Field goal, Garcia (2).
Michigan scoring: Touchdown, Seyferth. PAT, Coin. Field goal, Coin. Safety, Shuttlesworth tackled Ferguson in end zone.

1973

| USC | 7 | 0 | 21 | 14—42 |
| Ohio State | 0 | 7 | 3 | 7—17 |

USC scoring: Touchdowns, Swann, Cunningham (4), Davis. PAT, Rae (6).
Ohio State scoring: Touchdowns, Keith, Bledsoe. PAT, Conway (2). Field goal, Conway.

1974

| Ohio State | 7 | 7 | 13 | 15—42 |
| USC | 3 | 11 | 7 | 0—21 |

Ohio State scoring: Touchdowns, Johnson (3), Greene, Elia, Griffin. PAT, Conway (4 kicks); Greene (run).

USC scoring: Touchdowns, McKay, Davis. PAT, Limahelu (kick); McKay (pass from Haden). Field goal, Limahelu (2).

1975

USC	3	0	0	15—18
Ohio State	0	7	0	10—17

USC scoring: Touchdowns, Obradovich, McKay. PAT, Limahelu (kick); Diggs (pass from Haden). Field goal, Limahelu.

Ohio State scoring: Touchdowns, Henson, Greene. PAT, Klaban (2). Field goal, Klaban.

1976

UCLA	0	0	16	7—23
Ohio State	3	0	0	7—10

UCLA scoring: Touchdowns, Henry (2), Tyler. PAT, White (2). Field goal, White.

Ohio State scoring: Touchdown, Johnson. PAT, Klaban. Field goal, Klaban.

1977

USC	0	7	0	7—14
Michigan	0	6	0	0— 6

USC scoring: Touchdowns, Evans, White. PAT, Walker (2).

Michigan scoring: Touchdown, Lytle.

ROSE BOWL RECORDS

Through 1977
(Modern Records are
Considered
To Be 1947 To Present, Or
During
Period of Big-10–Pacific-8
Agreement.)

INDIVIDUAL
SINGLE GAME

TOTAL OFFENSE

Most Plays: 57, Ron Vander-Kelen, Wisconsin, vs. USC, 1963

Most Yards: 406, Ron Vander-Kelen, Wisconsin, vs. USC, 1963

Best Play Average: 21.6, Bob Jeter, Iowa, vs. California, 1959 (9–194)

Most Touchdowns Responsible For: 5, Neil Snow, Michigan, vs. Stanford, 1902

Modern: 4, Pete Beathard, USC, vs. Wisconsin, 1963; 4, Sam Cunningham, USC, vs. Ohio State, 1973

PASSING

Most Attempts: 48, Ron VanderKelen, Wisconsin, vs. USC, 1963

Most Completions: 33, Ron VanderKelen, Wisconsin, vs. USC, 1963

Most Had Intercepted: 3, Bob Celeri, California, vs. Ohio State, 1950; 3, Ron Vander-Kelen, Wisconsin, vs. USC, 1963; 3, Bill Siler, Washington, vs. Illinois, 1964; 3, Steve Juday, Michigan State, vs. UCLA, 1966

Most Yards: 401, Ron Vander-Kelen, Wisconsin, vs. USC, 1963

Most Touchdowns: 4, Pete Beathard, USC, vs. Wisconsin, 1963

Best Pct. (Min. 10 Att.): 90.-0%, Ken Ploen, Iowa, vs. Oregon State, 1957 (9–10) **(Min. 15 Att.):** 78.9%, Charles Ortmann, Michigan, vs. California, 1951 (15–19)

Long Pass: 70, Bob Dethman to Gene Gray, Oregon State, vs. Duke, 1942

Modern: 67, Clarence Peaks to John Lewis, Michigan State, vs. UCLA, 1956; 67, John Sciarra to Wally Henry, UCLA, vs. Ohio State, 1976

RUSHING

Most Attempts: 34, Ernie Nevers, Stanford, vs. Notre Dame, 1925 (34–114); 34, Vic Bottari, California, vs. Alabama, 1938 (34–137)

Modern: 32, Billy Taylor, Michigan, vs. Stanford, 1972

Most Yards: 194, Bob Jeter, Iowa, vs. California, 1959 (9–194)

Best Average: 21.6, Bob Jeter, Iowa, vs. California, 1959 (9–194)

Long Run: 84, Mel Anthony, Michigan, vs. Oregon State, 1965

Most Touchdowns: 5, Neil

Snow, Michigan, vs. Stanford, 1902

Modern: 4, Sam Cunningham, USC, vs. Ohio State, 1973

PASS RECEIVING

Most Receptions: 11, Pat Richter, Wisconsin, vs. USC, 1963 (11–163)

Most Yards: 164, Don Hutson, Alabama, vs. Stanford, 1935 (6–164)

Modern: 163, Pat Richter, Wisconsin, vs. USC, 1963 (11–163)

Most Touchdown Passes: 2, Johnny Mack Brown, Alabama, vs. Washington, 1926; 2, Harry Edelson, USC, vs. Pittsburgh, 1930; 2, Don Hutson, Alabama, vs. Stanford, 1935; 2, Bill Gray, USC, vs. Washington, 1944; 2, George Callanan, USC vs. Washington, 1944; 2, Hal Bedsole, USC, vs. Wisconsin, 1963; 2, Wally Henry, UCLA, vs. Ohio State, 1976.

INTERCEPTIONS

Most Interceptions: 3, Shy Hunington, Oregon, vs. Pennsylvania, 1917; 3, Bill Paulman, Stanford, vs. Southern Methodist, 1936

Modern: 2, Stan Wallace, Illinois, vs. Stanford, 1952; 2, John Matsock, Michigan State, vs. UCLA, 1954; 2, Joe Cannavino, Ohio State vs. Oregon, 1958; 2, George Donnelly, Illinois, vs. Washington, 1964; 2, Bob Stiles, UCLA, vs. Michigan State, 1966

Most Yards Returned: 148 Elmer Layden, Notre Dame, vs. Stanford, 1925 (78–70)

Modern: 67, John Matsock, Michigan State, vs. UCLA, 1954

Long Return: 78, Elmer Layden, Notre Dame, vs. Stanford, 1925

Modern: 54, Stan Wallace, Illinois, vs. Stanford, 1952

Long Non-Scoring Return: 77, George Halas, Great Lakes Navy, vs. Mare Island Marines, 1919

PUNTING

Most Punts: 21, Everett Sweeley, Michigan, vs. Stanford, 1902

Modern: 9, Len Frketich, Oregon State, vs. Michigan, 1965; 9, Larry Cox, UCLA, vs. Michigan State, 1966

Best Average: 52.7, Des Koch, USC, vs. Wisconsin, 1953 (adjusted to current state rules)

Long Punt: 72, Abrahamson, Great Lakes Navy, vs. Mare Island Marines, 1919; 72, Elmer Layden, Notre Dame, vs. Stanford, 1925; 72, Des Koch, USC, vs. Wisconsin, 1953

PUNT RETURNS

Most Returns: 9, Paddy Driscoll, Great Lakes Navy, vs. Mare Island Marines, 1919 (9–115)

Modern: 6, Rick Sygar, Michigan, vs. Oregon State, 1965

Most Yards: 122, George Fleming, Washington, vs. Wisconsin, 1960 (3–122)

Best Average (Min. 2 returns): 40.7, George Fleming, Washington, vs. Wisconsin, 1960

Long Return: 86, Aramis Dandoy, USC, vs. Ohio State, 1955

KICKOFF RETURNS

Most Returns: 5, Allen Carter, USC, vs. Ohio State, 1974

Most Yards: 178, Al Hoisch, UCLA, vs. Illinois, 1947 (4–178)

Best Average: 44.5, Al Hoisch, UCLA, vs. Illinois, 1947 (4–178)

Long Return: 103, Al Hoisch, UCLA, vs. Illinois, 1947

SCORING

Most Points: 25, Neil Snow, Michigan, vs. Stanford, 1902 (TD worth 5 pts.)

Modern: 24, Sam Cunningham, USC, vs. Ohio State, 1973

Most Touchdowns: 5, Neil Snow, Michigan, vs. Stanford, 1902

Modern: 4, Sam Cunningham, USC, vs. Ohio State, 1973

Most Field Goals: 2, James Roman, Ohio State, vs. USC, 1969; 2, Steve Horowitz, Stanford, vs. Ohio State, 1971; 2, Rod Garcia, Stanford, vs. Michigan, 1972; 2, Chris Limahelu, USC, vs. Ohio State, 1974

Long Field Goal: 48, Steve Horowitz, Stanford, vs. Ohio State, 1971

Most PATs: 7, Jim Brieske, Michigan, vs. USC, 1948

INDIVIDUAL CAREER

TOTAL OFFENSE

Most Plays: 80, Pat Haden, USC, 1973–74–75

Most Yards: 454, Cornelius

Greene, Ohio State, 1974–75–76

Most Touchdowns, Run and Pass: 6, Jim Hardy, USC, 1944–45

PASSING

Most Attempts: 63, Pat Haden, USC, 1973–74–75

Most Completions: 34, Pat Haden, USC, 1973–74–75

Most Had Intercepted: 5, Bob Celeri, California, 1949–50

Most Yards: 425, Pat Haden, USC, 1973–74–75

Most Touchdowns: 5, Jim Hardy, USC, 1944–45

RUSHING

Most Attempts: 79, Archie Griffin, Ohio State, 1973–74–75–76 (79–412)

Most Yards: 412, Archie Griffin, Ohio State, 1973–74–75–76

Most Touchdowns: 5, Neil Snow, Michigan, 1902

PASS RECEIVING

Most Receptions: 12, Ted Shipkey, Stanford, 1925–27; 12, John McKay, USC, 1973–74–75

Most Yards: 201, John McKay, USC, 1973–74–75

Most Touchdowns: 2, by several players

PUNT RETURNS

Most Returns: 7, Mike Battle, USC, 1968–69

Most Yards: 122, George Fleming, Washington, 1960–61

KICKOFF RETURNS

Most Returns: 6, Allen Carter, USC, 1974–75

Most Yards: 178, Al Hoisch, UCLA, 1947

INTERCEPTIONS

Most Interceptions: 3, Shy Hunington, Oregon, 1917; 3, Bill Paulman, Stanford, 1936

Most Yards: 148, Elmer Layden, Notre Dame, 1925

SCORING

Most Touchdowns: 5, Neil Snow, Michigan, 1902

Most Points: 25, Neil Snow, Michigan, 1902

Most PATs: 7, Jim Brieske, Michigan, 1938

Most Field Goals: 3, Chris Limahelu, USC, 1974–75

MISCELLANEOUS

Most Minutes Played: 180, Hollis Huntington, Oregon (1917, 20), Mare Island Marines (1918); 180, Bob Reynolds, Stanford, 1934–35–36

SINGLE TEAM

TOTAL OFFENSE

Most Plays, Rush and Pass: 87, Ohio State, vs. Stanford, 1971

Most Yards, Rush and Pass: 516, Iowa, vs. California, 1959

Best Play Average: 7.5 Iowa, vs. California, 1959 (69–516)

RUSHING

Most Attempts: 74, Ohio State, vs. USC, 1955 (74–305); 74, Michigan, vs. Stanford, 1972 (74–264) (Note: Michigan was credited with unofficial 90 carries in 1902)

Most Yards: 429, Iowa, vs. California, 1959 (55–429)

Best Rush Average: 7.8, Iowa, vs. California, 1959 (55–429)

Fewest Yards Rushing: 6, USC, vs. Alabama, 1946

PASSING

Most Attempts: 49, Wisconsin, vs. USC, 1963 (34–49)

Most Completions: 34, Wisconsin, vs. USC, 1963

Most Had Intercepted: 6, Southern Methodist, vs. Stanford, 1936

Most Yards: 419, Wisconsin, vs. USC, 1963

Most Touchdowns: 4, USC, vs. Wisconsin, 1963, and 4, USC vs. Pittsburgh, 1930

Best Avg./Pass: 21.7, USC, vs. Pittsburgh, 1930 (13–8–282)

Best Avg./Completion: 35.2, USC, vs. Pittsburgh, 1930 (13–8–282) (USC completed passes of 55, 25, 50, 6, 39, 31, 19, and 57 yards)

INTERCEPTIONS

Most Intercepted: 6, Stanford, vs. Southern Methodist, 1936

Most Yards Returned Int.: 148, Notre Dame, vs. Stanford, 1925

PUNTS

Most Punts: 21, Michigan, vs. Stanford, 1902

Most Punts, Modern Rules: 17, Duke, vs. USC, 1939

Best Average: 53.9, USC, vs. Wisconsin, 1953 (adjusted to current statistical rules)

PUNT RETURNS

Most Returns: 8, Michigan, vs. Oregon State, 1965 (8–85)

Most Yards: 124, Washington, vs. Wisconsin, 1960 (4–124)

Best Average (Min. of 2 returns): 31.0 Washington, vs. Wisconsin, 1960 (4–124)

KICKOFF RETURNS

Most Returns: 8, UCLA, vs. Illinois, 1947

Most Yards: 259, UCLA, vs. Illinois, 1947

Best Average (Min. of 2 returns): 33.8, Oregon State, vs. Iowa, 1957 (5–169)

MISCELLANEOUS

Most First Downs: 32, Wisconsin, vs. USC, 1963

Most Times Penalized: 12, USC, vs. Wisconsin, 1963 (12–93)

Most Yards Penalized: 98, Michigan State, vs. UCLA, 1956 (10–98)

Most Points: 49, Michigan, vs. Stanford, 1902; 49, Michigan, vs. USC, 1948

Most Points, Losing Team: 37, Wisconsin, vs. USC, 1963

Most Fumbles: 7, USC, vs. Ohio State, 1955 (lost 3)

Most Fumbles, Lost: 4, Michigan State, vs. UCLA, 1954; 4, Wisconsin, vs. Washington, 1960; 4, Stanford, vs. Michigan, 1972

TWO-TEAM COMBINED RECORDS

Most Plays, Rushing and Passing: 158, USC (74) vs. Wisconsin (84), 1963

Most Yards, Rushing and Passing: 855, Ohio State (499) vs. USC (406), 1974

Most Rushing Attempts: 115, USC (47) vs. Wisconsin (68), 1953

Most Yards Rushing: 643, Iowa (429) vs. California (214), 1959

Most Passing Attempts: 69, USC (20) vs. Wisconsin (49), 1963

Most Pass Completions: 44, USC (10) vs. Wisconsin (34), 1963

Most Passes Intercepted: 7, Oregon (5) vs. Pennsylvania (2), 1917; 7, Notre Dame (5) vs. Stanford (2), 1925; 7, Stanford (2) vs. Pittsburgh (5), 1928; 7, Stanford (6) vs. Southern Methodist (1), 1936

Most Yards Passing: 672, USC (253) vs. Wisconsin (419), 1963

Most Touchdown Passes: 6, USC (4) vs. Wisconsin (2), 1963

Most Points: 79, USC (42) vs. Wisconsin (37), 1963

Most First Downs: 47, USC (15) vs. Wisconsin (32), 1963; 47, Ohio State (20) vs. USC (27), 1974

Fewest First Downs: 2, California vs. Washington & Jefferson, 1922

Most Fumbles: 10, Illinois (5) vs. Washington (5), 1964

Most Fumbles Lost: 7, Michigan State (4) vs. UCLA (3), 1954

INDEX

Blue Devils. *See* Duke
Bobo, Hubert, 159, 160
Borton, John, 159
Boryla, Mike, 200
Boston (New England) Patriots, 206
Bowl Game Thrills, 52, 73
Bowls, other, 19, 20, 28, 110, 129, 137, 204, 226
Boyd, Red, 141
Breakenridge, Harold, 73
Brenkert, Wayne, 50, 52, 53
Brennan, Terry, 21
Brickhouse, Jack, 21
Brix, Herman, 91, 92
Brockington, John, 159, 164, 201, 202, 203–04
Brominski, Ed, 84
Brown (Univ.), 95, 134
Brown, Booker, 216, 222
Brown, C. C., 17
Brown, Jackie, 202, 204, 208, 210
Brown, Jim, 223
Brown, Johnny Mack, 91–92, 95, 144
Brown, Leo, 164
Brown, Paul, 149
Brown, Tom, 175–76, 177
Brown, Warren, 51, 65
Brown, Willie, 181, 182, 184, 186
Brubaker, Dick, 159, 162
Bruhn, Milt, 173, 180, 186, 187
Bruins. *See* UCLA
Bryant, Paul "Bear," 96–97, 98, 99–100, 155
Buckeyes. *See* Ohio State
Bull, Scott, 211
Bulldogs. *See* Georgia (Univ. of)
Bunce, Don, 197–98, 199–200, 206, 207–10, 212
Bundy, May Sutton, 24
Butcher, Ron, 182
Butler, Larry, 207
Butts, Wallace, 138, 140, 141, 142

Caen, Herb, 31
Cafego, George, 111
Cain, Jim, 184
Cain, Jimmy "Hurry," 96

Caldwell, Herschel "Rosy," 95
California (Univ. of), 20, 27, 34, 44, 45–48, 50–53, 61, 66, 68–74, 101, 121, 123, 130, 144, 145, 150, 159, 172, 175, 181, 191, 200, 201, 206, 207, 216, 217, 231
Camp, Walter, 45, 54, 61, 117
Campbell, Johnny Monk, 96
Cannavino, Joe, 164, 167
Cannon, Billy, 172
Cardinals. *See* Stanford
Carillo, Leo, 22
Carlisle, 56, 59, 104, 117
Carnegie, Ernie, 223
Carnegie Tech, 49, 60
Carpenter, Ken, 21
Carter, Allen, 15
Casanova, Len, 166, 168
Case, Ernie, 150, 151, 152–53
Cassady, Howard "Hopalong," 156, 157–59, 160, 162, 164
Centre College, 48
Chaves, Martin, 130, 133, 134, 136
Chicago (Univ. of), 118, 144
Chicago Bears, 38, 40, 107, 118, 119, 120–21, 125, 151, 177
Chicago Cardinals, 40, 56
Chicago Tribune, 55, 62
Christiansen, Jack, 199
Christman, Paul, 21
Ciampa, Al, 87
Cisco, Galen Bernard, 163–68
Clark, Don, 164, 166
Clark, G. H., 36
Clarke, Leon, 160, 162
Cleveland Browns, 116, 148, 151
Cleveland Rams, 140
Cobb, Marvin, 216
Coin, Dana, 207, 208, 209
Cole, Johnny, 94
College champions, in Rose Bowl, 20
College of Pacific, 174
Colletto, Jim, 193

Collier's (magazine), 46, 57, 60
Colorado (Univ. of), 171
Columbia, 76, 77, 78, 80, 81–82, 83–88, 99
Colzie, Neal, 217, 219
Considine, Bob, 21
Contratto, Jim, 160, 162
Conway, Blair, 217, 218
Conzelman, Jimmy, 40
Corbus, Bill, 86
Cornell, 48, 59
Cornhuskers. *See* Nebraska (Univ. of)
Corum, Bill, 76, 87–88
Cougars. *See* Washington State
Cox, Larry, 193, 194
Crabtree, Jack, 164, 165, 166, 167
Cranmer, Lee, 46
Creamer, Robert W., 143–44
Crimson Tide. *See* Alabama (Univ. of)
Crisp, Hank, 99
Cross, Eric, 202
Crowley, Jim, 54, 59, 60, 61, 62, 63, 64, 65, 83
Cuddeback, Murray, 62
Cunningham, Sam, 216, 217–18, 219, 221
Cvijanovich, Sam, 222–23

Daddio, Bill, 149
Dallas Texans, 177
Dana, Herb, 69
Dandoy, Aramis, 160
Danehe, Dick, 21
Danzig, Allison, 32, 57, 58, 59, 61, 103, 104
Darden, Tom, 207
Daugherty, Duffy, 190–91, 194
Davidson (college), 132
Davidson, Ben, 170, 174
Davis, Anthony, 15, 213–24, 229
Davis, Clarence, 216
Davis, George, 143
Davis, Glenn, 144, 149, 151
Davis, Lamar, 140
Davis, Tom, 134, 135
Davis, Van, 142